Luis Buñuel

Luis Buñuel

New Readings

Edited by
Peter William Evans and Isabel Santaolalla

 Publishing

First published in 2004 by the
BRITISH FILM INSTITUTE
21 Stephen Street, London W1T 1LN

The British Film Institute is the UK national agency with responsibility for encouraging the arts of film
and television and preserving them in the national interest.

Cover design by Ketchup
Cover image: Luis Buñuel and Catherine Deneuve on the set of *Belle de jour*
Set by Servis Filmsetting Ltd, Manchester
Printed in the UK by The Cromwell Press, Trowbridge, Wiltshire

British Library Cataloguing-in-Publication Data
A catalogue record for this book is available from the British Library

ISBN 1–84457–003–7 (pbk)
ISBN 1–84457–002–9 (hbk)

Contents

Acknowledgments

We would like to thank the School of Modern Languages, the Film and Communication Committee and the Department of External Relations and Communications (especially Nigel Relph) of Queen Mary, University of London, as well as the School of English and Modern Languages, the Research Office (especially Neil Taylor) and the Rectorate of the University of Surrey Roehampton, for various forms of support. We would also like to thank colleagues at our respective institutions, especially Jorge Díaz-Cintas and Lourdes Melcion, at Roehampton, on whose shoulders fell some of Isabel's responsibilities during her leave of absence. Thanks are also due to the Arts and Humanities Research Board for respective funded sabbaticals that enabled us to carry out the research and to put together this volume. Staff at the Filmoteca Española in Madrid especially Javier Herrera Navarro, were, as ever, extremely helpful in making available to us the Buñuel archive. We would like to thank Rob White and Sophia Contento, at the British Film Institute, for support and encouragement over this project. Finally, we would like to thank Juan Luis Buñuel, whose reminiscences have added a personal touch to our more scholarly reflections on one of the world's greatest film-makers.

Notes on Contributors

Juan Luis Buñuel was born in Paris in 1934. He graduated from Oberlin College, Ohio, with a Bachelor of Arts degree in English Literature. He was assistant director to Orson Welles, J. A. Bardem, Louis Malle, Hugo Butler, Jacques Doniol Valcroze and Luis Buñuel. He has made documentary, feature and TV films since 1963 starring Fernando Rey, Catherine Deneuve, Liv Ullmann and Michel Piccoli. He has had one-man exhibitions of sculptures and paintings in Mexico City, New York, San Francisco, Madrid, Barcelona, Palma de Mallorca, Ibiza and Arles. He was the co-founder, in 1968, of the Salón de Independientes, Mexico City.

Ian Christie has published mainly on British, Russian and experimental film, and has also curated exhibitions, including 'Eisenstein: Life and Work' (1988) and 'Spellbound: Art and Film' (1996), and contributed to many television and radio programmes about cinema. He also has a longstanding interest in Surrealism and in the work of Raúl Ruiz. Since working at the British Film Institute, he has held posts in Oxford and Canterbury and is currently Professor of Film and Media History at Birkbeck College, University of London.

Marvin D'Lugo is Professor of Spanish and Screen Studies at Clark University (Worcester, Massachusetts). He has written two books on Spanish film: *The Films of Carlos Saura: The Practice of Seeing* (Princeton University Press, 1991) and *Guide to the Cinema of Spain* (Greenwood Press, 1997). He has also authored more than a hundred essays and reviews on Spanish and Spanish American film topics, including Cuban, Mexican and Argentine film authors. He is currently working on a book on the transnational imagination in Spanish cinema.

Peter William Evans is Professor of Hispanic Studies at Queen Mary, University of London. He has published on Hollywood, British and Spanish cinema. He is the author of *The Films of Luis Buñuel: Subjectivity and Desire*

(OUP, 1995) (translated into Spanish as *Las películas de Luis Buñuel: la subjetividad y el deseo,* Paidós, 1998). He has recently completed a book on Bigas Luna's *Jamón jamón* (Paidós) and is writing another on Carol Reed (Manchester University Press).

Victor Fuentes is Professor of Spanish at University of California, Santa Barbara. His areas of interest are nineteenth- and twentieth-century Spanish narrative, cinema, and film and literature. He is the author of, among other books, *Buñuel en México, Los Mundos de Buñuel, Antología de la poesía bohemia española (temas y figuras)* and *La marcha al pueblo en las letras españolas 1917–1936* (Ediciones de la Torre, 1980). Under the name of Floreal Hernández, he has also published a novel, *Morir en Isla Vista* (Prames, 1999).

Paul Hammond is a writer, painter, translator and occasional curator who lives in Barcelona. His most recent books are *Constellations of Miró, Breton* and the third edition of *The Shadow and Its Shadow: Surrealist Writings on the Cinema* (both City Lights Books, 2000). Of late he has translated novels by Michel Houellebecq and Fernando Vallejo, plus Borde and Chaumeton's classic 1955 study of film noir. He is currently researching '1930s' Buñuel' and honing his scopophilia.

Stephen Hart is Professor in Hispanic Studies, University College London (PhD, Cambridge, 1985). His publications include *Religión, política y ciencia en la obra de César Vallejo* (1987), *White Ink* (Tamesis Books, 1993), *A Companion to Spanish American Literature* (Tamesis Books, 1999) and an edition of César Vallejo's poetry (2000). He has acted as consultant for Christie's, the BBC and Channel Four. He currently teaches Latin American literature and film.

Javier Herrera Navarro is keeper of the private library and personal papers of Luis Buñuel at the Filmoteca Española. His publications include articles in *Bianco e Nero, Secuencias, Nickelodeon* and *Goya.*

Mercè Ibarz teaches at the Univesitat Pompeu Fabra (Barcelona). Her most recent publication is *Buñuel documental. Tierra sin pan y su tiempo* (Zaragoza, 1999). She was the curator of the exhibition '*Tierra sin pan.* Buñuel y los nuevos caminos de las vanguardias' (IVAM, 1999–2000). She is also a novelist and essayist.

Laura M. Martins graduated at the Instituto Nacional Superior del Profesorado (Buenos Aires, Argentina) in 1983, and took her MA and PhD

(Latin American Literature and Film) at the University of Maryland in 1996. She has published a book, *En primer plano: literatura en Argentina, 1955–1969* (University Press of the South, 2000), and numerous articles on the relationship between Argentine literature and film and other semiotic systems.

Andrea Sabbadini, psychologist and psychoanalyst, works in private practice in London. A lecturer at University College London and Regent's College, he has published extensively in professional journals, and edited books on *Time in Psychoanalysis* (Feltrinelli, 1979), *Even Paranoids Have Enemies* (Routledge, 1998) and on *The Couch and the Silver Screen: Psychoanalytical Reflections on European Cinema* (Taylor and Francis, 2003). He is the founding editor of *Psychoanalysis and History* and the book review editor of *The International Journal of Psychoanalysis*. On behalf of the British Psychoanalytical Society he chairs the European Psychoanalytic Film Festival and an ongoing series of film presentations.

Vicente Sánchez Biosca is Professor of Theory and History of the Cinema at the University of Valencia. He has been the general editor of the film review, *Archivos de la Filmoteca*, since 1993. He is the author of various books, including *Shadows of Weimar: A Contribution to the History of German Cinema 1918–1933* (Verdoux, 1990), *A Fragmented Culture. Pastiche and Narrative in Film and Television* (Ediciones de la Filmoteca Valenciana, 1995), *Film Editing: Theory and Analysis* (Verdoux, 1996), *Luis Buñuel: Viridiana* (Paidós, 1999), and is currently working on an archive of No-Do documentaries for the Filmoteca Española.

Isabel Santaolalla is Reader in Spanish at the University of Surrey Roehampton, London. She has published on post-colonial literature and film, with special emphasis on the representation of ethnicity and gender, both in Anglophone and Hispanic cultures. She is the editor of *'New' Exoticisms: Changing Patterns in the Construction of Otherness* (Rodopi, 2000) and the author of *Los 'otros'. Etnicidad y 'raza' en el cine español contemporáneo* (Paidōs, 2004).

Foreword: A Desperate Call for Murder

Juan Luis Buñuel

'A desperate call for murder'. That was the meaning of *L'Âge d'or*. And now, as time goes by, people's vision of Luis Buñuel has been softened by this new mythological, museum-bound figure. Before, when one of his films came out, crowds would destroy the theatre, some liberal politicians would censure his works and others wanted to expel him from the country he was living in. That's what his films and writings were all about. To provoke, to shock, to destroy a society which he found corrupt and idiotic, to ridicule a religion which had oppressed millions of people, and continues to do so. 'The search for Truth is wonderful. Beware of the person who then claims to have found that Truth.'

Some towns in Spain are governed by rightist politicians who name streets after him. Don't they know what he thought of them? How he and his comrades fought against them during the Civil War, against their mentality? He has become these politicians' hero. It brings the tourists in … He told me once, as he looked up at the new 'Luis Buñuel' street sign: 'They name a street after me now; a few years ago they would have put me up against a wall.'

Now many of his books and belongings are on display in museums. He was never over-fond of museums. His last scenario was about a group of youthful terrorists who wanted to place an atom bomb in the Louvre Museum in Paris. Finally they didn't do it. They came to the conclusion that humanity didn't need any help to destroy itself. They were *dépassés* and disillusioned with today's society.

Buñuel must not be remembered as a politically correct individual. He was kind and good … but he was also violent and vengeful … against a bourgeois morality and social system that has always suppressed real freedom and love for Humanity.

I was just thinking what my father told me about Federico García Lorca. They had met at the Residencia de Estudiantes in Madrid. Both were very young men, very excited about the new world that was opening up to them. He said that Federico's real art was not his poetry or his music, but himself. He had never met someone who was so warm, outgoing and intelligent. His being was his art. He had laughter and humour.

One night, in the early 1960s, I was walking with my father through the narrow streets of Toledo. We arrived at a small square. One side gave out onto a cliff that dropped several hundred feet into the river Tajo. I leaned on the stone parapet and looked down. The moonlight made the river look like a slithering snake. Then I noticed that my father had tears in his eyes. I asked him what was the matter, if he felt all right. He also leaned on the stone railing and said, 'This is where Federico and Salvador and myself came to vomit when we were drunk.' Then he turned away. 'We used to laugh so much!' As we walked slowly back to our hotel, he said,

> I can only imagine the horror that Federico must have felt as he was being led away to his execution. He was such an exquisite being, so conscious of everything around him, of life! He knew what was going to happen to him.

Years later I went to the spot where García Lorca had been murdered. When I saw where it had happened, I was shocked. It stood fifty metres from some ugly modern buildings and several feet from a small road. On a sparsely wooded and dry hillside rested a nondescript concrete monument. Nearby stood an old splintered tree where, it seems, Lorca received his ultimate present. A few feet away, a pile of discarded garbage: ripped blue plastic bags, banana peels, rusty cans, a few letters, disintegrating cardboard boxes, sanitary napkin containers … It looked like this stuff had been lying around for quite a while. I thought of my father and of Federico. I also thought of the young Spanish Republic that had been refused help by the so-called Western democracies: England, France and the United States. Hitler and Mussolini did not hesitate in helping Franco.

What stands out most in my 'remembrances' are the evenings when old Republican refugee friends came over for dinner. My brother and I were young, so after supper we were sent off to bed. We were kept awake till three in the morning as they sat around the dining room table, the famous Spanish *sobremesa*, and the cognac was brought out. Then the violent discussions started: 'If at the Teruel front we had …', 'Franco, that *hijo de puta*!', 'The FAI, the CNT, the communists should have done, or didn't do, or did do …', their voices rising louder and louder. I heard this at every reunion, from 1938 when we reached New York till a few months before my father's death in 1983.

Introduction: Luis Buñuel – Twenty Years After

Peter William Evans and Isabel Santaolalla

Buñuel (1900–1983) died twenty years ago. This volume reconsiders, in Dumas's phrase, 'twenty years after', the legacy of twentieth-century cinema's most irreverent chronicler. His films have inspired some of the key film-makers of world cinema; their enduring popularity with audiences may be measured by lists of the twenty best films of all time, the number of revivals and DVD or video re-issues, and the worldwide events commemorating his birth. In the light of recent developments in film theory, as well as the discovery of new information and documents related to his work, the time is ripe for reviewing Buñuel's films, and to ask how and why they continue to hold the attention of film-makers and audiences alike.

Among the former, mention need only be made of Pedro Almodóvar and Whit Stilman. Stilman's homage in *Metropolitan* (1990), the film inspired by *Le Charme discret de la bourgeoisie* (1972), transforms Buñuel's *coterie* of bourgeois friends into the 'Preppie class' young Manhattanites who socialise together before their exhausted shared interests lead to the fragmentation of the group. Almodóvar's entire work could be said to have its roots partially in Buñuel's films. But the direct quotation in *Carne trémula* (1997) of a scene from *Ensayo de un crimen* (1955) draws attention to a common interest in black comedy, the contents and discontents in relations between the sexes, and the family as the crucible for the formation, and sometimes the perversion, of human personality.

There have, of course, been earlier admirers of Buñuel's films, none more so than Hitchcock, who constantly quoted and was himself quoted by Buñuel. Drawn together by Bazin (1975) as proponents of the cinema of cruelty, Buñuel and Hitchcock seem to have been permanently in dialogue with each other. In conversation with Buñuel at an event celebrating the latter's work, Hitchcock referred directly with envious approval to Tristana's prosthetic leg, but also often indirectly acknowledged him in many films, retaining that early interest in Surrealism and the oneiric poetry of *Un chien andalou* (1929) well into his career, as may be judged, for instance, not only by the famous Dalí dream sequence in *Spellbound* (1945), but also by the credit titles of *Vertigo* (1958). In invoking *Un chien andalou, Vertigo* identifies itself with the earlier film's surrealist exploration of the unconscious. As the Saul Bass-designed credits begin to roll, the fragmented face of a woman, supposedly – though not in actual fact – Kim Novak's, comes under the scrutiny of the camera. At first it focuses on rouged lips, then on both eyes, then on her left eye, now in huge close-up, as the word 'Vertigo' appears horizontally across it, slitting it, before the letters scatter away, leaving space for the rest of the credits that seem to spew out of the eye, which now disappears from view, before finally returning to be sliced again at the end of the sequence, this time by the words 'Alfred Hitchcock'. As in *Un chien andalou,* and its surrealist resonances of the eye closed to consciousness, where it is the director himself, not his name, as in *Vertigo*, who performs this act of sadism, the eye is the source of interiorised desire, a point elaborated in later scenes interrogating the Hitchcock hero Scottie's perceptions of his heroine, Madeleine. But again, as in *Un chien andalou*, it is the female perspective that is violated, in an ambiguous act that prefigures both release from Oedipal order and punishment for embodying its potential disruption.

The 'cruelty' of that early scene in *Un chien andalou* should be read, however, not as a taste for gratuitous sadism so much as Sadean clarity, or as the exposure of hypocrisy, sanctimoniousness and delusion. Indeed, in Buñuel's world, cruelty is inseparable from a humane and tolerant vision of *la comédie humaine*. The profane, almost adolescent humour of his films underlies an ultimately benevolent commentary on the confused social or psychological order under scrutiny.

His films combine the aesthetics of Surrealism with the politics of Marxism (although his actual relationship with the Communist Party remains a matter of some dispute). Both in practice and in theory – the early essays on film comedy (Buñuel, 2000, p. 124), and the later ones, such as the 1958 essay on the poetry of cinema (Buñuel, 2000, pp. 136–41) – Buñuel remained throughout his career true to his earliest instincts. This meant giving free rein to the imagination and to the unexpected, to what he and the other surrealists referred to as *'le hasard'*.

In purely film terms his clearest debts were above all to the silent Hollywood comedy stars, especially Harry Langdon, Ben Turpin and Buster Keaton – of equal fascination to his great friend García Lorca – and to the German cinema, particularly the expressionists, but also, as Agustín Sánchez Vidal has argued, to Lubitsch, mixed influences clearly noticeable in the Gothic ambience relieved by comedy in films like *Abismos de pasión* (1953), *Le Charme discret de la bourgeoisie*, or *Le Fantôme de la liberté* (1974). As regards the former category, with typical forthrightness, Buñuel wrote:

People are so stupid, and have so many prejudices, that they think *Faust, Potemkin,* and the like are superior to these buffooneries, which are not that at all, and which

I would call the new poetry. The equivalent of surrealism in cinema can be found only in those films, far more surrealist than those of Man Ray.

Buñuel, 2000, p. 24

His defence of the need for poetry in the cinema is equally robust in his attack on the well-made but, in his view, unimaginative, *Detective Story* (William Wyler, 1950):

> The structure of the story is perfect, the director is magnificent, the actors are extraordinary, the production is brilliant, and so on and so forth. But all this talent, all this know-how, all the complex activities that go into the making of a film have been placed at the service of a stupid and remarkably base story. It makes me think of that extraordinary machine in *Opus II* – a gigantic apparatus made of the finest steel, with a thousand complex gears, tubes, manometers, and levers, as precise as a watch and as imposing as a transatlantic liner – whose sole function was to post-mark the mail.

Buñuel, 2000, p. 137

In the same piece Buñuel advocates a cinema of mystery and fantasy, such as Lang's *Der müde Tod* (1921), the film he claims actually inspired him to be a film director himself, making the additional point that films should not treat human beings in isolation, but in relation to others, an observation that underlines the social consciousness of his films. In his autobiography, *Mon dernier soupir* (1982), his list of such films includes William Dieterle's haunting story about an artist's encounters with a beautiful woman at different stages in her earthly life. There is no mention of Lubitsch, but Buñuel's essay on Adolphe Menjou's moustache shows he was not ignorant of films like *The Marriage Circle* (1924) (the non-musical earlier version of *One Hour with You* [1932]). The sophisticated *liaisons dangereuses* of Buñuel's comedies of manners, such as *El ángel exterminador* (1962), and especially the late films like *Belle de jour* (1966), *Le Charme discret de la bourgeoisie*, *Le Fantôme de la liberté* and *Cet obscur object du désir* (1977), recall the ambience of films like *Trouble in Paradise* (1932) and *One Hour with You*, made by another of the cinema's stylish analysts of the relations between the sexes.

Comedy and fantasy are features of his films as well as of his writing. But beyond these debts to certain traditions in film-making, Buñuel's films also belong to a wider literary, philosophical and artistic heritage that includes the Spanish picaresque writers – especially Quevedo and Alemán (inspiring *Los olvidados* [1950]) – Cadalso (*Le Fantôme*), Goya (quoted in *Le Fantôme* and elsewhere), Sade (appearing as a character in *La Voie lactée* [1969]), Sacher-Masoch (the inspiration perhaps for *Tristana* [1970] and *Cet obscur objet*), the

Gothic novelists (*Abismos de pasión*) and, among his near contemporaries, especially the humourist Ramón Gómez de la Serna. Many scholars have commented on this *mélange* of influences, and although Buñuel's genius continued to be shaped throughout his life not only by constantly evolving interests and obsessions, but also by the taste and background of his collaborators – especially the scriptwriters Carrière, Alejandro and others – there are constant features that give his work its distinctiveness.

The attempts to claim Buñuel for Spain (where he worked from the early 1930s to the end of the Civil War in 1939), Mexico (from the making of *Gran Casino* in 1946, to the mid-1960s) or France (from the outset of his career and then from the mid-1960s up to 1977, and his last film *Cet obscur objet*) seem futile, especially in view of the fact that many films were co-productions (involving North Americans in *Robinson Crusoe* [1952] and *The Young One* [1960], and Italians in *Cela s'appelle l'aurore* [1955]). More seriously, though, no matter where and with whom Buñuel made his films, either those he called his 'películas alimenticias' (bread and butter films) or the more personal ones, he was the great *flâneur* of world cinema, drawing on his many backgrounds and experiences to produce conceptual and psychological dramas whose analysis of human desire has rarely been surpassed elsewhere. Cadalso's lugubrious grief-stricken lover forever stationed in *Noches lúgubres* by the tomb of his deceased beloved, the executed patriots of Goya's famous painting *El tres de Mayo*, the underclass ragamuffins of Quevedo's *El buscón*, the desire-crazed libertines of the *120 Days of Sodom*, Gómez de la Serna's comic characters, and Sacher-Masoch's cruel temptress, the Venus in Furs, find their ways into Buñuel's dark comedy of masochism. Their most vivid equivalents are the necrophiliacs Don Jaime (*Viridiana* [1961]), Alejandro (*Abismos de pasión*) and the chief of police (*Le Fantôme*); the mindless officer-class patricians in *Le Fantôme, La Voie lactée, La Fièvre monte à El Pao* (1959) and *Le Charme discret*; the desperate delinquents Jaibo and Pedro in *Los olvidados*; the fetishistic lovers in *Le Journal d'une femme de chambre* (1964) and *Cet obscur objet du désir*; and the '*belles dames sans merci*', Tristana, Susana, Séverine and Conchita. Their enigmatic beauty and unknown – and therefore threatening – identities lead to the traumas of their captivated male admirers. For all their ancient heritage, Buñuel's reformulations of familiar motifs and obsessions retain in their freshness and clear-eyed insights disturbing relevance for modern audiences looking for more than reassuring platitudes in the cinema. The power to shock of films like *Él* (1952)– with its explorations of male paranoid jealousy – or *Belle de jour* – and its analysis of female masochism – remains intact.

In all cases Buñuel's treatment of his flawed characters is sympathetic. This mixture of comedy and fantasy simultaneously reflects his attraction to the deep and invariably dark, often perverse, motivations of human desire and his compassion for fellow mortals whose victimisation by internal or external pressures and circumstances makes them a source of comedy and empathy rather than of satire or contempt. Even Buñuel's special loathing for political tyrants is usually expressed in comic form, the pompous minor figures of authority who include colonels, chiefs of police, head waiters and bishops who inhabit his imaginative social order. The rhetoric of his films naturally favours the oppressed (for example, the delinquents in *Los olvidados*, the political prisoners in *La Fièvre monte à El Pao*, the student activists in *Le Charme discret*), but even here there is no easy sentimentality in the representation of the marginalised. Buñuel's films concentrate on the wickedness as well as on the vulnerability of the innocent. There is chaos beneath the order not only of the well-to-do but also of the dispossessed. The former, of course, have no excuse. The privileges of power and wealth that come with status make tyranny less forgivable. The tyranny that is committed in the name of religion, along with the infamies justified in the name of the other pillars of society, the state and the armed forces, is a special target for Buñuel. If there is one undoubted legacy from his Spanish background it is the impact on his films of the central role of the church in Spain during his formative years:

> L'omniprésence de la religion se manifestait dans tous les détails de la vie. Ainsi je m'amusais à célébrer la messe dans le grenier de la maison, devant mes soeurs. Je possédais divers objets du culte en plomb, ainsi qu'une aube et une chasuble.

> (The presence everywhere of religion was noticeable in every detail of daily life. Thus I amused myself by celebrating mass in the granary of the house, in front of my sisters. I owned various liturgical objects made of lead, as well as an alb and a chasuble.)
>
> Buñuel, 1982, p. 19

'Athée grace à Dieu' (an atheist, thank God), as he famously described himself, Buñuel had an ambivalent attitude towards religion. His films are full of characters whose minds have been impaired by irrational faith: the priest and head waiter in *La Voie lactée* agonising over the mystery of transubstantiation, the self-mortifying Viridiana, the guilt-racked Séverine, or the hermetic Nazarín. In the name of religion, moralists, politicians and comparable figures of authority devise social orders that mean repression and misery for others: *Susana* (1950), *El ángel exterminador*, *Nazarín* (1958), *Simón del desierto* (1965), *La Voie lactée*, *Le Fantôme de la liberté* are only a handful of the many films that spin narratives out of this conviction. As always, though, Buñuel's sympathy lies with the victim, for even the perpetrators of tyrannies in the name of religion are casualties of faith. Beyond such considerations, though, as the above quotation indicates, Buñuel was also fascinated by the theatricality of religion. Its mysteries and doctrines intrigued him, but so too did its potential for masquerade and fantasy. Religion was, additionally, a familiar place, a refuge where, for all its dubious claims and practised barbarities, he could turn for inward meditation and sources of artistic creativity. Religious fanaticism, allied to political terrorism, as we go to press, seems no nearer extinction than it was in Buñuel's day. By the end of his own life, as the explosions in *Cet obscur objet du désir* demonstrate, he was beginning to be concerned about the devastations of political terrorism. *Un chien andalou* had been, admittedly, an invitation to murder, but the targets were bourgeois ideology and unjust social systems. The gratuitous killing of innocents did not fall into his category of justified calls to murder, and although Buñuel's attack in his last film on political terrorism had obviously specific targets in mind (such as ETA), his commentary on a world in moral and social chaos seems apt in modern times where, one feels, his condemnation of acts of barbarity would not have been divorced from acknowledgment of the causes that lead individuals to desperate measures.

This volume is both a reminder of Buñuel's status as one of the greatest directors in the history of cinema and a litmus test for assessing the validity of this claim. We take a fresh look at his films and career, attending as much to form as to content, to archival, previously unpublished material as well as to recent critical theory. The Buñuel who emerges is a film-maker who belongs to but also transcends the narrow limits of his time. In marvelling at his achievements we have no hesitation in noting his compromises, prejudices and omissions.

We began with a foreword by Juan Luis Buñuel, Buñuel's son and assistant director on some of his films, in which he evokes his father's unfailing belief in the pursuit of freedom and the overthrow of political and religious oppression, as well as his deep contempt for a bourgeois ideology that has ironically in recent years inspired attempts by some politicians and cultural bureaucrats to turn the politically incorrect Buñuel into a more acceptable, softened, even mythologised icon of Spanish culture. Following this introduction, the volume includes eleven chapters in which scholars from Europe (Britain, France and Spain) and the United States examine specific aspects of Buñuel's work in the light of current critical and theoretical debates, as well as of biographical material recently unearthed, always aiming to strike a balance between general discussions of key issues raised by Buñuel's work – for example, Surrealism, religion, exile, commercial and 'auteurist' tendencies, melodrama, narrative experimentation, sexuality – and analysis of individual films chosen from across the full range of his career, here represented chronologically by *L'Âge d'or*, *Tierra sin pan* (1933), *Los olvidados*, *Robinson Crusoe*, *The Young One*, *Belle de jour* and *Le Charme discret de la bourgeoisie*.

Initially, the volume adopts a chronological approach and concentrates on major films and issues, ranging progressively over Buñuel's career in Spain, Mexico and France. The first section focuses on his early phase, including membership of the Surrealist Group, his experiments in the documentary mode and his residence in the United States. Paul Hammond's chapter painstakingly traces the reactions of the Surrealist Group to Buñuel's *L'Âge d'or*, paying special attention to sources – press coverage, photos – scarcely analysed until now, concluding that reactions to the film can be viewed as a 'paroxystic figuration' of the complex and not always unambiguous relations that the surrealist and communist projects would nurture in the late 1920s and early 30s. Mercè Ibarz offers a fresh look at *Land Without Bread*, identifying the film's most notable experiment, the component that has suffered most manipulation over the years: its soundtrack. Ibarz argues that it is through the film's visual–aural counterpoint that Buñuel made his most subversive contribution to documentary film-making: although often described as a propaganda film for the Spanish Republic, *Land Without Bread* deliberately deconstructs the very mechanisms of propaganda by exposing the ambiguity of the documentary pact with the spectator. Javier Herrera Navarro's chapter throws new light on what until now has been one of the most obscure periods of Buñuel's life: his early years in the United States. Herrera's detailed analysis and commentary on the recently discovered correspondence between Buñuel and his friend Urgoiti between 1938 and 1940 discloses altogether novel details that provide invaluable insight on Buñuel's political, economic, artistic and personal activities and aspirations during his early years in the continent that would eventually become his home.

The second section of this volume is dedicated to Buñuel's Mexican phase. Through concentration on two specific motifs in *Los olvidados* – concealment and violence – Stephen Hart projects a new image of Buñuel, one precociously aware of the dangers in any attempt at speaking for the dispossessed, consciously staging in the act itself of representation the tensions inherent to even well-intentioned efforts to reveal the consciousness of the outcast, issues that have become extremely topical in recent years, within the field of subaltern studies. Marvin D'Lugo's analysis of *Robinson Crusoe* highlights the importance of sound as a strategy aimed at leading the spectator to a heightened awareness of the artificiality of the cinematic universe, and by extension, of the social and geopolitical ideology personified in the figure of Robinson. According to D'Lugo, the film's appeal to see beyond the constraints of pre-programmed frameworks – representative, psychological and geographical – give the film a fundamental transnational character that makes it thoroughly contemporary. For her part,

Isabel Santaolalla, referring to theories of space and post-colonialism, as well as noting the pattern of subversive intertextuality, argues that the somewhat neglected *The Young One* is a key film in the development of Buñuel's interest in questions of domination and appropriation in racial and sexual relations.

The third section concentrates on late Buñuel, specifically three of his most emblematic films, *Belle de jour*, *La Voie lactée* and *Le Charme discret de la bourgeoisie*. Andrea Sabbadini's psychoanalytic approach, concentrating here on perversion in a film that has already attracted much critical commentary, is an appropriate contribution to a volume on an author who together with fellow surrealists felt attracted from the very beginning to a discipline that aimed to explore the mysterious poetry of the unconscious. In his chapter on *La Voie lactée*, Ian Christie considers reasons why it is perhaps the most neglected of the late films. *La Voie lactée* represents an important stage in Buñuel's filmography, not only because of its characteristic interest in religion, formal experiment and political engagement, but also because of the way polarised interpretations of the film help place in focus the radical and contradictory nature of Buñuel's art. Finally, in his survey of Buñuel's representation of women, Peter William Evans contends that Buñuel, although hardly a feminist *avant la lettre*, was nevertheless far more sensitive to the problems faced by women – as, for instance, obscure objects of desire, Oedipal dragons or domestic harridans – than he has often been given credit for. A general discussion of the portrayal of women is followed by a detailed analysis of the women in *Le Charme discret de la bourgeoisie*.

The volume concludes with some general questions concerning key aspects of form and content raised by Buñuel's films. Victor Fuentes approaches Buñuel's work from the perspective of recent exile and diaspora studies. He carefully traces the characteristic marks of the exilic condition in Buñuel's films, arguing that the experience of exile worked as a creative force that decisively informed his film-making both thematically and formally. Vicente Sánchez Biosca demonstrates, through a detailed analysis of the use of the cinematic potential of Catholic rituals in *Él*, that Buñuel's denunciation of religion evolved from a somewhat external attack on Catholicism – for example, in *L'Âge d'or* – to a more personal, sophisticated critique expressed, in later years, precisely *through* – and not simply *against* – religion's own ritualised symbolic universe. Laura M. Martins continues the examination of Buñuel's iconoclastic practice through discussion of *Los olvidados* and its recurrent use of strategies that undermine the spectator's certainties and expectations. Buñuel's use of a 'dialectic image', Martins argues, goes beyond a mere rhetorical exercise, and aims instead to expose how social and cultural structures are inevitably built on unequal relations of power.

In a volume such as this there will inevitably be many gaps and much room for argument. Notable omissions include sustained discussion of key films like *Un chien andalou*, the lesser-known but fascinating minor Mexican melodramas like *Subida al cielo* (1951), *El bruto* (1952), *Abismos de pasión* and *La ilusión viaja en tranvía* (1953), or, from the marvellous late period, *Cet obscur objet du désir*. Mindful of this unavoidable negligence, our intention has nevertheless been to produce a volume that includes detailed analysis of specific films, as well as more general commentary, together providing a forum of discussion for a director who remains one of the undisputed masters of world cinema.

References
Bazin, A. (1975), *Le Cinéma de la cruauté. De Buñuel à Hitchcock,* Paris: Flammarion.

Buñuel, L. (1982), *Mon dernier soupir*, Paris: Éditions Robert Laffont.

—— (2000), *An Unspeakable Betrayal: Selected Writings of Luis Buñuel*, Foreword by Jean-Claude Carrière; a new Afterword by Juan Luis Buñuel and Rafael Buñuel; translated by Garrett White, Berkeley and London: University of California Press.

Sánchez Vidal, A. (1993), *El mundo de Luis Buñuel*, Zaragoza: Caja de la Inmaculada.

Wood, M. (2000), *Belle de Jour*, London: BFI.

PART ONE

EARLY YEARS

I

Lost and Found: Buñuel, *L'Âge d'or* and Surrealism

Paul Hammond

Created with half an eye to getting them into the exclusive, explosive fraternity they craved, *Un chien andalou* (1929) achieved its aims and shortly after its premiere Luis Buñuel and Salvador Dalí were invited to join the Surrealist Group. The movement they now pertained to, and which further empowered them, was, however, no metaphysical category called 'Surrealism', but a concrete entity engaging with its own aspirations as tempered by the times. Those shifting aspirations were hinted at by the substitution of one magazine, *La Révolution surréaliste* (1924–9), by another, *Le Surréalisme au service de la Révolution* (*LSAS-DLR*, 1930–3), in other words, by the gradual displacement of a post-Dadaist ultra-leftism whose creative axis was automatic writing and painting, dream description, hypnotic trance, psychosexual truth-telling and urban drifting, by a liaison with official communism (in the shape of the French Communist Party, the PCF), coupled with a systematisation of earlier discoveries, a materialist investigation of desire and irrational knowledge, and a de-alienated reconfiguring of the object world. This shift on the part of the brittle surrealist movement from marginal irresponsibility to instrumental responsibility can be seen as a changing, 'superstructural' response to the volatile political and social tensions of the Europe of those times, the Europe of the Treaty of Versailles and the League of Nations, with, to the East, the threat (or summons, depending on where you stood) that the evolving Russian Revolution posed to the *status quo*. Not only does the generalised economic collapse triggered by the Wall Street Crash of October 1929 mark both the end of a tacit peace between waxing totalitarianisms and waning capitalisms, and a critical mid-point between one world war and the next; it also, and here we come back to Buñuel (and Dalí), separates the ambitions of one proto-surrealist film from those of a second, absolutely authentic one: *L'Âge d'or* (1930).

Buñuel's first public outing as a bona fide surrealist is with his eyes shut in the famous Mark II group portrait *Je ne vois pas la … cachée dans la forêt*, published in the twelfth and final number of *La Révolution surréaliste* (15 December

1929). This montage – the three dots signify the self-effacing female nude in the Magritte oil the sixteen all-male, photo-booth 'sleepers' surround – is intercalated among replies to the enquiry 'What kind of hope do you place in love?' Buñuel's response is no more exalted (and parrot-like) than other surrealist testimonies – and probably equally at odds with real, individual 'love life'. His answer to one question, 'Do you believe in the victory of sublime love over sordid life, or of sordid life over sublime love?' possesses the ring of truth, however: 'I don't know,' he said (Surrealist Group, 1929, p. 71). The same issue also featured the scenario of *Un chien andalou*, the film thus being claimed by the movement as its own.

More importantly, this terminal *Révolution surréaliste* kicked off with Breton's 'Second Manifesto', the polemical text that marks the final end of the manic, millennial phase, limns in the whys and wherefores of the purging of the ranks – the Georges Bataille faction being the prime target – and announces the new 'politically correct' orientation of the movement. Prior to the manifesto being published in book form in June 1930, Buñuel was one of the signatories in March of a tract, 'Second Insert for the "Second Manifesto of Surrealism"'. Essentially a declaration of faith in Breton's trajectory, the text argues for supplementing the social critique of Marx and Engels, 'preserved by the world proletariat from the ravages of time', with a symbolic recuperation of individual psychic energies that draws on psychoanalysis and spontaneous creativity (Surrealist Group, 1930a). The vicissitudes of this ideological caduceus – Surrealism's maximum programme, and the key to its specificity – would define four years of fitful collaboration with the increasingly Stalinised and puritanical PCF. Of common accord as to strategy, but in disagreement over tactics, the PCF and the Surrealist Group had embarked on an inevitable collision course, the reef being the party's suspicion of heretical high modernism in general, and of Freudian depth psychology in particular. Serving the revolution, then, could only be achieved by the Surrealist Group kow-towing to the party apparatus and emasculating itself. After much worrying at the issue of proletarian realism among the Left, the adoption of socialist realism as the official communist aesthetic in 1934 was completely at odds with the surrealist project. A year later this dialogue of the deaf was broken off for all time, with Breton *et al.* allying themselves with, and making the front running in, the anti-Stalinist opposition, from the Souvariniens and the Socialist Left to, finally, the Trotskyists.

Turning the clock back to 1930: by the time the Surrealist Group divulged their telegram to the Moscow International Union of Revolutionary Writers (the UIER), putting themselves, 'should imperialism declare war on the Soviets', at the orders of the Third International (and as if they were members of the PCF), Buñuel had shot and cut *L'Âge d'or*, shown it to his patrons, Marie-Laure and

Charles de Noailles, and left Paris for a month's holiday in Spain – indeed, stills from the film appeared in the same issue of *LSASDLR* as the headlining telegram (Surrealist Group, 1930b, p. 1). We know that *L'Âge d'or* was a work of *bricolage*; that it grew segmentally from a twenty-minute short, a sort of sound remake of *Un chien andalou*, into a heterogeneous hour-long feature. (There are even a few lines of dialogue 'left over' from *Un chien* and used in its companion piece.) Aside from the febrile imagination of Buñuel – and of Dalí, who bombarded the director with ideas – assistant directors Jacques Brunius and Claude Heymann, hired for their experience of nascent sound cinema, helped the director compose his *découpage*. Among the players there were two who had made their own independent shorts: Gaston Modot and Pierre Prévert. Who knows what these and other collaborators – young and questing novices, in the main – may have offered the ductile Buñuel by way of ideas? Which begs the question: did the Surrealist Group proper put in its pennyworth, have its say? Éluard certainly warbled on the soundtrack, while Ernst snarled as a bandit (one day he would claim his 1930 collage novel *Rêve d'une petite fille qui voulut entrer au Carmel* partly inspired the film). Are we to imagine that Buñuel and Dalí hearkened to the

Amour fou in *L'Age d'or*

counsel of their comrades, and that they followed a preordained brief, that the Surrealist Group vetted the script, even? (Interestingly, Dalí would work on a didactic scenario between 1930 and 1932 about Surrealism and the unconscious, to have been made in collaboration with the group [Ades, 1982, pp. 198–91].) Is there a literal truth embedded in Buñuel's remark that *L'Âge d'or* is 'a clear, resolute film, without mystery. Zilch. Very Surrealist, of course, but there's no mystery to it. My ideas are clearly visible. Not mine, the ideas of the Surrealist Group are perfectly visible' (Aub, 1985, p. 134)?

Whatever the truth of the matter, the Surrealist Group themselves, sensing that the release of the film would be a major coup in publicity terms, presented their notions of its content in a tract prepared for the 28 November 1930 launch. Appearing in the Studio 28 souvenir programme, this broadside, 'L'Âge d'or', is a dense, often hermetic, Freudo-Marxist position paper that possesses little of the scatty brio of the movie, but does have the virtue of giving us an insight into how the Surrealist Group saw the film, and how they wished other people, especially the pro-communist intelligentsia, prone to dialectical subtleties, to see it (Surrealist Group, 1930c). A collage of thematic segments, the tract may be sum-marised thus: any artist (or film-maker) is the locus of instinctual conflict between the sex and the death drive, both of which are instincts of preservation. It is the artist's duty to critically consider the sublimation of these drives, which affirm themselves as 'amorous egoism' and 'passivity' respectively. If we wish to go beyond mere self-preservation and to reinvent the world, the baleful equilibrium of the instincts has to be upset by privileging one antithetical pulsion over the other. Given its frenzied violence and revolutionary dynamism, amorous egoism (or mad love, as it would later be called) is best suited to achieving this. The immense system of myths subtending society must be destroyed, and although these myths – the Golden Age, for instance – may penetrate as deep as the uncon-scious, it is the provident lawlessness of unconscious mentation that, rendered as language, can accomplish this destruction. New myths are needed, moral alle-gories that blend conscious and unconscious expression. Buttressed only by the clergy and the police, contemporary capitalist society is disintegrating, and the anti-clericalism and call to revolt of *L'Âge d'or* is an 'indispensable moral comple-ment to the stock-market scare' (Surrealist Group 1930c, p. 169). Buñuel's film takes its place in the surrealist movie pantheon, alongside Mack Sennett, Clair and Picabia's *Entr'acte* (1924), W. S. Van Dyke's *White Shadows of the South Seas* (1928), early Chaplin, *Battleship Potemkin* (1925) and, of course, *Un chien* itself.

The hoped-for attention was not long in coming, six days in fact: the fascist riot of 3 December, plus the ensuing moral panic and the intervention of Police Prefect Chiappe and the Board of Censors saw to that. Although the film would be more or less buried for fifty years, the Surrealist Group had achieved its immediate aims – to be bloodied in the class war, and to prove its revolutionary worth to the PCF. The latter was no stranger to Chiappe, of course: at the slightest hint of social strife, this rabid anti-communist would round up the militants – 4,000 were taken into preventative custody before the 1929 May Day Parade – and imprison the Party's leading lights (Cachin, Marty, Duclos and Vaillant-Couturier) for months at a time. Where cinema is concerned, Chiappe had ordered the closure, in October 1928, of 'Les Amis de Spartacus', a worker-oriented cineclub created fifteen months earlier by Paul Vaillant-Couturier, Léon Moussinac, Jean Lods, Francis Jourdain and Georges Marrane – all PCFers – after tumultuous showings of Eisenstein and Pudovkin. And Eisenstein in person had fared no better in Paris in February 1930 when, although the director was allowed to lecture, Chiappe had prohibited the projection of his new film *The General Line* (1929).

With the banning of Buñuel's masterwork the Surrealist Group moved into action once again, publishing a further tract in early January 1931, 'L'Affaire de "L'Âge d'or"', which neatly encapsulates the ideological, and hands-on, warfare being waged between the French Left and Right (Surrealist Group, 1931a). Laid out in the double-column format of *LSASDLR*, the six-page polemic consists of four sides of text – an 'Exposition of the facts', 'Programme extracts', and a 'Questionnaire' in the main column, with 'Press extracts' running alongside – and two of captioned photographs. Since the facts are now the stuff of history and the programme extracts are drawn from the 'L'Âge d'or' broadside, I will concentrate on the press coverage, the questionnaire and the photos.

Taking the last first: eight photos, four to a side, provide the visual argument. On one page, a brace of stills from *L'Âge d'or*, the bishops squatting their islet outcrop, 'restores' the two images excised from the film on 5 December by order of Paul Ginisty of the Board of Censors. The live bishops are captioned with a quote from early Marx: 'The criticism of heaven is transformed into the criticism of earth, the criticism of religion into the criticism of law, and the criticism of theology into the criticism of politics' (Surrealist Group, 1931a, p. 113). The post-mortem bishops are accompanied by a citation from the French Romantic poet Maurice de Guérin: 'There is no sweeter spectacle than the death throes of a priest.' Below, a still of the diminutive governor (Llorens Artigas) and his towering wife (Mme Hugo) is insidiously paired with a press photo of Victor Emmanuel III and his spouse. The former bears the legend: 'Apparently, this image from the film caused a protest to be made to the French Government by the Italian Ambassador, who feigned to recognise his sovereigns in it.' The latter: 'Their Italian Majesties, who have revolutionary workers killed – such as they are in sad reality.' The verso has two photos of the 3 December trashing of Studio 28. Among the debris of smashed furniture and picture frames one

recognises a pair of battered Tanguy oils, a slashed Dalí and a shredded pho-
tomontage of the Surrealist Group, accompanied by a quote from a protest
letter to Chiappe written by the Provost de Launay, city councillor for the
Champs-Élysées area: 'We who have decided to react against the by now systematic poisoning of French society and its young people are ever more
numerous.' A detail of the ink-stained Studio 28 screen is captioned: 'Christian
illiteracy'. Below it are both the pristine and lacerated states of Dalí's puzzle-
picture, *Invisible Sleeping Woman, Horse, Lion, etc.* (1930).

The press extracts are ideologically grouped, and open with plaudits from the
liberal papers. Writing in *Le Quotidien*, Lucie Derain likens *L'Âge d'or* to a
despair-filled manifesto or pamphlet, while a *L'Oeuvre* journalist remarks that
the film's repression bears comparison with that of Eisenstein's *The General Line*
and *Battleship Potemkin*. The centre-stage column inches are five snippets from
the PCF daily, *L'Humanité*. Moussinac, the paper's film and radio critic, and
author of *Le Cinéma soviétique* (1928), repeats the Buñuel/Dalí line about their
chagrin at *Un chien andalou*'s recuperation by Parisian 'snobs and aesthetes', but
cautions that this time round the sound of the audience gnashing its teeth will
reveal that the film-makers have attained their goal. The day after the revoca-
tion of the film's visa, *L'Humanité* wrote: 'Faced with such a crackdown, the
workers, too, must impose their "censorship" by preventing the showing of
nationalist rubbish and newsreels – weapons in the moral preparation of impe-
rialist war' (12 December 1930). The remaining extracts, some 50 per cent of
the total, come from the centre- and extreme-right press: *Le Figaro, Echo de
Paris, Journal des Débats, L'Ami du Peuple, Le Petit Oranais, L'Oeil de Paris*. As
this choice material is often quoted in the Buñuel literature, a résumé will suffice here, one moving – in accordance with the order of presentation – from
aesthetic outrage to vigilante xenophobia. *L'Âge d'or* is excoriated for its lack of
artistic merit, its poor workmanship, its motiveless and meandering scenario.
The film uses an old-hat avant-gardisme to display images that are pretentious,
deliberately off-putting, dreary, confused, stupid, low, repugnant, sacrilegious,
pornographic, anti-family and fatherland and revolutionary. It is the work of
imbecilic anarchists, foreign disciples of Lenin, *métèques* (wogs) who have
exploited their recently acquired French nationality to get the film shown in a
Judeo-Bolshevik cinema. The direct action of Christian patriots and anti-
Semites, coupled with the firm hand of police and censor, must rid the land of
such purulent, contaminating propaganda.

By insistently playing on the word *or* (gold) and *ordure* (lewdness/filth/shit)
the fascists demonstrated that they had involuntarily got the drift of the movie.
Indeed, their critiques demonstrated greater perspicuity than those of the communist press as to its content. For *L'Âge d'or* is a diatribe against a perennial

French fascism the roots of which can be traced back to the French Revolution, but which really took wing during the second and third decade of the Third Republic, in the guise of *revanchisme* against Germany for the defeat of 1871. Of the groups mentioned in 'L'Affaire de "L'Âge d'or"', the Ligue des Patriotes, founded by Paul Déroulède, went back to 1882 and the Boulanger crisis, and the Ligue Antisémite, the brainchild of Maurice de Guérin, to 1897 and the Dreyfus Affair. (This explains why the Surrealist Group quoted the *other* Maurice de Guérin.) With the formation of Charles Maurras' Action Française in 1899 the pre-1914 synthesis of pernicious 'isms' was in place: anti-republicanism, royalism, ultra-Catholicism, anti-parliamentarianism, patriotism, militarism and anti-Semitism, plus certain Socialist features (National Socialism, as per the teachings of Maurice Barrès). The fascist leagues proliferated after 1918 and, inspired by Mussolini's *squadrista* and peopled by ex-servicemen, became increasingly paramilitary and anti-communist. Two such were Pierre Taittinger's Jeunesses Patriotes (1924), which attracted many university students, and Colonel de la Roque's Croix de Feu (1927), with its rank-and-file made up of war veterans. Mussolini financed some of the French leagues, thus strengthening the Rome–Paris axis, an axis central to the narrative of *L'Âge d'or*.

Although the trigger for the 3 December fascist manifestation was the sequence of the ostensory taken from the limousine – perhaps owing to its juxtaposition with a shapely leg sheathed in 'Anitta' nylons – *L'Âge d'or* is replete with anti-fascist imagery: the blind man Modot boots is a war veteran; the note taped to the French windows of St Peter's is a gag about the Lateran Treaties of 1929 between the Pope and Mussolini; being Majorcan is a synecdoche for Italo-Spanish *Realpolitik*; the marble bust Modot drops in his final erotic delirium looks like the Duce, and so on (Hammond, 1997a).

The questionnaire included in 'L'Affaire de "L'Âge d'or"' is revealing of the group's adherence to the politics of the Comintern (the Third International, that is). After protesting the banning of the film by the police and their sanctioning of fascist anti-Semitism – and proposing retaliation against religious imagery in the shape of 'Catholic propaganda films, pilgrimages to Lourdes and Lisieux, centres of obscurantism like *Bonne Presse*, the Committee of the Index, churches, etc., the perversion of youth in church clubs and military training, radio sermons, shops selling crucifixes, Virgins, crowns of thorns' – the question is begged:

> Since this intervention is made under the pretext of protecting children, adolescents, the family, fatherland and religion, may it be momentarily assumed that the goal of this obvious fascisation is to destroy everything that tends to oppose the coming war? And especially the war against the USSR?
>
> Surrealist Group, 1931a, p. 116

The final sentence is the clincher. Taken together with the telegram to the UIER, it bespeaks the Surrealist Group's adherence to the Comintern's 'Third Period' line, which determined the mental horizon of most Western communists and fellow travellers between 1928 and 1934. An echo of the anti-religious campaign being waged in the USSR (as part of the dekulakisation campaign) subtended some of it, but its overriding thrust was the proscription of any united front with the Social Democrats, or 'Social-Fascists', as the catechism had it. The schizoid 'Third Period' strategy is now read as Stalin's attempt to *forestall* revolution in the West, since exacerbating the disintegration of the Depression-hit capitalisms might have unleashed an attack on a Soviet Union which was still pushing through its crash industrialisation (and weapons) programme, the Five Year Plan. In the case of the Surrealist Group, the virulent 'class against class' rhetoric requited their own extremism, but in terms of the instrumental clout of the PCF this Comintern diktat was disastrous.

The prelude and aftermath of *L'Âge d'or* can be read, then, as the paroxystic figuration, or symptom, of a polarisation that would determine the political landscape prior to World War II, and following the end of the Locarno era of *détente* (1925–30): the struggle between paired totalitarianisms, Stalinism and fascism. Returning to the two Surrealist Group tracts, one name is conspicuous by its absence: Luis Buñuel's. This is understandable in the first declaration since it is a homage to him, and in the case of the second we could argue for physical distance preventing his signing: from 28 October 1930 to 1 April 1931 the director was out of the country, mainly in Hollywood, time-serving at MGM. One who did put his name to both polemics, co-scriptwriter Dalí, would subsequently upbraid him, however, for not helping fight 'their' corner after the 3 December events. And Buñuel's distance from events didn't stop him trying to prevent Jean Mauclaire, the owner of Studio 28, from fighting against the banning of the film (this was done in the name of curtailing the distress suffered by the Noailles). While Surrealism was tantamount to a religious conversion for Buñuel, and while he gave the movement its cinematic jewel in the crown, creating a *sui generis* masterwork into the bargain, one gets the impression that, unlike Dalí, he was not one of the pacemakers in the group. After the scandal of *L'Âge d'or* – an impossible act to follow – and the deception of Hollywood, Buñuel spent three depressed years casting around for a viable project (and for paid work; he was on the breadline). His poetic writing remained a private affair, and the only contribution he made to a Surrealist Group magazine was 'Une girafe' in the final issue of *LSASDLR* (Buñuel, 1933). Neither does his name appear on any of the group's tracts, although he may have been one of the ten unnamed 'foreign comrades' who signed 'Au feu!' (their names are absent through fear of police reprisals, given their status as immigrants) (Surrealist Group, 1931b).

This violently anti-clerical squib was the Surrealist Group's response to the wave of church and convent burnings in Spain one month after the founding of the Second Republic. Penned by Louis Aragon and very 'Third Period' in tone, the squib pulled no punches:

> The quaking bourgeoisie [of the Republican-Socialist coalition government] will maintain the clergy on their lands because the partition of ecclesiastical property can only be the signal for a secular partition … They won't be able to separate Church and State. Only the terrorism of the masses can effect this separation.
>
> Surrealist Group, 1931b, p. 197.

And who but an atheist son of Zaragoza could have contributed this aside: 'May the Temple of the Pilar, where for centuries a virgin has served to exploit millions of people, be razed to the ground!' (Surrealist Group, 1931b, p. 196). (I would argue that this *anti*-Republican spirit coloured Buñuel's attitude towards Spain until the Comintern volte-face of 1934 and the making of common cause with the socialists). As to the day-to-day business of the Surrealist Group, sightings of Buñuel are rare, in part due to his extended stays in the United States and Spain. We know that he was present at Tristan Tzara's on 6 October 1931, when Breton read a first draft of *Les Vases communicants*, his gritty synthesis of Freud, Lenin and Hegel. The meeting also focused on the dispiriting fact that the first two numbers of *LSASDLR* had sold only 350 copies apiece. Things took an unexpected turn when, donning his 'proletarian' cap, Breton stated that he for one was capable of vulgarising his writing in order to reach a mass audience, even if it meant abandoning Surrealism. The session ended in turmoil, with Aragon proposing that a future discussion be devoted to 'dialectical materialism and its most far-reaching consequences'. Aragon, Breton, Éluard, Giacometti, Malet, Sadoul, Thirion and Tzara put their hand to this; Buñuel too (Thirion, 1972, pp. 323–4).

In early May 1932 the 'director of consciousness' (as his comrades dubbed him) quit the Surrealist Group. Truth to tell, his three-year sojourn in the movement was tensed between two crises: the scissions of late 1929 announced in the 'Second Manifesto' and the defections of spring 1932 occasioned by the 'Aragon Affair'. Or rather two moments in the same crisis: in 1929 the nucleus around Breton had ejected those who resisted the Leninist (read Stalinist) clarion call; in 1932 Breton *et al.* were marginalised by the communists for not being Leninist enough. Perhaps the *L'Âge d'or* image of Modot's hand casting feathers into the void in an endless ritual of self-purging, of Sisyphean self-abuse, could serve as a metaphor for this whole traumatic period …

The unfolding of the 'Aragon Affair' has been recounted often enough. In short, Aragon's role within Surrealism had become increasingly ambiguous ever since his appearance at the UIER Congress in Kharkov in November 1930. (Buñuel was invited to make the trip with Aragon, Elsa Triolet and Sadoul, but cried off, pleading poor health) (Bouhours and Schoeller, 1993, p. 78). There, pressurised by his Stalinist hosts, Aragon signed a document along with the future film historian denouncing the 'counterrevolutionary' ideas of Trotsky, Freud and Breton. Restored to Paris, and faced with the ire of the Surrealist Group, he and Sadoul recanted. In spring 1931 the two of them joined the PCF, along with Pierre Unik and Maxime Alexandre (for the second time in Aragon and Unik's case, since they had briefly been members in 1927, as had Breton, Éluard and Péret). It is probable that Buñuel became a member of the Spanish Communist Party, the PCE, at this time (Gubern and Hammond, 2001). In November the French police seized a magazine containing the poem 'Front rouge', Aragon's histrionic and doctrinaire paean to Stalin. In January 1932 he was indicted for 'demoralisation of the army and the nation'. A group tract in his defence, 'L'Affaire Aragon' (Pierre, 1980, pp. 204–5), was immediately issued, followed by another, more mitigated one six weeks later, written by Breton alone: 'Misère de la poésie. "L'Affaire Aragon" devant l'opinion publique' (ibid., pp. 208–22). While the first had, like the broadsides related to *L'Âge d'or*, attacked the proto-fascist justice of the bourgeois state, the second targeted PCF anti-modernist philistinism as well. Aragon departed the Surrealist Group the moment he denounced the 'Misère' tract in the 10 March edition of *L'Humanité*. Sadoul had already resigned on 7 March. Alexandre and Unik would exit the group a month later. And on 6 May Buñuel sent his letter of resignation to Breton. Henceforth Sadoul, Unik and Buñuel would walk in the shadow of the hyperactive and supine Aragon.

In this missive the director tells his erstwhile mentor that the very fact of becoming a member of the Surrealist Group led him to joining the PCE (given the frenetic Bolshevism of the movement after 1929 his argument is not without its logic). Only with the breaking of the 'Aragon Affair' has the incompatibility between group and party been brought home to him. Now, the mutual suspicion and irreducible will-to-power of the two has obliged him to choose. In aesthetic terms, while Buñuel admires Breton's 'closed' conception of poetry, as demonstrated in 'L'Union libre', he prefers the transparency of 'Front rouge', a poem that is 'less pure, which can be used as propaganda and which succeeds in directly touching the masses' (Thirard, 2000, p. 65; Herrera Navarro, 2000, p. 7). Buñuel's election of the proletarian- and then socialist-realist road would inflect – I repeat, inflect – his cultural activity during the 1930s and after. (I'm thinking of *Tierra sin pan* [1933], *Espagne 1937* [1937], *Los olvidados* [1950], *El bruto* [1952], *Robinson Crusoe* [1952], *El río y la muerte* [1954], *Nazarín* [1958], *Viridiana* [1961], *El ángel exterminador* [1962] and *Le*

Journal d'une femme de chambre [1964], plus those films that have always dis-comfited the critics: *Cela s'appelle l'aurore* [1955], *La Mort en ce jardin* [1956] and *La Fièvre monte à El Pao* [1959].) In any event, the socialist variety is one more realism at work in his oeuvre, along with 'super-realism' and the Spanish naturalist/grotesque tradition.

The 1930s, the decade of Buñuel's tryst with Stalinism, are still awaiting close study (Hammond, 1999). We need more detailed accounts of his bowdlerising of *L'Âge d'or*, of his defence of Soviet films of the Choumiatski era and his hopes of working as a director in the USSR, of his role in the Bolshevisation of Spanish intellectuals after 1933, the tracts he signed, the fronts he belonged to and the congresses he attended, and his *contienda* activities in the Spanish embassy in Paris – the city was home to Willi Münzenberg's Comintern media operation after Hitler's seizure of power – including espionage work.

Going back to 1932: the rift between the Breton and the Aragon camp under-mined the Surrealist Group's wish to participate in the Association of Revolutionary Writers and Artists (AEAR), the French (and later Spanish) off-shoot of the UIER in Moscow, launched in Paris in March 1932, and in which Aragon had a predominant role. A case in point: although Breton was invited to edit the AEAR's journal, *Commune*, the job went to the zealous Aragon. In July 1933 the increasingly ostracised Surrealist Group broke definitively with the association, the immediate cause being their harsh critique of recent Soviet cinema, in the shape of Nikolai Ekk's *Road to Life* (1931). Composed sometime between December 1931 and April 1932 (Hammond, 1997b), Buñuel's sur-realist text 'Une girafe', which appeared in the final issue of *LSASDLR* in May 1933, coincides with an ephemeral mending of bridges between the Surrealist Group and the AEAR prior to this final break (Buñuel, 1933). (Twinned with his appearance in *La Révolution surréaliste*, this textual swan-song neatly brack-ets an entire epoch.) Buñuel belonged to the AEAR's cinema section, and it is arguable that *Tierra sin pan* is an 'AEAR film'. With the Popular Front shift towards the *defence*, in the face of mounting fascism, of bourgeois culture on the part of the PCF/PCE and their mushrooming front organisations, the chasm between Surrealism and Stalinism grew ever wider. The nefarious activities of the Comintern during the Spanish Civil War were, along with the Moscow Trials, an object of fierce surrealist criticism.

Breton would never cease vaunting *L'Âge d'or* as the acme of surrealist cinema, and petitioned its director for a print in December 1934, a screening of the banned film being the precondition for his and Péret's invitation from the *Gaceta de Arte* surrealists to visit Tenerife in May 1935. In the book begun there, *L'Amour fou* (1937), Breton lauded the movie but lamented the rumour that Buñuel had produced an expurgated, worker-friendly version. It would seem that the surrealists saw neither *Tierra sin pan* nor *Espagne 1937* in Paris in 1937. Presenting *Un chien* in Mexico City in May 1938, during the trip on which he co-authored his famous manifesto with Trotsky, Breton alluded to Buñuel's Communist Party activities (Breton, 1938), and when *Los olvidados* put the director back on the map he repeated the charge within a generally positive memoir – a revamped interview – of Buñuel's brief Surrealist Group 'passage' (Breton, 1951). (The Surrealist Group linchpin refused to countenance the news, proffered by his journalist interlocutor, that Buñuel had recently boasted of carousing with Trotsky's assassin in his Mexican jail cell.) In *Entretiens* (1952) Breton would say that while

> *Los olvidados* marks a formal rupture with the oneirism of *Un chien andalou* and of *L'Âge d'or*, a film such as this, compared to the other two, demonstrates Buñuel's identity of spirit, something which is, *whether one wishes it or not*, a constituent part of Surrealism.
>
> (my italics) Breton, 1952, p. 207

Whenever Buñuel passed through Paris in later years, Breton would be peeved that as well as visiting him the director looked up Aragon.

Buñuel's kudos for Surrealism, post-1945, had its highs and its lows. In 1952 Benjamin Péret enthused about *Los olvidados* and his other films up to *Subida al cielo* (1951), while the young surrealist cinephiles of the magazine *L'Âge du cinéma* (five numbers in 1951) lionised the Mexican director, with two of their number, Robert Benayoun and especially Ado Kyrou, becoming his unswerving champions in the pages of *Positif*. Other members of the movement, however, were chary of the 'born-again Surrealism' of Buñuel's last six films, made after Breton's death in 1966. And the final cinematic controversy during the latter's lifetime – is this film 'surrealist' or not? – involved, not *Viridiana* (1961) but *L'Année dernière à Marienbad* (1961).

Surrealism's sinuous sublations over half a century frequently got the best out of those who were drawn to the movement, but it also consumed them, drove them away, and what they subsequently achieved was an extramural 'sort of' Surrealism adulterated by alien influences. In this essay I have argued for the historical specificity of *L'Âge d'or* as a work redolent with the intramural contradictions of the movement which spawned it, and as the figuration of more pervasive political and aesthetic tensions that would be worked through during the ensuing decade. Given its repression, *L'Âge d'or* proved to be a shock to Buñuel's system, a truly mortifying experience, and thus an inducement to seeking another path, one consonant with his commitment to an ideological apparatus 'objectively' – as the Stalinists were wont to say – at the service of the counterrevolution. Like all repressed material, however, *L'Âge d'or* would return time and again in the director's oeuvre, albeit in transmogrified form, as a compromise between the ideas which are repressed and those doing the repressing.

References

Ades, D. (1982), *Dalí*, London: Thames & Hudson.

Aub, M. (ed.) (1985), *Conversaciones con Buñuel. Seguidas de 45 entrevistas con familiares, amigos y colaboradores del cineasta aragonés*, Madrid: Aguilar.

Bouhours, J.-M. and N. Schoeller (eds) (1993), *L'Âge d'or. Correspondance Luis Buñuel – Charles de Noailles. Lettres et documents (1929–1976)*, Paris: Les Cahiers du Musée National d'Art Moderne. Hors-série/Archives.

Breton, A. (1938), 'Présentation de "Un chien andalou"', in A. Breton (1992), *Oeuvres complètes II*, Paris: Gallimard/Bibliothèque de la Pléiade, pp. 1263–7.

—— (1951), 'Sur "Los olvidados"', in A. Breton (1999), *Oeuvres complètes III*, Paris: Gallimard/Bibliothèque de la Pléiade, pp. 1124–30.

—— (1952), *Entretiens 1913–1952*, Paris: Gallimard.

Buñuel, L. (1933), 'Une girafe', *Le Surréalisme au service de la Révolution*, 6, pp. 34–6.

Gubern, R. and P. Hammond (2001), 'Buñuel: De "L'Union libre" au "Front rouge"', *Positif*, 482, pp. 63–7.

Hammond, P. (1997a), *L'Âge d'or*, London: BFI.

—— (1997b), 'Giraffa Camelopardalis Camelopardalis', in L. Buñuel, *Una jirafa*, Zaragoza: Libros Pórtico, pp. 7–12.

—— (1999), 'Hacia el paraíso de los peligros/To the Paradise of Pitfalls', in M. Ibarz (ed.), *Tierra sin pan. Luis Buñuel y los nuevos caminos de la vanguardia*, Valencia: IVAM/Centre Julio González, pp. 81–95, 211–17.

—— (ed.) (2000), *The Shadow and Its Shadow: Surrealist Writings on the Cinema*, third edition, San Francisco: City Lights Books.

Herrera Navarro, J. (ed.) (2000), 'Me adhiero al PCE, dejo el surrealismo', *El Cultural*, 13 February, pp. 6–7.

L'Humanité (1930), 12 December, in Surrealist Group 1931a, p. 112.

Pierre, J. (ed.) (1980), *Tracts surréalistes et déclarations collectives 1922–1939*, Paris: Le Terrain vague.

Surrealist Group (1929), 'Enquête', *La Révolution surréaliste*, 12, pp. 64–76.

—— (1930a), 'Seconde prière d'insérer du "Second Manifeste du Surréalisme"', in J. Pierre (ed.) (1980), pp. 151–2. The signatories are Maxime Alexandre, Louis Aragon, Luis Buñuel, René Char, René Crevel, Salvador Dalí, Paul Éluard, Max Ernst, Georges Malkine, Benjamin Péret, Georges Sadoul, Yves Tanguy, André Thirion, Pierre Unik and Albert Valentin.

—— (1930b), 'Question et réponse', *Le Surréalisme au service de la Révolution*, 1, p. 1. Although unsigned, the telegram was written by Breton and Aragon.

—— (1930c), 'L'Âge d'or', in J. Pierre (ed.) (1980), pp. 155–69. Translated in
    P. Hammond (ed.) (2000), pp. 182–9. The signatories are Alexandre, Aragon,
    Breton, Char, Crevel, Dalí, Éluard, Péret, Sadoul, Thirion, Tristan Tzara, Unik
    and Valentin.

—— (1931a), 'L'Affaire de "L'Âge d'or"', in J.-M. Bouhours and N. Schoeller (eds)
    (1993), pp. 111–16. The signatories are Alexandre, Aragon, Breton, Char, Crevel,
    Dalí, Éluard, Malkine, Péret, Man Ray, Sadoul, Tanguy, Thirion, Tzara, Unik and
    Valentin.

—— (1931b), 'Au feu!', in J. Pierre (ed.) (1980), pp. 196–7. The signatories are
    Alexandre, Aragon, Breton, Char, Crevel, Éluard, Malkine, Péret, Sadoul, Tanguy,
    Thirion and Unik.

Thirard, P. L. (2000), 'Colloque à Pordenone', *Positif*, 471, pp. 64–5.

Thirion, A. (1972), *Révolutionnaires sans Révolution*, Paris: Robert Laffont.

2

A Serious Experiment: *Land Without Bread*, 1933

Mercè Ibarz

Introduction

Buñuel's third film *Land Without Bread* (1933 and not, as commonly thought, 1932) may be regarded as one of the most important experiments of all his work and a decisive one in documentary cinema at the beginning of the sound era, as well as in documentary film development as a whole.

The film has been radically altered since its first release. A major change was the addition of a pro-Republican epilogue in both the French and English versions at the end of 1936, something that, while not affecting its intensity, nevertheless gave it an extra dimension. The effects of censorship in 1936–7 had more serious consequences. The changes made to the footage have been restored in the new French and English versions, but the alterations to the soundtrack remain a major problem.

Briefly, the story of the film's treatment is this: both the English and French versions underwent censorship. Because of protests from the area of Upper Savoy (France), indicated in the map at the beginning as an area containing other European 'Hurdes', the map disappeared in both versions. So too did the scene of the marriage rituals in La Alberca. Although they remain in some copies, these absences profoundly alter the film.

During the war the negatives were lost in France. In the 1960s, the film distributor Braunberger advised Buñuel to resurrect the film, as the censored scenes had been recovered. But it would mean a new soundtrack, as a complete version of the original was unavailable. A new version was made in 1965, which is when the new voice-over was added. On this occasion, one supposes that Buñuel agreed. But since 1995–6 new versions have appeared that completely nullify Buñuel's original intentions. The oratorical tone of the voice-over is even more compassionate and at some points the Brahms music has been omitted.

Few copies remain that retain the film's essential identity: the visual–aural counterpoint. If the film fails to shock today it is because in the copies currently available, at least in Spain, the narrator's voice assumes the fraudulent tone of compassion, something that characterises neither the French version of 1936 (for which actor Abel Jacquin stepped into the role), nor the English version of 1937 that reproduces the American newsreel tone of *The March of Time.*

As far as the film's title is concerned it is safe to say that in all drafts, both Spanish and French, stored in the Buñuel Archive (Filmoteca Española, Madrid), the film is entitled *Tierra sin pan*, and this is how it was released in both English and French, *Las Hurdes* being a title only used, informally, by Buñuel himself.

My discussion here focuses on the following characteristics of the film:

- As a surrealist documentary that explores the relationship between cinema and history's radical changes. It carries out this experiment through a multi-layered and unnerving use of sound, the juxtaposition of narrative forms already learnt from the written press, travelogues and new pedagogic methods, as well as through a subversive use of photographed and filmed documents understood as a basis for contemporary propaganda for the masses. It is at a revolutionary moment and with a revolutionary crew that Buñuel films in Las Hurdes, a place already exploited at the time by still photography and the press.
- Its specific lessons in sound and documentary *mise en scène*. These are experiments that situate *Land Without Bread* as one of the key texts of film and television history. If the event doesn't happen naturally, it must be provoked. Besides, the film warns us, the spoken word can be more powerful than visual imagery. Acknowledging the film's experimental use of sound and its treatment of the death of the goat, many later films have gestured to *Land Without Bread*'s dual nature as conscious revelation (*cinéma du réel*) and subconscious icon (propagandistic image).

Pedagogy in sound

Through an introductory written text the film proclaims its nature as a 'cinematic essay in human geography' at the beginning of the 1930s. A map of Europe points out other 'Hurdes' on the continent, and then draws the viewer's attention to the location of las Hurdes on the Iberian Peninsula, very near to Salamanca, the home of Spain's first university.[1] A shot of a village street initiates the story. We are in La Alberca. The commentator speaks in the first person plural, in the name of the film's crew who, through La Alberca, will enter the valley of Las Batuecas, a place with strong echoes of prehistoric culture and long submission to the Catholic Church. Through this valley we will arrive at Las Hurdes.

But before this we pause at La Alberca and visit a local *fiesta* with strong feudal and sexual overtones. Men who have married that year must compete with one another on horseback to cut off the heads of as many roosters as marriages that have taken place. The live roosters are hung upside down. Each rider must cut a rooster's neck and may not give up until he has done so. La Alberca's main street is decorated, and the participants, mainly males, take part with glee and much wine. The riders are dressed in traditional costume and the camera dwells time and again on their attacks on the roosters' necks and heads, while a woman observes the proceedings with a wild look in her eyes.

From the onset we hear Brahms's Fourth Symphony and the voice-over speaks with a register similar to that of cinematic newsreels of the time: indifferently, frivolously and at a rapid pace. The spectator is witness to a relentless array of images and sounds: the dense commentary, read at an exhausting pace in a cold and distant voice, is underlined by the austere and 'cultured' music of Brahms while the images appear in short, sharp shots at an equally frantic pace. It is a device used throughout the film, a work devoid of even a moment's silence.

In the valley of Las Batuecas, the second stop on the journey, our attention is continually drawn to the presence of Catholic architecture in the territory's convents and churches. Only one monk remains: an elliptical allusion to the limitations on the church's property that were imposed, not by the Republic, but by earlier liberal governments in the nineteenth century. From here we enter Las Hurdes through a wide shot of the mountains that will again be used to close the film.[2] We are guided by the suffocating visual–sound composition to one of its villages, where narrative detachment is overcome by despair. First we focus on the school, 'a white, recently constructed building'. Later on we move into the streets, where children and adults resemble the living dead. From here the film guides us through the core activities of human experience: food, work, education and the rituals that mark our collective culture in hunger, sickness and death. It lingers on the school, types of work and death rituals. An old woman's prayer for the dead, set against a panoramic shot of the mountains of Las Hurdes, closes the film. The voice-over brusquely bids farewell in the name of the crew. The End.

The death of the goat

Some of the film's incidents – such as those concerning different types of work, the collective rituals of death and the presence of animals in everyday life – parallel autobiographical stories from Buñuel's childhood in Calanda, referred to in the first chapter of his memoirs (1982a).[3]

Here a goat acts as the metaphor and as the leitmotif of the film's strategy of communication. The story highlights the impossible living conditions in Las Hurdes. Even goats throw themselves off mountaintops. The camera follows a goat that (as we see later in a discussion of the cut footage) was savagely pursued by the crew. Buñuel ended up by shooting the goat himself, which falls from a position where we can see the smoke from his revolver in the middle right-hand side of the screen – a decision that reflects Buñuel's radical style in *mise en scène* composition.

The visual evidence of the goat's death and the overall decisions concerning the visual–sound montage make *Land Without Bread* a film that is always viewed in the present, a strategy that allows it to make its direct impact upon the spectator while retaining its historic value. It is as if everything it wants to abolish continues just the same, even now and, if not in present-day Las Hurdes, in other parts of the world. In his lecture at Columbia University (Ibarz, 1999b, p. 235) Buñuel referred to this condition as 'relentless pain'.

A mythic story

Land Without Bread is shaped by press photography of Las Hurdes published in 1922, by press articles published in 1929 (Arcelu and Benítez-Casaux, 1987) by scholarly research (Legendre, 1927), and by travelogues, newsreels and avant-garde cinema. Its power derives from its documentary nature as much as from the timelessness of Flaherty, the political agendas of Ivens or Storck and above all the poetic and erotic drives of Vigo.

This film's construction is extremely elaborate and obvious, and is related to popular narrative forms, particularly oral folk tales, that maintain tension through exaggeration, contradiction and reiteration, to arrive at a story that can be termed 'mythic'. It has similarities with Flaherty's first films and his 'out of time' camera that narrates the past more than the present.

It is an oral work about a people who keep no written record of their history, whose songs, although composed, are not heard. Buñuel altered the sociological aspect and one could say that he made the film *a tiros* (with a gun), to use an expression that an old woman made to the poet, journalist and co-writer of the commentary, Pierre Unik. Someone, she said, should get them out of Las Hurdes *a tiros*. 'À coups de pistolet', wrote Unik in his articles for *Vu* in 1935.[4]

These gunshots (in the scenes of the goat and donkey) are physical as well as metaphorical. Today, seeing is no longer believing, a truism Buñuel anticipated in the 1930s.

The place of words

The voice is dominant in the narrative, often contradicting the images, as in the case of the sick young girl in the street, or the baby in the house. Shots and themes are linked together at great speed: the voice-over nearly always speaks with neutrality, but sometimes with annoyance or astonishment. It concludes a scene abruptly, with indifference, and then continues.

The importance of this radical use of sound has been stressed in critical commentary, above all, in relation to the Brahms music, but it is worth emphasising again. The surrealists' use of imagery and text, in the interests of creating shock, as may be seen, for instance, in the paintings of Ernst or Magritte, has its magnified reflection in Buñuel's film. Sometimes what the narrator says fails to correspond to what the images portray; at other times, we credit what he says, not what we see, in the same way that a photo caption dictates how we read a visual image.

Neither the sick girl nor the baby is dead: the narrator tells us they are but the images contradict him. The deliberate ambiguity of the documentary pact with the spectator is here exposed, relying on communicative strategies that would subsequently become common practice in publicity, propaganda and television. In this sense, *Land Without Bread* is a forerunner.

If in the scene of the death of the goat Buñuel did not dispense with the shot that shows smoke coming from the gun that killed the animal, thus drawing attention to the ambiguity of documentary, similarly, with the voice-over, he underlines the pitfalls in the use of sound. It is the answer to the challenge Buñuel faced after his first two films. In deciding to shoot a documentary, Buñuel's guiding principle was not to look for 'exotic' places that would be unknown to the spectator. He did not set out on a search for the Other/Different, as did the makers of travelogues or documentaries in the style of *Nanook* (1922). Buñuel went in search of the Other/Same.

But not the Other/Same of the kind sought in two other key documentary themes of the time: the cities of Vertov, Ruttmann or Vigo, or the labour of the working classes of Ivens, Grierson or Strand. He went in search of an Other/Same excluded from progress, the images of which were already engraved in the spectator's minds thanks to photography and other mass media, and by the historic visit to Las Hurdes by King Alfonso XIII in 1922 and its subsequent impact on the media (Ibarz, 1999a, pp. 33–9). Here lies the originality of the project.

He filmed from within the very heart of the countryside – from the viewpoint of his own childhood in Calanda – in order to achieve the sort of image Walter Benjamin demanded in his analysis of the surrealist image: an image that can no longer be 'measured contemplatively' (Benjamin, 1980, p. 53), and instead becomes a moral metaphor and a new type of political action.

The place of memory

We are in the spring of 1933, a few weeks after the electoral victory of Hitler and when the Liberal-Socialist Spanish Republic was living its most insurrectionary moment. The anarchists of the CNT (National Workers' Confederation) were being imprisoned, stripped of their rights of association. Among them is Ramón Acín, the producer, who after the filming is accused of subversion for his participation in numerous political and cultural activities. The socialists confront a government that in part represents them and that at the same time, incited by the anarchists, pushes them to radical revolution. It is a time of great social upheaval that in the months ahead leads to the formation of a fascist movement that becomes the Spanish Falange.

But luck was on Buñuel's side, in the form of a lottery won by Ramón Acín in December 1932. Thanks to this stroke of luck Buñuel saw an opportunity to make the film and assembled a remarkable crew appropriate for these historic times.

As well as Acín, he called up as assistant director Rafael Sánchez Ventura, another Spanish anarchist who was no stranger to Spanish cultural and political controversies. Both Sánchez and Acín formed part of the Surrealist Group of Zaragoza (Aranda, 1981, p. 126). Buñuel added two more members of the Parisian movement: the camera operator Eli Lotar and the photographer Pierre Unik.

The choice of crew, as surprising as everything else about this film, prefigures the film's future course of events. In life, as in the cinema. Before, during and after filming, and on into the present. Avant-garde movements express trauma (White, 1996, p. 32) and, one might add, often seem capable of mixing the causes of illness and cure. Today Las Hurdes owes much to the lasting effects of Buñuel's film, to the point where it may even now be seen (a view that would not displease Grierson) as a revolutionary film that has left its mark on that land and its people. Also unforgettable was the co-operation between members of the crew, whose inevitably different attitudes and opinions would divide them during the war and subsequent dictatorship.

Acín came up with the 20,000 pesetas necessary to launch the project. He had his own reasons. He was starting out in film-making, having already put on magic lantern shows, and written a script for a surrealist film that never went into production (Ibarz, 1999a, pp. 50–60). A known anarchist and Bohemian, he was assassinated in Huesca, Northern Spain, in early August 1936, and could thus be plausibly considered the 'García Lorca of Aragón' (Torres Planells, 1998, pp. 35–41). He was most at home in the fine arts, deeply interested in popular culture and visual anthropology and attracted to Las Hurdes because of its representation of Spain at its most difficult and extreme. He went there with two intentions: to prepare the film, and to introduce Freinet methodology into some of its schools.[5]

The school is the only specific attack on the Republic that remained in the film (heavily altered by Buñuel between 1933 and 1936), an attack that was prompted by the view of both Buñuel and Acín that the Republican school curriculum was wholly inappropriate. This is implicit upon arrival at Las Hurdes ('the white building, *of recent construction*, is the school,' says the voice-over [my

A child without bread in *Las Hurdes*

emphasis]) and explicit in the classroom scene. At that time the Republic did keep one of its political promises: the building of schools and the reform of teacher training.[6]

The children enter and go to their desks. The voice-over comments: 'Here hungry children are taught the same as children everywhere, that the sum of three angles of a triangle equals the sum of two right angles.' Naturally! Why wouldn't they be taught this basic fact? It's only normal. Maybe it is, says the film, but in Las Hurdes this kind of education has no place or purpose. Here, as Freinet would say, they need to learn about themselves and their way of life. The film also shows the astonished faces of two children when one of them writes on the blackboard a rule from a book shown to them by their teacher: 'Respect other people's property.' But everything in Las Hurdes – the incessant commentary tells us – belongs to somebody else. The beehives are the property of another village, employment opportunities, food, hygiene and health may be found in other parts of Spain, but here, only the land is theirs – because nobody else wants to cultivate it.

The film focuses on the subversive pedagogic restlessness of the time and thus sheds new light on Buñuel's cinema. It is an aspect that has been largely overlooked in studies of his films. It has not gone unnoticed by Godard, though, whose works *Histoire(s) du cinéma* (1998) and *Origine du siècle xxi* (2000) include a brief overview of the first sequence of *Land Without Bread*, where two young girls in close-up remain silent and with a wild and questioning look.

The place of propaganda

The film's history mirrors that of the Second Spanish Republic. When it was ready for release, the Republic had already fallen into the hands of the anti-Republican right that banned it. At the end of 1934, Buñuel decided in the text of the commentary (Buñuel, n.d., p. 5) to date the film 1932. It was not released until late 1936 in Paris and early 1937 in Rotterdam, London and a couple of cities in Belgium, hitting the cinema club circuit and then later becoming popular on the back of a general surge of interest in social documentaries. It was previewed with an epilogue in favour of the Republic.

Land Without Bread became a propaganda film for the Spanish Republic, one that nevertheless deconstructs the very mechanisms of propaganda. It is narrated in the first person plural. It is a work that does not avoid acknowledging that its main subject is its crew. It says so again and again. The use of sound, as already argued by Ado Kyrou (1962, pp. 62–8), creates a strong sense of unease in the viewer.[7] His observations on the use of sound need to be emphasised: words are denser than images, and dangerous when launched onto the masses, as is all too clear nowadays in television. We believe what they tell us. This is – precisely in the year 1933 – the key mechanism of audiovisual propaganda, from Goebbels to Roosevelt and Franco.

In its international relations from the end of 1936, the Spanish Republic eliminated all references to anarchism. It is not known whether or not Buñuel was too concerned about including in his film the epilogue in favour of the Republic. The fact is that he agreed to the epilogue and removed Ramón Acín's name from the credits.[8] It is highly plausible that he knew the epilogue would barely alter the uncompromising nature of the film, something recognised over and over again, whether by students, documentary historians or museums.

Subversion of information codes

Although later on some of its original points of reference changed through Buñuel's own political evolution and the censorship the film suffered, Surrealism and a sense of libertarian communism make *Land Without Bread* an aesthetic artefact that rises to some of the challenges of the time: the agrarian reforms of the Spanish Republic, Hitler's Europe, the political and cinematic demands of the avant-garde across Europe, the new wave of cinematic activism, and the long and arduous economic crisis of the 1930s.

After the difficulties of his first two films, he was finally able to shoot again. Much of the film's credit goes to the crew. Without the talents of Acín and

Sánchez Ventura and their sensitive treatment of their under-privileged subjects the film would not exist. Nor would it without the talent of cameraman Eli Lotar (once criticised for being the photographer of unpleasant subjects), who had tried unsuccessfully a year earlier to film in Las Hurdes with Yves Allégret. Lotar brought the same qualities he deployed in Joris Ivens's film *Zuyderzee* (1929). The poet Unik was Buñuel's link with the Parisian surrealists, and Lotar had contacts on the European avant-garde film circuit.

But despite the politically committed nature of the crew – that mixture of anarchist-surrealists and surrealist-communists – *Land Without Bread* operates under its own surrealist and libertarian cinematic order.

The visual–sound composition of the film is in effect a way of complicating the informative political codes of a budding society of mass communication that was promoted as much by the graphic press as by cinematic newsreels. Buñuel obeyed the strong sense of pedagogic duty of the avant-garde movement, and injected a dose of political will power.

The tone is similar to *Un chien andalou* (1929) and *L'Âge d'or* (1930). The first of Buñuel's collaborations with Dalí confronts the viewer with the repressive ideological framework of the individual bourgeois unconscious, and affronts the collective unconscious of the dominant classes. These films have already been commented on from an anthropological viewpoint. In *Land Without Bread*, without Dalí, Buñuel goes one step further and develops a formula (a landmark in documentary film-making) that above all challenges the social unconscious: that which binds people together in a hostile land. Like its predecessors, particularly *L'Âge d'or*, it is conceived as a commentary on and provocation to its generic equivalents: the 'urban symphony', newsreels, travelogues, scientific films and the ethnographic ideas of the Parisian surrealists.

It is interesting to note that while Buñuel was in Las Hurdes confronting the collective, Dalí was pushing on with his exasperating criticism of the surrealist crisis in Paris, which culminated in his naming it 'the surrealism of Hitler' in 1934 (Éluard, 1984, p. 198). Buñuel kept a close watch on Dalí and the transformation of the Parisian surrealists, as he did on the spread of fascism in Europe and the alternatives the Left proposed in confronting the advance of Stalinism. But his attention was focused mainly on Spain. Buñuel's militancy in the emergent Communist Party in 1932 has not been fully demonstrated. If he had been a committed communist at this time, the choice, for *Land Without Bread*, of a mixed anarchist-communist crew would only show that there were no sectarian prejudices on the part of Buñuel or the members of the crew. Buñuel had total control over the film. The script and the editing were his work. The commentary, although written by Unik with a substantial input of ideas by Acín, is very different from the pieces Unik did for *Vu*. In these, Unik was concerned with a Marxist analysis of the social inequalities between the people of Las Hurdes, while the film's commentary presents them not in Marxist terms but as a social collective. Unik and Lotar were communists and Acín and Sánchez Ventura were libertarians, but their militancy and differences did not prevent them from working together. Thus, *Land Without Bread* is a touching, intimate experience of what history tends to bury: collective co-operation. In the words of Godard (1995, p. 69) the film is a 'moving experience in the interior of history'.

Change of date and commentary

Buñuel's decision to change the date of the film to 1932, even though he shot and edited it in 1933, requires commentary.[9] Dating it 1932 ensured that the film became a sharp critique of the liberal-socialist Republic, which governed from April 1931 to November 1933, when the anti-Republican Right won the elections and the film was banned. It should be emphasised that this ban took place in the pre-fascist phase of the Republic. But the change of date enabled Buñuel to leave it up to the spectator to reach conclusions about the historical sequence.

Between 1933 and 1936 Buñuel experienced one of his most acute political crises. *Land Without Bread* is the testimony. Between 1934 and 1936, when together with Unik he wrote the French commentary (probably to read it to André Gide to whom they would also show the film in Paris in 1936), he changed the text several times, reducing its most specific references. The changes made the work more abstract, and finally, gave it a timeless quality. This has contributed to its stasis and durability, its modern Goyaesque character.

The soundtrack could have been added when Buñuel joined Filmófono, one of the first production companies to use sound in 1934, but it was not until the spring of 1936, when the Popular Front won the elections, that there was some campaigning for the film's release. It was shown only once, at the Cine-Studio Imagen in Madrid. In any case, at the end of 1936, when the film premiered in Paris, Buñuel was in a different political frame of mind to that of 1932–3 when the film was made.

Perhaps because of this Buñuel – towards the end of his life – made his most personal statement about the film, a work from which he had always distanced himself: 'Nothing is gratuitous in *Las Hurdes*. It is perhaps the least gratuitous work I have made' (Pérez Turrent and de la Colina, 1993, p. 37).

About the unused footage

The unused footage is of notable interest and has been insufficiently studied. It is stored in the Cinémathèque de Toulouse, where it was deposited by Marcel

Oms after being found by Buñuel's family in the early 1960s. It runs for thirty-seven minutes and offers valuable insight into the aims of *Land Without Bread*.

The people of Las Hurdes were directed at every given moment, posing in front of Lotar's camera in a way that repeatedly confirms the co-operative spirit of the film. Used to the camera's gaze – having been photographed since the beginning of the century – they willingly agreed to work with Buñuel and his crew. Lotar also filmed some beautiful panoramic shots of the intricate Hurdean landscape, with its trees moving in the wind, images that, had Buñuel decided not to omit them, would have given his harsh portrait of the area a certain vitality.

The sense of the collective in the film (the school, the agricultural workers, the child's funeral) was aimed at highlighting the very lack of the collective life in question. When the inhabitants look at one another, the shot is cut and they are left as individuals, in front of the camera, looking at the spectator.

The camera lingers on two occasions: the death of the goat and the ritual of the cocks in La Alberca. In the case of the goat, the unused footage lasts more than four minutes. Here one observes Buñuel (with a revolver) and the assistant director Sánchez Ventura inciting the goats to jump off the side of the cliff until the gun finally makes one of them do so.

The smoke from the fired gun that Buñuel finally decided to leave in one of the shots acts as a central metaphor for this mythic tale about revolution: the filmed violence is a metaphor for real violence, for political violence. This is, after all, a film made *a tiros* (at gunpoint). It is as if Buñuel wanted to leave the remark made by the old woman – possibly the same one that closes the film with her prayer for the dead – as an appeal to the Hurdeans to leave their homes in search of a better life.

The unused footage in La Alberca lasts more than six minutes. In this sequence, the inhabitants do not pose in front of the camera; instead, Lotar films them following the *fiesta*. In the final editing process, however, Buñuel eliminates the collective to concentrate on the symbolism of the marriage ritual and its unmistakably erotic-social overtones. Lotar's first shots of the phallic-like neck of the cock – strung up and feather-less, until severed by a hand – do not appear in the final cut and are testimony to the radicalism with which Buñuel came to *Las Hurdes*. It is radicalism in the service of Surrealism, an essential combination as outlined in the pages of *Documents* (1929–30) by Bataille and Leiris. Buñuel softened it in this visual montage, opting instead for radicalism in sound.

The film in Spain

Tierra sin pan was one of those films that repeatedly made the rounds of the cinema club circuits during the Spanish dictatorship (Gubern, 1999, pp. 9–11).

These were anti-Franco cinema venues where the Republican epilogue failed to cause a stir. It was not known that it had been added during the war and nobody seriously questioned why the Republic had prohibited it. It seemed to form part of the film and did not detract from its radicalism. And although later discussions alluded to the final rays of hope that Franco's victory extinguished, at the end of the film everyone was so perturbed by what they had seen that attention was rarely paid to the epilogue.

Never released commercially in Spain, the film belongs in specialist cinemas, television and museums. But it is also in some ways, in his own country, Buñuel's most 'jinxed' film. Revolutionary and reformative, the Hurdean symphony that Buñuel composed when his counterparts were making documentaries about urban spaces, the working class or the exotic, continues to disturb.[10]

Cavalcanti, Buñuel, Rouch

The key influences on *Land Without Bread* begin at the transition from silent to sound cinema. Many film-makers – from Lubitsch to Hitchcock – transported their experiments in sound and image from Europe to Hollywood. In exile, they managed to popularise the accomplishments of the avant-garde from the old continent. Others, like Alberto Cavalcanti, following his relocation to London, applied their experiments to documentary film-making. Bill Nichols (1991; 2001) has analysed the oratory, poetry and rhetoric of documentaries in the 1920s and 30s. Somewhat sternly, he rebuked an ageing John Grierson for his 'repression' of the 'spirit of constructivism of the avant-garde' (Nichols, 2001, p. 90) that films like *Land Without Bread* represent. But delving even further than Nichols's discussion of sound experimentation, we see similarities between Buñuel, Cavalcanti and the British school.

In 1926 Cavalcanti filmed *Rien que les heures* in Paris, a film much admired and commented on by Buñuel (1927). His book of press clippings, now in the Buñuel Archive, in Madrid, contains some of Cavalcanti's articles. Buñuel closely followed the work of this Brazilian who had emigrated to Europe. In London, together with John Grierson, Cavalcanti later laid the foundation for modern documentary sound that, in the state-run studios of the GPO, would acquire a MacLuhanian tone, even though the Grierson school is characterised by experimentation more than by dynamism. In 1933, the year Buñuel shot and edited *Land Without Bread* using a preconceived soundtrack as a base, Cavalcanti was advocating the same in London. In this they coincided.

Buñuel never made another documentary. However, following his Hurdean experience, the documentary mode remained a feature of subsequent work, deeply influenced throughout by the visual and aural experiments of *Land Without Bread* as well as by those of his previous two films. Like Cavalcanti, he continued to work towards allowing for the release of the voices of the ordinary citizen, poetry, music – and even the State. Sonority, then, becomes a powerful link between reality and its documentary representation, a link that Rouch would also later exploit.

After everything that had happened in Europe and Japan, Jean Rouch followed Buñuel's and Cavalcanti's examples in his African films, most notably *Moi, un noir* (1958). Cameras still had not been synchronised, but Rouch had already decided to make a film *with* his main characters, not *about* them, which is why he says in the prologue 'je leur passe la parole'. Just as Buñuel had killed the goat, so Rouch provoked situations in the film (1995). He too rose to the challenge of sound. The monologues and dialogues could only be put together in the editing room, dubbed over the image. The characters' spoken words were reactions to the sight of their own images on screen. This is a fundamental lesson in sound, inspired by the Soviets and developed by Buñuel and a Grierson-influenced Cavalcanti. Today this is a key element of the representation of reality. When it fails, it sharply exposes the mechanisms of modern propaganda. Much of the continuing impact of *Land Without Bread* is owed to this, as may be seen in its creative effects on the political documentary, most notably in contemporary Latin America.

I would like to conclude with a reflection on Buñuel's relationship to *Land Without Bread*. It is probably the film where he exercised greatest control. All key decisions were his. He wrote the script, the commentary (his input was greater than Unik's), and carried out the sound and image editing process, aided by the Republican Spanish ambassador in Paris at the studios of Pierre Braunberger (whom he had previously helped out with a camera and some metres of film). He went into exile with a copy of the film. It opened the doors to the Museum of Modern Art (MOMA) for him and gained him esteem in the eyes of Flaherty, who was inspired by it to shoot *The Land* (1942), another banned film.

Buñuel lived through the changes in the film, including the Republican epilogue. He wrote and rewrote the commentary according to the moment and his political persuasions between 1933 and 1936. He accepted the fact that a new soundtrack had to be made in 1965 (when he was again filming in Spain) and kept the unused material. There is really nothing gratuitous in *Land Without Bread*; it was adapted time and time again for specific reasons, but still retained what mattered most: the articulation of the compelling reasons why people become trapped by the things they love, as well as a testimony to the barbarity that lives side by side with the camera.

Translated by Suzanne Wales

Notes

1. From the very beginning, Miguel de Unamuno is one of the most implicit references of the film. He had already reported on his travels through Hurdean lands in 1913 in Madrid's press. The articles were collected in book form in 1922, coinciding with the trip made by King Alfonso XIII to Las Hurdes (Unamuno, 1988). Unamuno was then perhaps the most significant personality of Spain's political regeneration. He had greatly contributed as a sounding board for republican ideas that finally became a political reality in 1931. *Land Without Bread* would carry out its Hurdean voyage in reverse order to Unamuno's. The film starts where Unamuno ended his journey, in La Alberca, and ends in the mountains of Las Hurdes, its poorest area, where Unamuno never went (Ibarz, 1999a, pp. 22–6).

2. This frame is exactly the same as the photo from the beginning of the twentieth century by Maurice Legendre (1927, appendix) to whom Buñuel always expressed his gratitude.

3. The relationship is even more evident in the preceding text of this first chapter, titled *Recuerdos medievales del Alto Aragón* published first in 1976 (Buñuel, 1982b, pp. 237–44).

4. Pierre Unik published two reports on *Las Hurdes*, not in *Vogue*, as Buñuel stated in his memoirs, but in *Vu*. His text, with photographs by Eli Lotar, was not published until 1935, in the January and March issues (Unik, 1935). They were published in a shortened version, according to a letter that Unik wrote to Buñuel a few weeks later, that is now stored in the Filmoteca in Madrid. Some of the pages of the Unik–Lotar reportage can be consulted in Ibarz (1999a, pp. 75–81).

5. Three villages in lower Las Hurdes were having a Freinetian experience. The children made the books: *Vida hurdana. Lo que escriben los niños.* The books are preserved at the Néstor Almendros' Archive, at the Fundació Soler i Godes at the Universitat Jaume I in Castelló (Spain). Some of the images can be seen in Ibarz (1999b, p. 113).

6. Criticism was also aimed at the forced 'Pedagogic Missions' of the Republic, that brought theatre, books, photography and even cinema to the most remote places.

7. In his critique of 1937, Basil Wright (1971, p. 146) doubted that the music and sound montage was Buñuel's work.

8. Buñuel always tried to make amends for Ramón Acín's absence in the credits. He is the only one he continually cites in every single text or interview that refers to the film and its crew, the conference at the University of Columbia already mentioned being an example. In the 1960s, when he returned to Spain to film *Viridiana,* he paid Acín's daughters various sums for the film's rights.

9. The date of the film has been established from documents found in *L'Âge d'or* (1993).

10. Both the epilogue and the international premiere of the film during the war had a

great influence on the area, especially with regard to the reforestation projects and other changes that Franco imposed on las Hurdes in 1940. From then on, although it has adversely marked its history, the people of las Hurdes have benefited from the film, in the form of numerous reforms and privileges that they have received from European and Spanish governments both then and now.

References

Aranda, J. F. (1970), *Luis Buñuel. Biografía crítica*, Barcelona: Lumen.

—— (1981), *El surrealismo español*, Barcelona: Lumen.

Arcelu, J. I. and Benítez-Casaux (1987 [1929]), 'Una semana en Las Hurdes', *Estampa de Castilla y León*, Salamanca: Diputación de Salamanca (edition of *Estampa*, Madrid, 20 August–10 September 1929), pp. 39–50.

Benjamin, W. (1980 [1929]), 'Surrealismo, la última instantánea de la inteligencia europea', *Imaginación y sociedad. Iluminaciones I* (notes and translation by Jesús Aguirre), Madrid: Taurus, p. 53.

Buñuel, L. (1927), 'Una noche en el Studio des Ursulines', *La Gaceta Literaria*, 2, 15 January, p. 6.

—— *Documents* (1929–30), 1991 (facsimile edition by J. M. Place), Paris: Bibliothèque du Musée de l'Homme.

—— (n/d), *Tierra sin pan*, (typewritten script), Buñuel Archive, Filmoteca Española, Madrid.

—— and P. Unik (1934), 'Terre sans pain', (typewritten script), Buñuel Archive, Filmoteca Española, Madrid.

—— (1982a), *Mi último suspiro*, Barcelona: Plaza y Janés.

—— (1982b), *Obra literaria* (introduction and notes by Agustín Sánchez Vidal), Zaragoza: Ediciones del Heraldo de Aragón.

Éluard, P. (1984), *Lettres à Gala*, edited by Pierre Dreyfus, Paris: Gallimard.

Godard, J. L. (1995), 'JLG/JLG', *Archipiélago*, 22, p. 69.

—— (1998), *Histoire(s) du cinéma*, Paris: Gallimard.

—— (2000), *Origine du siècle xxi*, Canal +.

Gubern, R. (1999), 'Tan cerca, tan lejos', in M. Ibarz, 1999a, pp. 9–11.

Ibarz, M. (1999a), *Buñuel documental. Tierra sin pan y su tiempo*, Zaragoza: Prensas Universitarias de Zaragoza.

—— (ed.) (1999b) Tierra sin pan. *Buñuel y los nuevos caminos de las vanguardias* (exhibition catalogue), Valencia: Instituto Valenciano de Arte Moderno.

Kyrou, A. (1962), *Luis Buñuel*, Paris: Seghers.

L'Âge d'or. Correspondance Luis Buñuel–Charles de Noailles. Lettres et documents, 1929–1976 (1993), Paris: Centre Georges Pompidou.

Legendre, M. (1927), *Les Jurdes. Étude de geographie humaine*, Bordeaux and Paris: École des Hautes Études Hispaniques.

Nichols, B. (1991), 'Strike and the Genealogy of Documentary', *Blurred Boundaries*, Bloomington: Indiana University Press, pp. 107–16.

—— (2001), 'Documentary Film and Modernism, 1919–1939', *Critical Inquiry*, 27 (4), pp. 580–610.

Pérez Turrent, T. and J. de la Colina (1993), *Buñuel por Buñuel*, Madrid: Plot.

Rouch, J. (1995 [1975]), 'El hombre y la cámara', in E. Ardévol and L. Pérez Tolón (eds), *Imagen y cultura. Perspectivas del cine etnográfico*, Granada: Diputación Provincial, pp. 95–122.

Torres Planells, S. (1998), *Ramón Acín. Una estética anarquista y de vanguardia*, Barcelona: Virus.

Unamuno, M. (1988 [1922]), 'Viaje a Las Hurdes', *Visiones y andanzas españolas* (foreword by Luciano G. Egido), Madrid: Alianza Editorial, pp. 142–60.

Unik, P. (1935), 'Chez le Sultan des Hurdès', *Vu*, 362 (January), pp. 218–20, and *Vu*, 364 (March), pp. 291–3.

Vida hurdana. Lo que escriben los niños (1933), Vilafranca del Penedès: Ediciones de la Imprenta en la Escuela.

White, H. (1996), 'The Modernist Event', in Vivian Sobchack (ed.), *The Persistence of History: Cinema, Television and the Modern Event*, New York: Routledge, pp. 29–42.

Wright, B. (1971 [1937]), 'Land Without Bread', in L. Jacobs (ed.), *The Documentary Tradition. From Nanook to Woodstock*, New York: Hopkinson & Blake, pp. 146–7.

3

The Decisive Moments of Buñuel's Time in the United States: 1938–40. An Analysis of Previously Unpublished Letters

Javier Herrera Navarro

For Luis Buñuel, as for so many Spaniards, the fateful date of 18 July 1936 marked a clear dividing line in his biography. In his personal life, for example, Buñuel went from being the potentially wealthy owner of the convent Las Batuecas[1] (which he had used just three years earlier as his centre of operations for filming *Tierra sin pan/Land Without Bread* [1933]) and property holder[2] to living a nomadic life. Often hard pressed to survive, Buñuel sometimes had to depend on loans from friends and relations to support his wife and children. The sharp contrast between two such different ways of life and the unwelcome necessity of facing up to adversity would, from this moment on, affect his professional trajectory and, consequently, his filmography. These little-known years of his life lasted exactly one decade, from 1936 to 1946, the time from the moment he left Spain for the embassy in Paris to his arrival in Mexico. There he would be able to rebuild his life slowly and to develop his art. Until now, what little was known of this obscure period came primarily from his own testimony. Thus, the recent discovery of a series of letters which Buñuel exchanged during those years with his friend Ricardo Urgoiti, a fellow exile in the Americas (Herrera Navarro, 2001–2), whose papers were donated to the Filmoteca Española by his heirs in 2001, is of extreme importance. These letters allow us to verify or refute information from previously known sources as well as learn new facts about the eight years he spent in the United States.

Within the limits of an enforced exile, one can describe the early years of Buñuel's time spent in the Spanish embassy in Paris as relatively quiet and secure. From an artistic point of view, he was able to stay in contact with the cinema even though he was also busy producing propaganda, working in intelligence and spying. Also, the 'montage' documentaries he made about the events of the Spanish Civil War to some extent continued the kind of work he had started with *Land Without Bread*. Nevertheless, this would no longer be the case after 20 September 1938, when Buñuel was on board the *Britannic*, headed for New York.

> Here I am headed for America with my distinguished wife and lovely child. I am going officially, although in an honorary capacity as I'm paying my own way, or rather a few friends I borrowed money from are paying.[3] I'm going to Hollywood in the hope of possibly finding work on films they are making there about Spain. I have enough to live on for four months and to get a car. If I haven't made any money by then I'll end up on the other side of the world with no way back, since I've already used up all my credit with friends. From now until then, the world might come to an end.[4]

These remarks are important because they reveal both Buñuel's intelligence and his hidden strategies at a moment when he had to face very serious problems. 'I am going officially, although in an honorary capacity', is an obvious contradiction in terms that sounds like a pretext or excuse for running away from a continent preparing for war. Although the motive of the trip ('finding work on films they are making there about Spain') sounds reasonable, other sources offer contradictory information concerning the initiative behind the trip. While *Mi último suspiro*[5] suggests that it was the Spanish ambassador Pascua's idea, Max Aub's version claims that it was Buñuel's.[6] This latter possibility seems even more plausible if we consider the advice that Buñuel gives Urgoiti in the letter's next paragraph. He tells him not to leave his exile in Buenos Aires under any circumstances:

> Just before leaving I gave a dinner for friends. Gremillon was there and he told me he'd received a letter from you which by the way had bad news. Really? According to them, you're discouraged and ready to return to Europe. Don't do it, not under any circumstances. You can't imagine how much confusion and rot there is there. You must have some news of it over there in the papers. Such baseness, such cowardice, such infamy have now taken over! They believe that they're keeping the war at bay when all they're doing is losing any advantage and paving the way for it to be yet more awful.

Thus we have here a confirmation of the danger which hung over Europe and of Buñuel's extraordinary sense (those 'premonitions' which Aub constantly refers to in his work), which was already sounding an alarm, of impending danger. The impression that he is running away from the scene of war is confirmed in an earlier letter in which he writes:

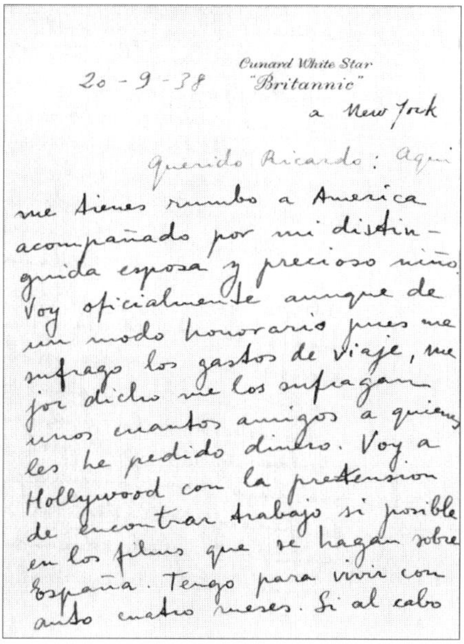
Cunard White Star
"Britannic"
20 - 9 - 38
a New York

Querido Ricardo: Aquí me tienes rumbo a America acompañado por mi distinguida esposa y precioso niño. Voy oficialmente aunque de un modo honorario pues me sufrago los gastos de viaje, mejor dicho me los sufragan unos cuantos amigos a quienes les he pedido dinero. Voy a Hollywood con la pretensión de encontrar trabajo si posible en los films que se hagan sobre España. Tengo para vivir con ahorro cuatro meses. Si al cabo

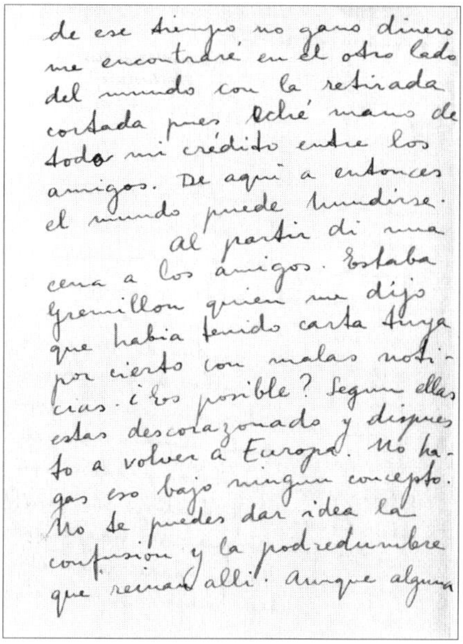
de ese tiempo no gano dinero me encontraré en el otro lado del mundo con la retirada cortada pues eché mano de todo mi crédito entre los amigos. De aquí a entonces el mundo puede hundirse.

Al partir di una cena a los amigos. Estaba Gremillon quien me dijo que habia tenido carta tuya por cierto con malas noticias. ¿Es posible? Segun ellas estas descorazonado y dispuesto a volver a Europa. No hagas eso bajo ningun concepto. No te puedes dar idea la confusión y la podredumbre que reina allí. Aunque alguna

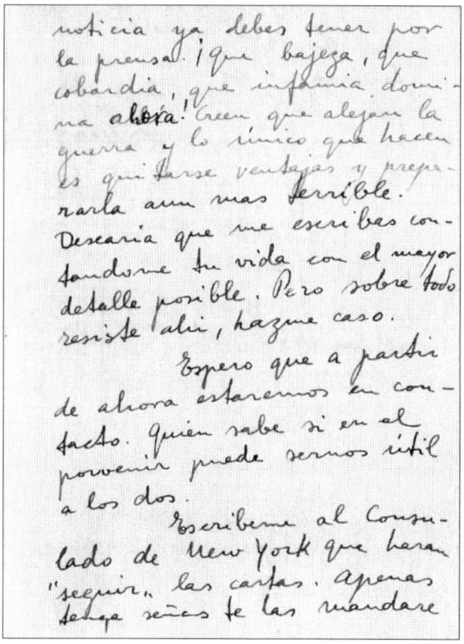
noticia ya debes tener por la prensa. ¡Que bajeza, que cobardia, que infamia domina ahora! Creen que alejan la guerra y lo único que hacen es quitarse ventajas y prepararla aun mas terrible. Desearia que me escribas contandome tu vida con el mayor detalle posible. Pero sobre todo resiste allí, hazme caso.

Espero que a partir de ahora estaremos en contacto. Quien sabe si en el porvenir puede sernos util a los dos.

Escribeme al Consulado de New York que harán "seguir" las cartas. Apenas tenga señas te las mandaré

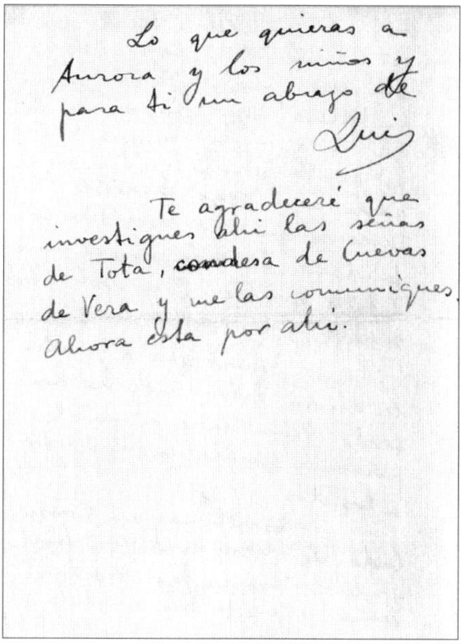
Lo que quieras a Aurora y los niños y para ti un abrazo de

Luis

Te agradeceré que investigues allí las señas de Tota, condesa de Cuevas de Vera y me las comuniques. Ahora está por allí.

Letter from Buñuel to Ricardo Urgoiti, 20 September 1938

From a personal point of view, things were going badly and *it's possible my draft year will be called up soon.* If that's to be the case, I want to leave a few matters settled, among them our official or commercial affairs, since our friendship will remain the same. You must understand that in saying this I'm thinking of my wife and son. Two things could happen: your affairs could go badly and in that case so much the worse for us all, or, as I hope and desire, they could go well for you. Therefore I want to leave it very clear and agreed upon what amount or percentage I, or my family, would receive from your films which are already in circulation.

Buñuel to Urgoiti, 11 August 1938, p. 1, my emphasis

The facts appear incontrovertible: on 11 August he says to Urgoiti that his draft year will be called up, and little over one month later he is on board a ship to New York. (Significantly, his friend writes back to him, 'I see that you're still a fast decision maker,' which suggests that this kind of reaction was typical of him [Urgoiti to Buñuel, 14 December 1938, p. 1].) Other published evidence also confirms this reading of the event.[7] Thus we can clearly see that in case he was called into service, he intended to be as far away as possible to make returning difficult. At the same time, he headed for a safe place (Paris and Europe no longer were) where he had real opportunities to get by working at something he knew how to do.

On the other hand, as one can deduce from the '*Britannic*' letter, it is also clear that Buñuel is beginning to make use of all potentially helpful contacts. As he reveals to Urgoiti, his hope is, 'that we'll stay in touch from now on. Who knows whether in the future we might be useful to one another' (Buñuel to Urgoiti, *Britannic*, 20 September 1938, p. 1). At the same time Buñuel asks him to look up Tota, the countess of Cuevas de Vera, who was also in Buenos Aires. She had been René Crevel's last 'lover'.[8]

It seems, then, that Buñuel foresees that the solution to his problems might lie in going back to collaborating with his friend the businessman. Nevertheless, despite appearances to the contrary, owing to his flair for giving them an eso-teric appearance, Buñuel's forebodings were always based on reality. In this case, they are based on one of Urgoiti's suggestions found in an earlier letter written from Mexico in which he tells Buñuel: 'Let's see if you could get out of your present commitments and come back to serving as "Administrator." You'd love Mexico. I don't remember if you went for a visit when you were in Hollywood, but it's worth it' (Urgoiti to Buñuel, Mexico City, 22 February 1938).

In other words, the one with real foresight is the businessman whose goal from the very start of his exile is to restart his production activities in Mexico and Argentina. He dangles this poisoned offer to his old chief of production, who, as we will see, would soon take the bait. In fact, there is a later instance of

Urgoiti's insistence on the same idea. When he answers Buñuel's first four letters written from the United States, he writes with news of friends from Filmófono and refers to the fortunes of the musician Fernando Remacha.

> *Remacha*. I just received a letter. *He tells me I should encourage you to come and work as a producer with me.* I was considering a production which had commercial potential but the national star got away from me. She was one of the key elements, but I didn't have the 'dough', as they say here, and she signed a contract with a Hispanic producer, Ramos-Cobián.
>
> Urgoiti to Buñuel, Buenos Aires, 14 December 1938, p. 1, my emphasis

The prospects of work Buñuel hoped to find in Hollywood did not materialise, as he reveals in a later, and also important, letter:

> I'm still idle here. I have a lot of possibilities for work and the hard thing is getting started. Still, I trust first in my lucky star and second, once I actually have a job, in my own energy. By March everything has to work out since I've got $350 left to live on and the car. Of course there's no doubt about being able to work, and it's just a question of hanging on, of stretching my finances until I get started. If by the end of March I haven't found anything, I'll find myself for the first time in my life in huge and terrible peril. Almighty God will provide and I hope that the Virgin, whom I've always remembered in my prayers, will effectively plead for me.
>
> Buñuel to Urgoiti, Los Angeles, 2 January 1939, p. 1[9]

The following paragraph of this letter is also priceless and a good example of Buñuel's volatile and impetuous character, as well as of his attacks of generosity for his friends:

> I often remember my friends, I miss them terribly. If everything goes well for me here and I make money I'll consider myself as the father of them all (they aren't many) and provide for their survival if things go badly in Spain. *This motive made up about 70% of my decision to come to Hollywood.* Certainly, Remacha is part of this little family.
>
> My emphasis

In this same letter, one can guess that Buñuel is considering something important as he asks for information about Enrique Pelayo, a Filmófono worker who owed him some favours. Pelayo was then in Bolivia working in the lumber business. Buñuel writes to Urgoiti, 'it is extremely important that you send me his address as soon as you get this letter, since I have something important to write to him about'. We will see what this project consists of as we go along.

The fact is that nothing was working out as he had hoped, that money was running out, and that the future looked bleaker than ever, especially given that this period coincided precisely with the last months of the Spanish Civil War, with his friends on the losing side and the Republic practically defeated. This mood can be seen in his next letter, which he wrote towards the end of the month, before receiving a reply from Urgoiti.

> Dear Ricardo: What's the use of talking about the terrible current events or the tragedy of so many good friends! The absolute solitude in which I find myself here has made these days that much more bitter. Now my only desire is to be able to live and to be useful to my friends, to my few lifelong friends, although at the moment things aren't going as well as I might wish.
>
> Here everything continues to be promises and *bluff* [*sic* in the original]. Spanish productions which have been announced for months as something big never material-ise. Right now in Hollywood just one movie in Spanish is being made with a Mexican director and cast.[10] I've been just about to start at MGM as a *technical adviser* [*sic* in the original] but I haven't got past the 'just.'[11] The Chaplin film[12] has failed me too, the same as a number of other things. If I had money to hang on I'm sure I could do something but now I've only got the car and enough to hang on for another month.
>
> Buñuel to Urgoiti, Los Angeles, 30 January 1939, p. 1

Thus there are contradictions between what the facts show and what Buñuel says he wanted: between working for free or looking for a contract, and between being sent by the Spanish Republic or going of his own accord. The fact is that in this letter there are already signs of desperation in his tone, and not only because he has already made a firm decision to revive Filmófono, as we see in this paragraph:

> I am ready to leave here as soon as my money runs out and if there are possibilities and if you're going to do something I'd like to be part of Filmófono again but now as a director or as anything else. Buñuel is dead and I can be like a mere Durán, just a director. Without my artistic prejudices I think I can be more useful than before. As soon as we have a success, which will be with our first film, we could split the cost of getting Remacha to come.
>
> Buñuel to Urgoiti, Los Angeles, 30 January 1939, p. 2

This is reinforced, with Buñuel's usual mysteriousness, by a marginal note: 'I'm not telling you something important that I'm pursuing here and which would give us money to start production in Argentina. I'll tell you about it only if it works out' (ibid.). His desperation is also apparent in his now explicit appeal for money. 'If you're not doing anything and you can't even "sign me on," send me any money you can, from $10 on up [and] if it's not possible for you to either "sign me on" or send me money, write back and tell me so and send me the addresses I asked you for: Tota's and Enrique's' (ibid.).

Only a few days later Buñuel goes on the attack again and reveals part of his mystery:

> I'm writing to ask you for information about production conditions there since I have in theory started up a business to go and make movies there with you, Ugarte[13] and Kilpatrick,[14] who is a screenwriter and is the one who would supply the money. I talked to him the day before yesterday and he liked the idea a lot. At present he's waiting on a Paramount contract. If he gets it the business would get started up within six months. Can you hang on that long? If not, much sooner.
>
> We want to know if there are studios, if they're often available, and a complete list with the average amounts paid there: studio, film, developing, actors, etc. Kilpatrick knows a 'director' there named Borcosque who used to work under him, as did Ugarte, at MGM. All three are friends. Kilpatrick has already written to Borcosque and I'm writing to you. If the deal is closed it might be very worthwhile as there will be dollars. Write back soon. [PTO]
>
> Also tell me *when* [*sic*, really meaning 'how much'] a commercial film costs there and especially pretend you're well connected with contacts, distributors, etc.
>
> Still, in spite of everything I've said, what I wrote in my letter of a few days ago still stands. I believe more than ever that things will work out for me here, but in the meantime …
>
> If you can, get in touch with Borcosque whom Kilpatrick has in turn been asking about.
>
> Buñuel to Urgoiti, Los Angeles, 3 February 1939, p. 1

Buñuel's request for financial help from Dalí, who was then in New York, must be from around this time, and this request would as a consequence precipitate Dalí's enmity (Filmoteca Española, Buñuel Archive, AB-572.49).[15] The fact is that such was Buñuel's desperation at Urgoiti's eloquent silence that he even began to think Urgoiti had returned to Europe without telling him and that the reasons were perhaps political in nature. However, through a mutual friend, he found out that Urgoiti was still in Buenos Aires and he wrote a new letter which expressed the fears he had for Urgoiti as well as for other Filmófono workers who were in exile. In this context of despair, he wrote as follows:

> I'm still not busy here. I'm close to great possibilities but they haven't materialised yet. I'm working a lot and my career and my immediate future are the only things

that concern me at the moment. The Rockefeller Institute has asked for me and I've already presented all the documents, a biography, etc. that they wanted from me. I'm waiting for their acceptance. It seems that they want to pressurise me into making 'psychological' documentary cinema by giving me a free hand and a lot of means. Although such a job wouldn't make me a millionaire, it fits in perfectly with my background as an independent film-maker and it's a good start in the USA.

Although up until now we haven't lacked for anything, I keep on living almost by a daily miracle. French friends, some sales of personal items, etc. have given us our daily bread. It's impossible for my family to help me. I must insist once again on what I asked you in my unanswered letter. If you have just enough to live on, I withdraw my request. But if you have anything extra, I am claiming, officially and as a friend, my share of the movies you have made money off in south america [*sic*]. Leaving aside my part as an investor, I'm asking for the 3% that corresponds to me from each of them except for *La hija de Juan Simón* which comes to 5%. It's your turn to speak even if it is only to allow me to hear from you.

Buñuel to Urgoiti, Los Angeles, 11 August 1939, p. 1

A few points from these three letters are worth commenting on in more detail because they introduce important nuances in our knowledge about Buñuel's development. On the one hand, it seems that his complicated family situation makes him become more pragmatic, although not without a certain amount of resignation (he is about to turn forty years old), even to the point of accepting a job 'as a director or as anything else'. In other words, he begins to think seriously about changing direction, something he defines quite graphically with the phrase 'Buñuel is dead and I can be like a mere Durán, just a director.' By this he seems to put an end to his youthful capriciousness, his avant-garde and destructive tendencies, and it also shows his willingness to adapt himself to any situation (like his friend Gustavo Durán),[16] any, that is, within his profession of film-maker. This, along with his subsequent comment 'without my artistic prejudices I think I can be more useful than before', suggests the total abandonment of his Marxist and surrealist theories, at least in their most doctrinaire forms. It suggests the beginning of a new creative period in which his work will show signs of his having fully assimilated these theories rather than merely mechanically reflecting them. In fact, this phase of his life is the culmination of the process begun in 1933 with *Land Without Bread* which would lead him, although with false starts and irregular results, into documentary film-making in all forms. Surely this is what he was hoping for when he mentions the Rockefeller Institute's proposal to make 'psychological' documentaries.[17] As we well know, things will work out differently, but Buñuel at least is quite certain that his reputation as an independent film-maker has to be linked to documentary film-making. As he states in his biography of that year, documentaries (among which he makes a distinction between 'descriptive' and 'interpretive' films) are the heirs of independent productions. What there can be no doubt about is his intention to make a qualitative leap and to surpass the transcription or interpretation of social or natural reality by trying to penetrate into the psychological nature of the human being, as much of the performer as of the spectator, and by investigating a totally different kind of reality. Oddly enough, this coincides with what Hitchcock was also thinking about at this time.[18] The fact is that Buñuel, helped along by Iris Barry and her husband Dick Abbot, undertakes a new adventure in New York.

Urgoiti had remained silent until, finally, on 19 March 1940, he writes back, asking Buñuel in affectionate terms to excuse his long silence. He attributes it to, among other things, 'the impossibility of remedying your problems' (Urgoiti to Buñuel, Buenos Aires, p. 1). Buñuel answers right away and after giving him some news about mutual friends, he updates him on his situation:

> Thanks to the great vitality that gives me life, I haven't yet been driven to despair. Since arriving in America, I haven't made a single cent. I've survived thanks to good friends. In Hollywood it was absurd to try to do anything. After spending a year there, I moved to New York last November and here, although I haven't got anything yet, I'm very hopeful. It's better not to talk about it in case nothing works out. I can tell you that it has to do with cinema and with radio.
>
> Buñuel to Urgoiti, New York, 1 April 1940, p. 1

His hopes were for once well founded. They had to do with Iris Barry's proposal that he should work on *The March of Time* newsreels. Although first, as we know, he would get *Land Without Bread* shown at the McMillan Academic Theater and at the MOMA. Even so, he continues to be wary and just in case keeps alive the idea of reviving Filmófono with his friend:

> If between now and June [he continues in the same letter] my situation is not clear, I plan to go to Argentina to 'make films' *à la* Urgoiti. I'll set myself up right in front of Filmófono Argentina and I'll make movies for half the price and much shabbier than the famous *Daughter of Juan Simón*. The characters will call each other 'vos' instead of 'tú' and that will be the only difference. I hope you'll come soon so that we can merge the two companies, but I may not want to by then. Seriously now: there's a good chance I'll have capital available to produce films and surely if it is going to happen, it would be with the money in advance. I'll get in touch with you in time …
>
> I forgot to tell you before that the way I would get started in business in Argentina would be to ask for a small advance of capital to survey for three

months the possibilities in Buenos Aires. I would certainly get in touch with you immediately, and I would be greatly pleased if we could go back to working together. *I've changed a bit in practical terms, in ways that would suit any production company, although morally I'm still as stubborn as I was at twenty. I owe this notion of a practical sense of life in part to our 'Juansimonesque' scheme in Madrid and to the rough patches I've gone through here in this country.* The fact that we could work together as we did in Madrid seems like a reward to me and would give me the greatest satisfaction.

Buñuel to Urgoiti, New York, 1 April 1940, p. 1, my emphasis

Buñuel's recognition of a change in practical matters ('in ways that would suit any production company') owing to the 'rough patches' of his time in the United States confirms what is suspected in the earlier letters, anticipates the artistic turn his work would take after 1946 in his Mexican films, and implies his acceptance of the industry's conventions. Although morally, as he affirms, he would like to remain 'as stubborn as I was at twenty'.

After this letter the relationship between the two friends seems to stabilise in spite of the fact that Urgoiti's words suggest that he is somewhat reticent about Buñuel's coming:

I read with great interest your account of past, present, and future projects, and I'll envy you if they work out and turn into a 'job' in the United States. That would be my ideal … if you persist with your idea of coming here, let me know in advance, and I'll get you up to date on the production scene. I'm a little bit pessimistic, since I did my productions without money and without 'bluff.' With a bit of money and another bit of 'bluff,' for which a North American source would be very favourable, one can get things done … and I'll tell you again if you're thinking seriously about coming here – and I wouldn't advise you to do it without a base – I'll quickly send you the information which you might find useful for your 'investors', as long as you promise me a job as assistant or 'script boy' in the productions you take on.

Urgoiti to Buñuel, Buenos Aires, 12 April 1940, p. 1

As providentialist as Buñuel was, the birth of his second son must have made him burst with euphoria, as this event brought along in its wake the signing of a contract 'although temporary, well paid, in *The March of Time*. Besides, there are even more interesting prospects in view' (Buñuel to Urgoiti, New York, 19 July 1940, p. 1).[19] It is obvious that things start to improve for him; one sees in his letters a tone of optimism and joking good humour with his friend. The next letter is exultant:

I've found capital in dollars to produce there, capital which I could have available in November. Of course I would like to join you. Before going into details I wish you would write to let me know about the production possibilities there: the cost of films, availability of studios, chances for success, your thoughts on the matter, etc. Whether I will definitely set myself on the path towards production in Argentina or whether I stay here in a new enterprise to make pan-American cultural films which Rockefeller has just founded and they've made me propositions about, although they haven't discussed salaries, etc. yet, *depends* on your letter. The Argentina idea, which includes the capital found, would be to make three films, and for that a little more capital would be necessary. Although I believe that with your experience there that wouldn't be difficult. Also, Tota Cuevas de Vera who is around here has promised to help me in my search.

Buñuel to Urgoiti, New York, 4 October 1940

For Buñuel, the moment of decision, of urgent crisis has arrived: should he return to his past and the old times with good friends or should he turn to the future of new friends from a new culture? This path would be filled with uncertainty and for this reason he leaves in his friend's hands the terrible responsibility for deciding his fate. Although here we also find the auspicious reappearance of the figure of Tota Cuevas de Vera. Urgoiti answers him some twenty days later with all kinds of details about costs and strategies for production in Argentina (Urgoiti to Buñuel, Buenos Aires, 28 October 1940).

Buñuel's subsequent reply is fundamental to understanding the rest of his career. This is the letter in its entirety:

Dear Ricardo: I received your letter a few days ago and today I finally find myself ready to give you the details you asked me for. The items that I can bring to our possible collaboration are as follows: 1, Ricardo Urgoiti as associate producer and head of work; 2, 40,000 Argentine pesos in cash; 3, Luis Buñuel as director; 4, Rosita Díaz[20] as star, although this would not hinder the participation of other local stars according to the demands of the market and; 5, as much help and collaboration as we need from Tota Cuevas de Vera who to start with has already contributed 5,000 pesos which I have included in the 40,000.

Regarding the plot, a crucial point, we'll discuss it Filmófono style as soon as our meeting is arranged. I think that the distributor you talked about will have to be part of the agreement and, as you say, should have a wide commercial range. In Cuba Polaty got United Artists as distributor. I can't promise the same because I'm not a businessman so it would be your responsibility to find a good one there. I never considered producing independently, so we're in agreement there.

The bases of my collaboration are succinctly expressed here. If you can attract

Letter from Buñuel to Urgoiti,
New York, 4 October 1940

Señas para un año: { 301 E. 83 St
                     New York City

new York 4 - Octubre - 40

Querido Ricardo: Voy al grano. He encontrado capital en dolares para producir ahí, capital del que podré disponer en Noviembre. Es claro que quisiera unirme contigo. Antes de entrar en detalles desearía que me escribieses dándome detalles de la posibilidad de producir ahí: coste de peliculas, estudios libres, probable exito, tus ideas sobre el asunto, etc. De tu carta depende el que me encamine definitivamente hacia la produccion en Argentina o me quede aqui en una nueva empresa para producir films culturales panamericanos que acaba de fundar Rockefeller y para la que ya me han hecho proposiciones, aunque aun no hablado de sueldos, etc. La idea, contando con argentina, con el capital encontrado, sería producir tres films y haría falta para

ello algo mas de capital, que con tu experiencia ahi no seria dificil segun creo. Ademas, Tota Cuevas de Vera que esta por aqui me ha prometido apoyo en esa búsqueda.

Espero que esta vez tu carta no se hara esperar: me urge mucho tomar una decision.

Un abrazo de
Luis

Se termino la dictadura de Filmofono. Como yo poseeré el 51% de las acciones seré el manejeador y Dn. Ricardo un humilde "assistant" del Sr. Buñuel. Asi son los tiempos: unos subimos y otros bajais.

En mi proxima, respuesta a la tuya, te daré todos los detalles y precisiones que me pidas.

other investors, so much the better. In any case Tota will help us look for others and she's setting an example by putting up some money. She's told me she can't put up more because it's materially impossible *at the moment*. She's been around here for a couple months. I thought she might have more available but that's not so. In any case, given the times it's quite a little feat.

Now I'll tell you what I've been offered as a job in the US. The State Department has created an institute for pan-American propaganda which is based in Washington and is directed by Nelson Rockefeller. Cinematography is among the many activities of the institute and the well-known millionaire John Whitney is in charge of this. In addition to being the king of American Airways and other things, this gentleman finances David Selznick of Hollywood. I've already been introduced to those who proposed me to him. They are his collaborators in this matter, the directors of New York's Museum of Modern Art Film Library. They've offered me a position in that organisation as something like a technical adviser and occasionally as a director. Whitney leaves for South America in January and it seems like I would be part of the trip. The offices haven't started up yet as they're still being organised now. They have $6 million to work with.

Normally this job would seem like winning the grand prize in the lottery to me. Not now. Every last person believes that America will enter the war next year and I hope to be at a distance from it. I can see myself defending the American flag in Hong Kong or resting for a few years in a concentration camp, and of course I'm getting out of here.

I'm waiting for your immediate, categorical reply so that I can make bold decisions.

[hand-written, in the left margin]

What I've told you about my job wasn't just for the pleasure of digressing. I happen to have a project that is compatible with our production and Whitney's. I'll see him this week to talk about it. If it works out I'll let you know. If not, what I've written is enough.

Buñuel to Urgoiti, New York, 12 November 1940

It is clear from a first reading of this letter that he has already decided to go to Argentina and in this sense his proposals to Urgoiti are quite reasonable. However, the real novelty is found in another important and well-known theme, which is the offer to work for Nelson Rockefeller's committee for propaganda for Latin American countries. Until now the details of the offer were unknown, especially insofar as the network of powerful interests (Selznick and Whitney) which could have been brought into play. In particular, Whitney's project, which Buñuel already saw himself involved in, turns out to be the decisive spark which unmasks his true intentions at the time and always, especially with regard to

LUIS BUÑUEL
30I E. 83 St.

New York City I2 Noviembre I940

Querido Ricardo : Recibi tu carta hace unos dias
y ya hoy me hallo en condiciones de darte los detalles que me pides. Los elementos que puedo aportar para una posible colaboracion entre nosotros son los
siguientes: I°Ricardo Urgoiti como productor asociado y organizador del trabajo.
2°, 40.000 pesos argentinos cash;3°,Luis Buñuel como director;4°, Rosita Diaz como
estrella aunque esto no impida la intervencion de otras estrellas indigenas segun
lo exija el mercado y 5°,la ayuda y colaboracion para cuanto nos haga falta de
Tota Cuevas de Vera la cual contribuye para empezar con cinco mil pesos que ya he
incluido en los cuarenta mil.

Respecto al argumento punto este de importancia
capital ya lo discutiriamos estilo Filmofono una vez nuestra reunion efectuada.
Tendria que intervenir,creo yo,en el acuerdo la distribuidora de que me hablas
que debera ser como dices de gran radio comercial. Polaty ha obtenido en Cuba la dis-
tribucion por United Artists . Yo no me comprometo a eso por no ser hombre de ne-
gocios de modo que quedaria a tu cargo el encontrar ahi una buena indigena. Yo nunca
he pensado en producir independientemente asi que de acuerdo contigo.

Sucintamente expuestas quedan las bases de mi co-
laboracion. Si tu puedes atraer a otros capitalistas tanto mejor. Tota en todo caso
nos ayudara a buscar otros y ella al ejemplo poniendo algo de dinero. Me dice que
no pone mas po que le es materialmente imposible por ahora. Hace un par de meses
que se halla por aqui. Yo crei que podria disponer de mucho mas pero no es asi.
De todas maneras y como estan los tiempos es una pequeña proeza.

He aqui ahora lo que me han propuesto como job en
U.S.A. El State Department ha creado un organismo de propaganda pan-americana
que radica en Washington y se halla dirigido por Nelson Rockefeller. Entre las mil
actividades de ese organismo esta la cinematografica de la que se encarga el cono-
cido millonario John Whitney. Dicho Sr. ademas de ser el rey de los American Airways
y de otras cosas es el financiero de David Seltznik de Hollywood. Ya me lo han pre-
sentado los que me propusieron a el,que son sus brazos en el asunto:los directores
del Museo de Arte Moderno Film Library de New York. Me han ofrecido un puesto en
dicha organizacion que seria algo asi como technical advisor y ocasionalmente director. En Enero sale Whitney para Sud America y segun parece formaria yo parte de la
expedicion. Las oficinas no han comenzado aun a funcionar hallandose ahora en el mo-
mento de la organizacion. Hay seis millones de dolares para actuar.

En tiempos normales me pareceria ese empleo una loteria
y el premio gordo. Hoy no. America como cree aqui ya hasta el gato entrara en guerra el año proximo y yo procuro poner desde ahora tierra de por medio. Me veo defen-
diendo la bandera americana en Hong Kong o descansando en un campo de concentracion
por unos años,y claro es me largo.

Espero tu respuesta inmediata,categorica,para tomar
decisiones energicas.

A Aurora nuestros mas cordiales saludos lo mismo
que a tus hijos. No me atrevo a decir besos porque deben estar hechos ya unos hombres.

Abrazos para ti   Luis

Reparas el de Filmofono
llega esta semana! Intentaré verlo.

Letter from Buñuel to Urgoiti, New York, 12 November 1940

the war. In this sense, the last paragraph is a true revelation. He must 'be at a distance', he must 'get out of here', so that he does not get caught up in American involvement in World War II. It is obvious then that first his leaving for Paris and then for New York later are really flights from the scene of war which point to an instinct for survival that turns out to be key to understanding his life and work. On the other hand, it is also characteristic of high intelligence to be playing with three options at the same time: the certain (everything connected to Iris Barry), the probable (Argentina) and the possible (the unknown factor he prefers not to reveal). It is also characteristic of him that he prefers to escape by taking 'the middle road' or what is effectively the same thing: to run away from commitment, from everything that could disturb personal interests.

Urgoiti does not wait long to answer (Urgoiti to Buñuel, Buenos Aires, 20 November 1940, p. 1) as he knows the importance of his information, which is in itself quite interesting and realistic about how to face up to guaranteeing the commercial success of film production in Argentina by a Spanish company. What is certain is that the correspondence ends at this point,[21] that in January 1941 Buñuel begins working at MOMA's Film Library in New York, that in March he is hired as adviser and chief of editing for the propaganda office, that in May of the same year he regularises his immigration status and that the following year he applies for United States citizenship. In other words, he does the opposite of what he had wanted to do, just in case. It is obvious that once things begin to go well for him his friend's help is no longer necessary. Not until June 1946, when Buñuel is once again in Hollywood and Urgoiti is then in Madrid, do they take up their correspondence again. By then he has just returned from Mexico where they have made him an offer to direct his first Mexican film with Jorge Negrete. The change is complete, but that is another story.

Translated by Lisa Jarvinen

Notes

1. This is according to Max Aub. There is an unpublished letter of 21 December 1935 written by José Hernández Barrera, the owner of an inn in the village of Batuecas, which shows some of the negotiations made in this matter (FE Buñuel papers 435). Yasha David confirms that between 6 and 8 June 1936 he went with Pepín Bello to Las Batuecas to buy the convent (David, 1997, p. 312) but the transaction was not completed, since the outbreak of war spoiled the plans.

2. Another unpublished letter of 6 June 1936 by one Luis Gómez, of nearby La Alberca, talks about a request to bring him 'an animal [in reference to a pig] like

the ones you saw here'. One must suppose from these letters that Buñuel made a trip to the area in early December.

3. In his memoirs, this is how he refers to the event: 'I had a little bit of money left from the salary I'd received for three years. Various friends, among them Sánchez Ventura and an American woman who had done a lot for the Spanish Republic, added the rest to pay for the trip for me, my wife and my son' (Buñuel, 1982, p. 173). Nevertheless, with Max Aub he is even more explicit:

> Ione Robinson, who was the mistress of both Quintanilla and the American Secretary of the Treasury at the same time, lent me 100,000 francs, and Sánchez Ventura gave me, I believe, $1,400, which is what he had saved, on condition that I returned it to him when I could. By then, he also supposed that all that couldn't last much longer, and preferred to have the money in the United States.
>
> Aub, 1985, p. 87

4. Buñuel letters, Urgoiti Archive, letter of 20 September 1938. Henceforth all references to Buñuel's letters in the Urgoiti Archive kept at the Filmoteca Española will be given parenthetically after the quotation, indicating place and date of origin.

5. 'At that time they were making films in the United States which showed the war in Spain … At times these movies contained gross errors as far as local colour. This was why Pascua suggested I should return to Hollywood and get a contract as a *technical* or *historical adviser* (*sic*, English in the original) (1982, p. 173). This version is corroborated in the interview with Pérez Turrent and de la Colina (1993, p. 41).

6. 'In Hollywood at that time, they were making films in favour of the Spanish Republic, but with some tremendous errors of facts … Therefore I proposed to Pascua – and to Vayo – going to Hollywood for free, as an adviser. They thought it a very good idea' (Aub, 1985, p. 87).

7. 'Anyway, when I arrived in Hollywood they called up my draft year. I wrote to Cruz Marín, who was in Washington as minister, to see what I should do, and he told me to wait, or rather, to wait for orders. Naturally they never arrived, and I stayed there' (Aub, 1985, p. 93). Cf.

> At that time I got news that my draft year had been mobilised. I had to go to war. I wrote to our embassy in Washington to offer him my services, asking him to repatriate me along with my wife. He answered saying that it wasn't the best moment. The situation wasn't clear. When they needed me, they'd let me know.
>
> Buñuel, 1982, p. 174

Cf. 'I wrote a letter to our government's ambassador in Washington, offering him my services to go to the front when they called up my draft year' (Pérez Turrent and de la Colina, 1993, p. 41).

8. René Crevel is known to have been a homosexual and, since the surrealists did not accept homosexuals, he tried to become Tota Cuevas de Vera's lover when they first met in Venice on 20 September 1931. However their relationship was so stormy that Crevel finally committed suicide. Tota would be tormented by this for the rest of her life. Buñuel was her shoulder to cry on, confidant, and possibly even lover.

9. The providentialist tone of this paragraph, and its cynical sarcasm, is worth pointing out, as it shows Buñuel's character as he looks at the world through his friend's Catholic point of view – a strange attitude for a supposedly convinced atheist.

10. The only film made in Spanish which corresponds to these characteristics is *Los hijos mandan*, directed by Gabriel Soria, produced by Rafael Ramos Cobián for 20th Century-Fox, based on a work by López-Pinillos and starring Blanca de Castejón and Arturo de Córdova in the lead roles. See Heinink and Dickson, 1990, pp. 269–70.

11. Here is what is known up until now about this episode:

> My old supervisor Frank Davis [he refers to his earlier stay in the United States: Davis supervised the Spanish productions for MGM] was going to produce *Cargo of Innocents*. He accepted me immediately as historical consultant … I was ready to start working, when an order from Washington arrived … it was purely and simply prohibited to make any movie about the war in Spain.
>
> Buñuel, 1982, p. 174

> I arrived in Hollywood … and I went to see the producer Frank Davis, a communist, who was going to make a movie, *Blockade*, which was the story of how an American ship was rescuing children from Bilbao which was under siege. But two days later the Cinematographic Center of Washington gave the order that no films could be made either in favour of or against the Republic. So I ended up out of a job.
>
> Aub, 1985, p. 87

> When I arrived, I introduced myself to the producer Frank Davis, who was very leftist, and I told him that I wanted to work for free for them as a technical advisor, because my government was paying me.
>
> Pérez Turrent and de la Colina, 1993, p. 41

12. One supposes he is referring to the gags he was hoping to sell him. See Buñuel, 1982, p. 174. Buñuel's opinion about him: 'Chaplin, as a person, was a pathetic human being' (Aub, 1985, p. 90).

13. Eduardo Ugarte was a screenwriter. See Ríos Carratalá, 1995.

14. I believe this refers to Tom Kilpatrick (1898–1962), author and screenwriter, creator of Dr Cyclops (indeed for Paramount) in 1940, and whom Buñuel had already met during his first trip to Hollywood. He mentions it in Aub (1985,

p. 75) in reference to the notoriety he gained there, and that had not helped him at all in finding work on this occasion.

15. It seems clear that Dalí was getting revenge on him for the offences he had suffered in relation to the two films they made together. As he reminds him in the final paragraph: 'In the past our collaboration has been bad for me. Remember that I had to make an effort so that my name be included in *Un chien andalou*', and the only thing that occurs to him to relieve his friend's economic situation is to suggest that he ask for money from Noailles.

16. Gustavo Durán (1906–1969) is one of the most curious and zany characters in contemporary Spanish culture. Musician, pianist, writer, member of the Communist Party, during the war he undertook a military career, went into exile in London where he married Bonté Crompton, became a spy for the United States, and a bureaucrat at the United Nations from 1946 on, from where he was sent to several different countries. His relationship with Buñuel began in the Residencia de Estudiantes and culminated in the United States while working at the MOMA in New York for a time. Buñuel refers to him in this manner for his capacity to 'change his colours' because he could not understand how a militant communist could, during the Civil War, become an enemy spy. Horacio Vázquez Rial in *El soldado de porcelana* (1997) tells his interesting and exciting biography.

17. This is the reason he would write an autobiography that was very illustrative of this period. It can be found in its entirety in David (1997, pp. 285–92). I believe that, as this reading reveals, the offer, if there was one, would have been to make documentaries in general.

18. 'Documentary films usually bore the non-specialist public. More material than is necessary is usually used to point out details whose only value is visual or dynamic. The majority of documentaries lack any psychological value.' Cf. David (1997, p. 292).

19. Urgoiti's answer in a telegraphic style was sent on 29 August. After the usual congratulations he asks him if he intends to continue with his idea of going to Argentina.

20. In the margin, a hand-written note in pencil, surely by Urgoiti: 'watch out'.

21. There is an undated telegram from the Western Telegraph Company sent from New York by Buñuel in which he asks Urgoiti to donate a copy of the film *La hija de Juan Simón* to the MOMA. He suggests that this request would do credit to Filmófono, and that the museum would underwrite the costs of copying and sending the film.

References

Aub, Max (1985), *Conversaciones con Buñuel. Seguidas de 45 entrevistas con familiares, amigos y colaboradores del cineasta aragonés*, Madrid: Aguilar.

Buñuel letters, Urgoiti Archive, Filmoteca Española, Madrid.

Buñuel papers, Filmoteca Española, Madrid.

Buñuel, L. (1982), *Mi último suspiro*, Barcelona: Plaza y Janés.

Dalí letters, Buñuel Archive, AB-572.49 and 572.53, Filmoteca Española, Madrid.

David, Y. (1997), *Buñuel! La mirada del siglo*, Madrid: Museo Nacional Reina Sofía.

Heinink J. B. and R. G. Dickson (1990), *Cita en Hollywood. Antología de las películas norteamericanas habladas en español*, Bilbao: Mensajero.

Herrera Navarro, J. (2001–2), 'El cine y el exilio español en América Latina: Ricardo Urgoiti y los inicios de Filmófono-Argentina', *Histoire et Sociétés de l'Amérique Latine*, 14, pp. 53–66.

Pérez Turrent, T. and J. de la Colina (1993), *Buñuel por Buñuel*, Madrid: Plot.

Ríos Carratalá, J. (1995), *A la sombra de Buñuel y Lorca: Eduardo Ugarte*, Alicante: Servicio de publicaciones de la Universidad.

Vázquez Rial, Horacio (1997), *El soldado de porcelana*, Barcelona: Ediciones B.

PART TWO

MEXICO

4

Buñuel's Box of Subaltern Tricks: Technique in *Los olvidados*

Stephen Hart

Luis Buñuel's cinema is enigmatic and palimpsestic, and a paradigm of that multilayeredness is the scene in *Belle de jour* (1966) when an Oriental client takes a box into a brothel. Buñuel describes viewers' reactions to this scene in his memoirs:

> Of all the senseless questions asked about the movie, one of the most frequent concerns the little box that an Oriental client brings with him to the brothel. He opens it and shows it to the girls, but we never see what's inside. The prostitutes back away with cries of horror except for Séverine, who's rather intrigued. I can't count the number of times people (particularly women) have asked what was in the box, but since I myself have no idea, I usually reply, 'Whatever you want there to be'.
>
> Buñuel, 1983, p. 243

Buñuel knows that we want to see what's in the box, and he teases us, inviting us to guess. But we will never know the answer.

Buñuel's life, like his films, was also full of surprises. When he went to Mexico in 1946, nursing his wounds after a disastrous experience in Hollywood, it looked on the surface as if his career had hit rock bottom. He had no illusions about what Latin America had to offer:

> I had so little interest in Latin America that I used to tell my friends that should I suddenly drop out of sight one day, I might be anywhere – except there. Yet I lived in Mexico for thirty-six years and even became a citizen in 1949.
>
> Buñuel, 1983, p. 197

Mexico in the 1940s was anything but a centre of bustling, innovative cinematography. That it was successful in commercial terms, though, there is no doubt. The Mexican movie industry had been going through a boom period under the administration of Miguel Alemán (1946–52), based on the Hollywood model. As Carl J. Mora notes:

> The major factor sustaining such a movie industry was the 'star system'. Mexican producers and directors were indeed fortunate in that during the 1940s and 1950s a fortuitous confluence of talented, charismatic, and attractive performers appeared who could assure commercial success for even the worst of films. The problem with this was that a motion picture became a vehicle for the star and consequently the director and the script became of secondary concern. This was the situation faced by Luis Buñuel when he arrived in Mexico in 1946 to work for Oscar Dancigers.
>
> Mora, 1982, p. 75

Mora's spin is a positive one but it does not hide the fact that the actors and actresses were in the driving seat, the directors subservient to the exigencies of the show.

It was perhaps inevitable that Buñuel – a vulnerable foreigner down on his luck – would be enticed into making some Mexican melodramas of his own for purely commercial reasons: films such as *Gran Casino* (1946), *El gran calavera* (1949), *Susana* (1950), *La hija del engaño* (1951), *Subida al cielo* (1951), *El bruto* (1952), *Abismos de pasión* (1953) and *La ilusión viaja en tranvía* (1953). But he also bucked the trend by producing some extraordinary films such as *Los olvidados* (1950) and *Nazarín* (1958), which reflected the 'more personal interests and obsessions of the Surrealist auteur' (Evans, 1995, p. 36; for more information on Buñuel's Mexico period, see Pérez Turrent, 1995). In his more auteurist works Buñuel sought to hollow the Mexican melodrama out from within. The relationship he had with his cameraman neatly illustrates the point.

Gabriel Figueroa El Indio was by far the most famous cinematographer of the time – so much so that he once declared: 'I am Mexican Cinema' ['El cine mexicano soy yo'] (quoted in King, 1990, p. 48) – and the aesthetically beautiful landscapes in his films were seen as paradigmatically Mexican. The following comments of a contemporary critic are typical of the awe in which he was held at that time:

> Languid *maguey* plants, crepuscular love on the banks of the river, *charros* more macho than those in *Allá en el Rancho Grande* … All that seemed to characterise the 'national' was dramatised in El Indio's films, making up the cinematographic image of a nation.
>
> Quoted in King, 1990, p. 48

Mora provides a more balanced assessment of the techniques that formed the
basis of El Indio's repertoire:

> Gabriel Figueroa's photographic preciosity incorporated all of the Eisensteinian
> techniques: low-angle long shots in silhouette that emphasize the stark landscape
> and sky and the smallness of the human figures before them; the close-ups of
> Indian faces and shrouded women; and the 'dead tree framing' in which long shots
> are composed between the gnarled branches of a dried-up tree.
>
> Mora, 1982, pp. 79–80

Carlos Fuentes recalls that, when Buñuel and El Indio worked together in the
1950s, Figueroa would set up his rather precious camera shots and Buñuel
would at the last minute divert the camera towards a barren landscape in the
distance:

> While *Nazarín* was being filmed on location near Cuatla – or so the story goes –
> Gabriel Figueroa carefully prepared an outdoor scene for the director Luis Buñuel.
> Figueroa set up the camera with the snow-capped volcano Popocatépetl in the
> background, a cactus at the right-angle of the composition, a circle of clouds
> crowning its peak and the open furrows of the valley in the foreground. Looking at
> the composition, Buñuel said: 'Fine, now let's turn the camera so that we can get
> those four goats and two crags on that barren hill.'
>
> Quoted in King, 1990, p. 130

In effect in *Los olvidados* Buñuel turned from the sky to the stones, from the
lush landscape of rural Mexico to the dry concrete jungle of Mexico City, from
the noble Indian savage to the real Mexico City savage, Jaibo (Roberto Cobo).
Rather than an antiphonal structure balancing stylised long shots with epic close-
ups of Indian faces, Buñuel employed a breathtakingly rapid narrative
sequentiality mediated, as Edwards has pointed out with regard especially to the
opening sequences of the film (1982, pp. 89–91), by the dissolve which, by keeping the old frame in focus as the new frame emerges, tended to promote an
atavistic mindscreen, an Oedipal obsession with the preterite.

Made on schedule in twenty-one days – Buñuel had no leeway for error, as
his autobiography indicates (1983, p. 200) – *Los olvidados* has a robust storyline
about some criminals in an urban setting which has led some critics to see the
film as the revamping of a picaresque tale.[1] While acclaimed at the Cannes Film
Festival, its uncompromising view of the down-and-outs in Mexico City aroused
fierce reactions from some Mexicans: 'Many organizations, including labor
unions, demanded my expulsion, and the press was nothing short of vitriolic in

its criticism. Such spectators as there were left the theatre looking as if they'd just been to a funeral' (Buñuel, 1983, p. 200). After a private showing of the film, Diego Rivera's wife, Lupe, refused to speak to him, and León Felipe's wife tried to maul him:

> Bertha Gamboa, León Felipe's wife, arrived; she was Mexican and with her nails all sharpened up, she was absolutely livid, like a harpy, intent on scratching my eyes out (I got scared, but I couldn't back down), she was shouting at me with her nails in front of her eyes: 'You scoundrel! You bastard! You swine! Those kids aren't Mexican! I'm going to get you deported! You low life!' She'd flipped.
>
> [Llegó Bertha Gamboa, esposa de León Felipe, mexicana, con sus uñas afiladísimas, hecha una furia, una harpía, decidida a sacarme los ojos [yo tuve miedo, pero no me podía echar para atrás], gritándome con sus uñas delante de los ojos: '¡Miserable! ¡Canalla! ¡Puerco! ¡Estos niños no son mexicanos! ¡Voy a pedir que le apliquen el treinta y tres! ¡Granuja!' Fuera de sí.]
>
> Quoted in Aub, 1985, p. 119, my translation[2]

Buñuel's close friend, Sadoul, burst into tears at the premiere (Aub, 1985, p. 128). Faced with evidence such as this, we find ourselves asking: what was it about this film that evinced such a visceral reaction in the audience?

Los olvidados expressed a paradigm shift, since Buñuel brought with him a different mindset – European, surrealist – and Mexican cinema was, at the beginning of the 1950s, still playing out the last runs of its Golden Age years, the time of the Mexican melodramas, in which men were strong, women beautiful and love a word with a romantic aura. This was, perhaps, the main reason for the shock, since the characters in Buñuel's film are anything but stars. In fact, it would be difficult to think of a film in which the characters are more un-star-like; it is, as Octavio Paz pointed out, 'a star-less film' ['una película sin "estrellas"'] (1994, p. 223).[3] Both Jaibo and Ojitos were played by non-actors, after all. But its un-star-like quality went deeper than this. It is not that films do not portray unpleasant characters; they have to, if they want to create a sense of verisimilitude. It was simply that there are no redeemable characters in this film – with the possible exception of Julián (Javier Amezcúa) who is consigned to the oblivion of death early on anyway. Jaibo is instantly recognisable as the archetypal young villain, a Mexican version of Hollywood's Babyface.

Even the characters whom we expect to be good are just as corrupt. We expect sympathy to be engineered on behalf of Carmelo (played superbly by Miguel Inclán) when he is cruelly beaten up by the local gang, spearheaded by Jaibo, early on in the film. But then, later on, he shows himself to be just as quick to kick others when they are down, given half a chance. A latent paedophile, he tries to grope the young girl, Meche (Alma Delia Fuentes), when she sits on his lap, and he jumps at the chance to turn in Jaibo to the police. Pedro's mother, Marta (Stella Inda) also deviates from contemporary film mores. In his essay on the various mythologies of Mexican cinema, Carlos Monsiváis notes how women were depicted during the Golden Years: 'for a married woman, monogamy is the only guarantee of your existence; for a single woman, your honour is your only justification; for the prostitute, tragedy is your punishment and your only chance for glory; for the daughter, in your hymen I have deposited my honour and your future' (1995, p. 121). Yet Marta disrupts the codes of melodrama; she is beautiful, sensual and prepared to have a sexual relationship with Jaibo just, it appears, for the hell of it. And, in one of the most disturbing scenes of the novel, the dream sequence, when she offers her son some meat, and if we accept Peter Evans's convincing interpretation that she is offering him her 'torn vagina' (1995, p. 86), then she is offering sex to her son. Clearly we are poles apart from the victimised princess served up in the Mexican melodrama of the time. Even the staff behind the camera were adversely affected by episodes such as these. During the scene in which Pedro's mother rejects her son after he comes home looking for food, in Buñuel's words, 'one of the hairdressers quit in a rage, claiming that no Mexican mother would ever do such a thing'. One of the technicians asked him 'why I didn't make a real Mexican movie instead of this pathetic one', and Pedro de Urdemalas, 'a writer who collaborated with me on the script, refused to allow his name in the credits' (Buñuel, 1983, p. 200). Even his professional peers were shocked. The comments made by the Italian neo-realist, De Sica, after seeing the film, sound like those of a concerned relative: 'But, Buñuel, has society done something to you? Has it mistreated you? Have you suffered a lot?' ['Pero, a usted, Buñuel, ¿qué le ha hecho la sociedad? ¿Le ha tratado mal? ¿Ha sufrido mucho?'] (Aub, 1985, p. 126). He even stayed behind to ask Buñuel's wife, Jeanne, if he was a wife-beater. Lastly, and no doubt the final straw for those who had their doubts, the moral of the film seems quite clearly to indicate that social violence is perpetuated by example, and is inescapable. The closing sequence of Los olvidados, rather than enacting catharsis or promoting social justice, is simply the working out of the inevitable consequences of societal evil.

It is clear that the specific cinematic depiction of the Mexican subaltern in Los olvidados also has something to do with the violent reaction it caused in the audience. Here Gayatri Spivak's theory of the subaltern helps to elucidate the dynamics at work in Buñuel's film. In her important essay, 'Subaltern Studies: Deconstructing Historiography', Spivak begins by acknowledging the innovatory nature of the work carried out by the Subaltern Studies collective, headed by Ranajit Guha, in its aim to rewrite the history of colonial India from the

The plight of the subalterns in *Los olvidados*

bottom upwards. She goes on to argue that the group's notion of the 'consciousness' of the subaltern, though, is problematic:

> Because of [the] bestowal of a historical specificity to consciousness in the narrow sense, even as it implicitly operates as a metaphysical methodological presupposition in a general sense, there is always a counterpointing suggestion in the work of the group that subaltern consciousness is subject to the cathexis of the elite, that it is never fully recoverable, that it is always askew from its received signifiers, indeed that it is effaced even as it is disclosed, that it is irreducibly discursive.
>
> 1985, p. 212

This means, as she goes on to suggest, that the retrieval of subaltern consciousness is mediated by what she calls the 'subaltern subject-effect':

> A subject-effect can be briefly plotted as follows: that which seems to operate as a subject may be part of an immense discontinuous network ('text' in the general sense) of strands that may be termed politics, ideology, economics, history, sexuality, language, and so on … Different knottings and configurations of these

strands, determined by heterogeneous determinations which are themselves depen-
dent upon myriad circumstances, produce the effect of an operating subject. Yet
the continuist and homogenist deliberate consciousness symptomatically requires a
continuous and homogeneous cause for this effect and thus posits a sovereign and
determining subject. This latter is, then, the effect of an effect, and its positing a
metalepsis, or the substitution of an effect for a cause.

Ibid., p. 213

This, she contends, is an example of 'positivistic essentialism', even if it is politically 'strategic' (ibid., p. 214). *Los olvidados*, as we shall see, in articulating the
consciousness of the Mexican subaltern, brings to the fore the indeterminacy
and uncertainty involved in quantifying the observable. While ostensibly seeming to 'retrieve' the consciousness of Mexican subalternity for the benefit of its
viewers, Buñuel's film simultaneously intimates that that very consciousness is,
to quote Spivak, 'never fully recoverable' for it is 'effaced even as it is disclosed'.
The film creates a 'subaltern subject-effect', whereby, as in *Belle de jour*, we see
the external surface of the box but not its contents.

In *Los olvidados*, the role of the subaltern is occupied by the criminal class in
Mexico City, epitomised by Jaibo, the (homin)id of Buñuel's pantheon of villains, at once a degraded *homo sapiens* and an expression of the animal, the id,
the beast within. In this sense, we can see Buñuel's film as an intellectual product of an investigator who compiles information about his object of study, and
subsequently promotes the knowledge thereby created for consumption by
society at large. Buñuel, the researcher, creates knowledge about the forgotten
remnants of society, that is he brings those sections of the society which are pre-
conscious to consciousness. In fact he spent a number of months travelling
around the shanty towns of Mexico City, watching, listening, thinking about the
subject of his film:

> For the next several months, I toured the slums on the outskirts of Mexico City –
> sometimes with Fitzgerald, my Canadian set designer, sometimes with Luis
> Alcoriza, but most of the time alone. I wore my most threadbare clothes; I
> watched, I listened, I asked questions. Eventually, I came to know these people,
> and much of what I saw went unchanged into the film.

Buñuel, 1983, p. 199

He sorted through records in a women's prison and a lunatic asylum: 'I went
to mental asylums, I looked at a lot of files on beggars' ['Fui a clínicas de defi-
cientes mentales, vi muchas fichas de mendigos'] (quoted in Aub 1985,
p. 118). In one sense, thus, the film can legitimately be described as sociologi-

cal study. So much is suggested by the voice-over just before the establishing scene of the film:

> Big modern cities such as New York, Paris, London, hidden away behind their magnificent buildings, have poverty-stricken homes which contain ill-nourished, dirty children who do not attend school – breeding grounds for the delinquents of the future. Society attempts to remedy this evil but with limited success. It is only in the not too distant future that the rights of children and adolescents will be respected in order to make them useful members of society. Mexico City is no exception to this universal law. That's why this film, based as it is on real-life events, is not an optimistic one and sees the responsibility for solving this problem falling to the progressive forces within our society.
>
> [Las grandes ciudades modernas, Nueva York, París, Londres, esconden tras sus magníficos edificios hogares de miseria, y albergan niños mal nutridos, sin higiene, sin escuela, semilleros de futuros delincuentes. La sociedad trata de corregir este mal pero el éxito de sus esfuerzos es muy limitado. Sólo en un futuro próximo podrán ser reivindicados los derechos del niño y del adolescente, para que sean útiles a la sociedad. México no es excepción a esta regla universal. Por eso esta película, basada en hechos de la vida real, no es optimista y deja la solución del problema a las fuerzas progresivas de la sociedad.]

The tone adopted here suggests that we are being presented, in the words of one critic, 'not with a fiction but with a closely observed picture of the real world' (Edwards, 1982, p. 92). We are, thus, initially lured into sympathising with the 'progressive forces of our society' – as epitomised by the director (Francisco Jambrina) of the reform school where Pedro finally ends up – which will contrive to 'remedy' the 'evil' depicted in the film. It is significant too that the cities chosen as an illustration in *Los olvidados*'s prologue are remarkably similar to those selected by Oscar Lewis in his later study of *The Children of Sánchez* to illustrate a point about the pervasiveness of the culture of poverty. According to the American sociologist, there are 'remarkable similarities in family structure, interpersonal relations, time orientations, value systems, spending patterns, and the sense of community in lower-class settlements in London, Glasgow, Paris, Harlem, and Mexico City' (1965, p. xxvi). Like Lewis, Buñuel was depicting a social problem and thereby bringing it to public notice.

Despite the apparent similarity between the subject matter and its treatment in *Los olvidados* and *The Children of Sánchez*, is it fair, however, to see Buñuel's film simply in terms of the positivistic measurement of sociological observables? The extensive role played by the motif of concealment alerts us to the fact that this film does not offer untrammelled access to the Mexican criminal mind; the consciousness of the subaltern is, as we shall see, 'never fully recoverable' for it is 'effaced even as it is disclosed'. A clue is couched within the opening voice-over of the film which refers to how the poverty-stricken homes are 'hidden away' behind the magnificent buildings of the modern city. Even as the film displays the lives of Jaibo and his accomplices before us, it also hides them away.

The motif of concealment is more than simply a prelude to a later act of discovery, for it is at the centre of the film's rhetorical staging. Thus Jaibo conceals the rock with which he will kill Julián in a sling. When Jaibo has to flee from the police, he chooses to hide himself away in a disused slum by the railways. When Pedro runs away he has to conceal himself in the same area. Whenever Pedro is caught up by Jaibo, the latter invariably emerges from his hiding-place in the shadows. Similarly the juncture in the film when the viewer sees Meche's legs as she bathes them in milk (a scene echoed when Marta washes her legs), is revealed to be Jaibo's furtively voyeuristic point of view; immediately after the point-of-view shot Jaibo emerges from the shadows.

The dwellings inhabited by the various people in the story – Meche's household, Carmelo's house – are always depicted in semi-darkness. This could be an example of verisimilitude (the houses of the lower classes in the 1950s in Mexico City, of course, did not enjoy the luxury of electricity), but it is remarkable how consistently Buñuel chooses to depict interiors as dark and threatening, so much so that it becomes a leitmotif of the film. As viewers, we often struggle to see who is in each bed as the camera pans around the room. Even the interior of the knife grinder's shop where Pedro works is dark, whereas the furnace could have led to a brighter interior if the film director had desired such an effect. A high proportion of the scenes takes place at night, crucially at the beginning, when Ojitos (Mario Ramírez) is seen waiting all day for his lost father, and at the conclusion, when darkness becomes the natural accomplice to Pedro's murder. Paz's astute comment that *Los olvidados* depicts 'the nocturnal slice of life' ['la porción nocturna de la vida'] (1994, p. 233) betrays an awareness that Buñuel has consistently used the darkly lit stage set as a shorthand to express the darker, evil side of the human personality. Buñuel's cinematic enlightenment is counterbalanced by a gradual process of nocturnalisation whereby the brighter the light that shines on the subaltern the darker it appears.

These features, when taken together, suggest that concealment is a seminal rather than incidental component of the film's rhetorical strategy. It is surely significant that Carmelo should be blind. On a superficial level his disability makes him – like the amputee on the trolley – vulnerable to the predatory designs of villains such as Jaibo, and he therefore illustrates the tragedy of social inequality.[4] But his blindness is, I would argue, the outward manifestation of the underlying motif of concealment. Carmelo gradually grows in stature and symbolic density as the plot unfolds. Simply a vicious, blind old man at the beginning of the film, he is transformed by its conclusion into the conscience of society; his blindess thereby takes on a resonant, mythical quality. He enlists the help of the police, tells them where Jaibo lives (something, that no one with perfect vision would have been able to do), and, when the boy finally returns to his lair, Carmelo advises the police as to where to lie in wait: in an eerie way, he becomes, in effect, Jaibo's judge and executioner. As we hear the shots off-screen which finish Jaibo off, the camera cuts to a medium close-up of Carmelo's face as he pronounces the triumphant words: 'One less, one less. If only they could all die before daybreak' [Uno menos, uno menos. Ojalá mueran todos antes de la llegada del día]. Since this is a structurally important scene – the climax – we are drawn into seeing Carmelo as a Tiresias figure who, despite his blindness, is blessed with second sight.[5]

A number of critics have argued that Carmelo's blindness makes him an Oedipal figure. In the classical myth, Oedipus killed his father, Laius, unknowingly married his mother, Jocasta, and put out his own eyes when he discovered what he had done. His blindness signified the punishment meted out by the gods for his misdeeds. The Greek script, as filtered through Freud's epistemology, though, has been subjected to a number of important changes in *Los olvidados*, which might be expressed as follows:

1. Pedro (who is not quite Oedipus) does not sleep with his mother, though, as his dream suggests, he has harboured Oedipal fantasies about her, and is instead rejected by her.
2. Jaibo (who is not quite Oedipus) does not kill his father or sleep with his mother, but he does sleep with his friend's mother, at which point he becomes the surrogate father of his friend.
3. Pedro (who is not quite Oedipus) does not kill his father (Jaibo), although he attempts to do so; instead he is killed by his own father (Jaibo).
4. Carmelo (who is not quite Oedipus) nevertheless suffers his blindness; it is, perhaps, transferred – metaphorically speaking – to him from Jaibo as a result of the latter's misdeeds.
5. Marta (who is not quite Jocasta), does not hang herself. In fact, she simply walks calmly past while Pedro's body is transported on a donkey to the rubbish tip.

At a number of key junctures, therefore, the Greek/Freudian myth has been disrupted, transformed, ironised. The irony resides in the gap between the characters of *Los olvidados* and those of, say, Aeschylus's *The Oresteia*. The *grand récit* of the House of Atreus has become the miserable tale of a hovel in Mexico City.

The most intriguing patchwork character, though, is Carmelo, since he puts us in mind of not only Oedipus but also (as mentioned) Tiresias. In that final scene in which he mouths his triumphant words, Carmelo becomes the voice of society which, via the juridical system, condemns 'los olvidados' to death, and – metaphorically speaking – to societal invisibility. The rather enigmatic message contained on the invalid's trolley – '*me mirabas*' – draws attention to the ways in which, as viewers of films or as spectators of the social fabric, we sometimes cannot see what we are/were looking at. *Los olvidados* hints at the idea that we are often blind to what we do not want to see (for example, the physically deformed, the mentally deformed, the subaltern).

Given the enigmatic symbolism attached to the realm of the visual in general and the eyes in particular in Buñuel's work (one has only to think of the slitting eye sequence in *Un chien andalou*),[6] it is significant that the character who is designated as the outsider early on in the film should be called 'Ojitos' (Big Eyes). There is an important scene in the film when Ojitos, who is bewildered and sad because his father seems to have abandoned him to his fate, is bullied by the street gang, first, because he is a foreigner (a '*forastero*') and, second, because he stares at one of the street boys. This sequence is important because Ojitos is given prominence as a displaced projection of the camera eye, which studies others and, in effect, 'stares' at them. The gang's aggression towards Ojitos is, indeed, a projection of the aggression of the subaltern when threatened by the gaze from without, a gaze that, as we shall see, includes the camera eye.

In order to understand the nature of the gang's aggression towards Ojitos I need to make some preliminary comments about the role of violence throughout the film. The overwhelming presence of physical violence in *Los olvidados* has been noted by various critics. Francisco Aranda has argued that violence in this film is both excessive and monotonous, and indeed that, for this reason, the film has been overrated (Edwards, 1982, p. 19). Most of the violent scenes are unadorned in terms of musical accompaniment (there is hardly any), backdrop (there are never stylised stage sets), or filler scenes (the onward march of the plot has a Racinian nakedness to it). Violence, which Buñuel has admitted as being the 'central theme' of his work (Aub, 1985, p. 151), is presented in Sadean terms as having its own justification, that is, a *raison d'être* based on the voice of nature. As we read in *La Philosophie dans le boudoir*: 'What voice other than that of nature incites our personal hatred, our desire for vengeance, war, in a word, the constant motive for murder? If, therefore, she advises us thus, she has her reasons for doing so' ('quelle autre voix que celle de la nature nous suggère les haines personnelles, les vengeances, les guerres, en un mot tous ces motifs de meutres perpétuels? Or, si elle nous les conseille, elle en a donc besoin') (Sade, 1909, p. 240).

The worst, and possibly the most famous, violent scene is the one which occurs just eight minutes into the film: out of revenge for grassing on him, Jaibo kills Julián, hitting him on the back of the head with a stone, and then pounding him to death with a stick. The audience is not prepared by visual or aural clues, and the murder is made all the more horrific because of Julián's dull scream. The action is filmed in a sequence of medium shots without graphic close-ups, in a typically Buñuelian manner: 'There are hardly any close-ups in my films. It's unnecessary to go beyond the medium shot' ['no ... hay casi *close-up* en mis películas. No hace falta pasar del busto'] (quoted in Aub, 1985, p. 156). The sequence possesses symbolic resonance since it is framed by an establishing shot of urban decay (a dilapidated building) at the beginning and by the black cock at the end. By wrapping these two apparently unconnected images – one expressing violent urbanity, the other aggressive animality – around the film's central act of violence (since all the other crimes spring from it), Buñuel in effect shows that the human and the animal worlds are linked by their mutual predication on violence.

Other images of violence are similarly unadorned. When Carmelo, for example, is beaten up, the desire for vengeance is shown in all its nakedness. 'Go on, tough nut, let him have it!' ['¡Anda, Pelón, desquítate!'], as Jaibo says to his friend, Pelón (Jorge Pérez), throughout the scene. And the scene in which Pedro is murdered by Jaibo when attempting to hide in the barn where Meche's family lives, is stylistically raw; once more we see Jaibo hitting Pedro's head off-screen, and this time we see his blood-covered face. What is most disturbing about these scenes is that, as viewers, we are provoked into taking up the Sadean position of deriving pleasure from the visual experience of the suffering of others, those passions which, according to Saint-Fond, are 'the most delicious to experience within a man's heart' ['les plus délicieuses que puissent naître au coeur de l'homme'] (Sade, 1909, p. 101).[7] This is uncomfortable for the average viewer.

The last scene of violence I wish to focus on is the one in which Pedro attacks his peers in the reform school and subsequently, out of frustration, two hens. It is at this point that the viewer realises that the cycle of violence has passed from one generation to the next and, furthermore, that Pedro cannot escape Jaibo's evil influence. The pious words which feature in the opening voice-over are shown – ultimately – to be a nonsense. This scene brings together a number of different strands which had been weaving their way through the film. Thus Pedro re-enacts not only Jaibo's violence (remember that he stopped Jaibo, or tried to stop him, from killing Julián, early on in the film), but also, more importantly, his mother's, since he is mimicking her violence when she killed the black cockerel which had been fighting with the hens in the barn. An unusual feature of this scene occurs when the camera lens is suddenly brought into focus and then gets splattered by the egg yolk hurled angrily at it by Pedro. Marcel Oms describes this action in terms of aggression against bourgeois perceptions of reality.[8] It can also legitimately be seen as that juncture when the subaltern attempts to destroy the control that the camera eye exerts over the characters' lives, breaking down the system whereby art produces scopophilic pleasure, allowing, just for a moment, the violence of the subaltern to be expressed precisely because it fights against disclosure.

There is clearly, thus, a tension operating in *Los olvidados* whereby it mimicks the positivistic essentialism of the sociologist who exposes poverty on a superficial level, while simultaneously hinting that the consciousness of the subaltern will always remain hidden, even when it is being disclosed. The subaltern in *Los olvidados* deliberately absconds from that epistemic violence which, in one guise, is the omniscient and non-forgiving panopticon of the legal code and, in another, is the all-seeing eye of the camera. The film, thus, draws attention to the mechanics of its own production and, in particular, the means by which the subaltern is imaged and transmitted to a larger public. The subaltern at the conclusion of *Los olvidados* is shown to be actively involved in the process by which it remains unknown.

These three scenes are important, I suggest, because the central motif of the film is that the cardinal law of subaltern culture is that it is forbidden to be a 'grass' (*soplón*). Squealing on your neighbour is met with the most rigorous of punishments. Jaibo first of all kills Julián because he believes him to be a grass, and then he kills Pedro, his accomplice, for the same reason. Grassing is equivalent to breaking up that unity to which Jaibo alludes – just after murdering Julián, and pointing to the shared possession of the spoils of the kill – when he says to Pedro: 'so now we're more united than ever' ['así que estamos más unidos que nunca']. To break down that fraternity – the self-sufficiency of the subaltern classes – is to blow the whistle, and this transgression can only be met with death. Pedro has learned this lesson; again it is not by chance that the reason he attacks the boy in the *Correccional* is because the latter is a *soplón*.

This is, indeed, one of the delightful paradoxes of the film. While Buñuel is revealing the plight of the subaltern classes, he also allows their aggression at the thought of being disclosed – imaged variously as closing doors, keeping your neighbours out, killing people who grass – to rise to the surface in the film. Buñuel is thereby able to show both sides of the coin simultaneously. He displays the subaltern in that carefully constructed cage of publicity epitomised by the language of film but he also demonstrates, at crucial junctures in *Los olvidados*, how the forgotten react with hostility towards the camera's all-seeing eye. The forgotten actively collude with society's desire that they be for ever consigned to oblivion: the subaltern remains hidden inside the box.

Notes

1. Octavio Paz refers to Carmelo in the following terms: 'That blind beggar is already familar to us from the Spanish picaresque' (Ese mendigo ciego ya lo hemos visto en la picaresca española) (1994, p. 224).

2. Henceforward translations from texts in languages other than English are mine.

3. Though Paz was impressed by the film: 'I found the film moving: it was infused with the same violent imagination and the same implacable logic as *L'Âge d'or*, but Buñuel, in a very controlled way, had created an even more concentrated final product' ['La película me conmovió: estaba animada por la misma imaginación violenta y por la misma razón implacable de *La edad de oro*, pero Buñuel, a través de una forma muy estricta, había logrado una concentración mayor'] (1994, p. 230).

4. Carmelo and the nameless amputee are also linked by the central image of sight; the latter has the unusual phrase, 'you were looking at me' ['me mirabas'], on his trolley; see a still in Agustín Sánchez Vidal (1988, pp. 311–12).

5. Tiresias was the most renowned soothsayer of all antiquity, despite being blind from his seventh year; he carried a golden staff, which, in Carmelo's case, becomes a stick with a nail at the end.

6. For further discussion of eye imagery in Buñuel's work, see Sandro, 1987, pp. 23–9.

7. Octavio Paz has commented on how *Los olvidados* is redolent of 'a passage from Sade' (un pasaje de Sade), and even points to Sade as being one of Buñuel's most important literary sources (1994, pp. 226, 229). Peter Evans refers to Buñuel's 'Sade-dominated attraction' to the Gothic (1995, p. 80).

8. Quoted in Evans 1995, p. 85. Evans also offers the following interpretation of this act:

> Like Oedipus he [Pedro] plucks out, albeit figuratively, his own eye, symbol of sexual as well as other types of knowledge, and hurls it at the viewer, a gesture of rage and defiance aimed equally at his mother – and through her, all mothers – and at the social, moral, and metaphysical order of which he is the helpless and (invoking Freud's explanation of eye symbolism in the essay on the uncanny), in various cases, the castrated victim.
>
> 1995, p. 86

References

Aub, M. (1985), *Conversaciones con Buñuel. Seguidas de 45 entrevistas con familiares, amigos y colaboradores del cineasta aragonés*, Madrid: Aguilera.

Buñuel, L. (1983), *My Last Sigh: The Autobiography of Luis Buñuel*, translated by Abigail Israel, New York: Vintage.

Edwards, G. (1982), *The Discreet Art of Luis Buñuel*, London: Marion Boyars.

Evans, P. W. (1995), *The Films of Luis Buñuel: Subjectivity and Desire*, Oxford: Clarendon Press.

King, J. (1990), *Magical Reels: A History of Cinema in Latin America*, London: Verso.

Lewis, O. (1965), *The Children of Sánchez*, Harmondsworth: Penguin.

Monsiváis, C. (1995), 'Mythologies', in P. A. Paranaguá (ed.), *Mexican Cinema*, translated by Ana López, London: BFI, pp. 117–27.

Mora, C. J. (1982), *Mexican Cinema: Reflections of a Society 1896–1980*, Berkeley: University of California Press.

Paz, O. (1994), *Fundación y disidencia*, Mexico City: Fondo de Cultura Económica.

Pérez Turrent, T. (1995), 'Luis Buñuel in Mexico', in Paranaguá (ed.), pp. 202–8.

Sade, Marquis de (1909), *L'Oeuvre du Marquis de Sade*, edited by Guillaume Apollinaire, Paris: Bibliothèque des Curieux.

Sánchez Vidal, A. (1988), *Buñuel, Lorca, Dalí: el enigma sin fin*, Barcelona: Planeta.

Sandro, P. (1987), *Luis Buñuel and the Crises of Desire*, Columbus: Ohio State University Press.

Spivak, G. (1985), 'Subaltern Studies: Deconstructing Historiography', in Donna Landry and Gerald Macclean (eds), *Selected Works of Gayatri Chakravorty Spivak*, New York: Routledge, pp. 203–35.

5

Hybrid Culture and Acoustic Imagination: The Case of *Robinson Crusoe*

Marvin D'Lugo

> We have auditory obsessions just as we have visual obsessions. I believe, as well, that the auditory speaks more to our imagination than does the visual.
>
> Luis Buñuel (in de la Colina and Pérez Turrent, 1986, p. 108)[1]

> The techniques of sound editing and mixing make sound the bearer of a meaning – and it is a meaning which is not subsumed by the ideology of the visible. The ideological truth of the sound track covers that excess which escapes the eye. For the ear is precisely that organ which opens onto the interior reality of the individual.
>
> Mary Ann Doane (in Doane, 1986a, p. 61)

Cultural hybridity, co-productions and sound

Of Luis Buñuel's twenty-two films shot in Mexico between 1946 and 1965, none was more successful commercially nor more widely distributed at the time of its release than *Robinson Crusoe* (1952). Though much praised by critics in the US and Europe (García Riera, 1993, p. 227; Taylor, 1964, p. 99), it eventually became an 'orphaned' film,[2] eclipsed in the eyes of those commenting on Buñuel's Mexican period by *Los olvidados* (1950), *Él* (1952) and *Ensayo de un crimen* (1955). Yet, more than any of his work over the decade of the 1950s, *Robinson Crusoe* demonstrates an essential transnational mobility that few of his other films of the period achieved. That is, the ability to circulate beyond the framework of the national cinema within which it was produced and to operate as a mainstream commercial commodity within international markets.

While most of Buñuel's Mexican films have come to be read as part of the director's effort to negotiate the tension between the commercial Mexican cinema and European auteurist cinema (Evans, 1995, p. 4), *Robinson Crusoe* is one of the very few to actually achieve that goal, principally by cultivating forms of hybridity that reposition the narrative of the famous shipwreck within transnational contexts that undermine the meaning of the story it purports to tell. In essential ways, hybridity, in its multiple forms, constitutes the film's central theme. I am using the term in the sense that Néstor García Canclini defines it. That is, not simply syncretism or the admixture of races (1995, pp. 15–16), but a textual process that involves its audience in a rethinking of the hierarchy between centre and periphery (ibid., p. 241), whereby territorial identities are blurred but, importantly, the focus is not on some meaningless blending, but rather a redressing of the powerful asymmetry of the cultural core/periphery (ibid., p. 266). This is precisely the concept that gradually emerges from *Robinson Crusoe*.

The film highlights those conditions of the story that mirror the terms of its own production – transnational exploitation of the periphery by the economic and cultural machinery of the core, encounters between civilised and presumed primitive peoples, finally, a productive collaboration across cultures that redefines the nature of national cultural identity.[3]

Buñuel's version of Defoe's hero seems to embody García Canclini's view of Latin American experience of cultural hybridity 'where traditions have not yet disappeared and modernity has not yet completely arrived' (1995, p. 1). This Crusoe continually enters and exits modernity, bringing his European technical ingenuity to the pristine tropical island in order to survive. In the process, however, he assumes postures of superiority only to confront the raw nature of the physical world that ultimately sabotages that pose.

Robinson Crusoe was Buñuel's ninth film in Mexico and the first of a cycle of four international co-productions he directed there in the 1950s.[4] The director's opening gambit for this, the fifth cinematic remake of the Daniel Defoe novel, serves to underscore the duality of the textual operations that will guide the subsequent reworking of the Defoe narrative. The post-credit scene begins with an image of an eighteenth-century frigate being tossed by a tropical storm. As the hull smashes against the rocks and the voice-over of Robinson (Dan O'Herlihy) explains the general circumstances that led to his shipwreck, we clearly see the ship's name, the *Ariel*. Buñuel has, in fact, embellished details of the famous Defoe novel with an intertextual reference that does not appear in the original work. For an Anglo-American audience, the reference to *Ariel* may cast this as a version of the opening scene of *The Tempest* and thus be read as an invitation to view the subsequent narrative as a reworking of the Shakespearean text. Yet in the Latin American context within which the film was produced and within which it eventually circulated in a Spanish-language version, the Shakespearean allusion may conversely invoke the anti-colonialist symbolism of José Enrique Rodó's well-known 1900 essay, 'Ariel', a denunciation of US and European commercial imperialism in Latin America (Vaughan and Vaughan, 1999, pp. 98–9).[5]

This intertextual duality points up the asymmetry between the two sides of

the cultural equation that produced this version of *Robinson Crusoe*: the dominant anglophile culture (the English source novel and the Hollywood style of its
genre adaptation) and its Hispanic mode of production (director, technical crew,
joint funding and locations).[6] Shot in Mexico in 1952 as a collaboration between
the recently established Ultramar Studios and its US partner, United Artists, this
was Buñuel's first English-language film, his first colour production, and the first
film of the Mexican period to use a mixture of English- and Spanish-speaking
actors. Though Buñuel frequently asserted indifference to the idea of an adaptation of the Defoe novel, material abounds to suggest that this was much more
than a routine shooting assignment for him. Indeed, he penned one version of
the shooting script himself.[7]

Though *Robinson Crusoe* is only looked at, if at all, as simply another part of
Buñuel's auteurist production, the film also poses in its own right a prescient
characterisation of hybrid culture precisely at the moment when the sense of the
global reach of motion pictures was beginning to make itself felt through international co-productions. It does this by rewriting the popular myth that
surrounds the figure of Crusoe, the quintessential agent of mercantile capitalism, crossing geographical and cultural borders, and, through the process of his
journey, unmasking the ideology that belies the very idea of globalisation.
Buñuel's script underscores the series of assumptions about the superiority of
civilisation that are insistently juxtaposed against the primitive world, showing
global commerce confronting Latin American cultures on the margins. This version of *Robinson Crusoe* enables us to see the global as something more than
merely the encroachment of transnational commerce on communities on the
periphery of modern industrial society.

As the opening images of the film suggest, Buñuel's strategy is to maintain
the impression of a narrative fidelity to the Crusoe narrative but to undercut and
reposition the story through seemingly minor details and embellishments, all of
which serve as a means through which to interrogate the social and political
nature of the hybrid cultures formed through global processes.

As John Baxter contends, the production of *Robinson Crusoe* coincides with
Buñuel's growing desire to break out of the patterns of the Mexican film
industry and somehow to enter either a European or, better, an American
market (1995, p. 218).[8] He found that opportunity in a project proposed by
George Pepper and Hugo Butler, two 'Hollywood Marxists in exile' (de la Vega
Hurtado, 1998, p. 238) who had fled to Mexico after being named in the 1947
California Un-American Activities hearings. Pepper worked in Mexico under the
name 'George P. Werker'. The two operated under the recently founded
Ultramar Productions and worked closely with Buñuel's long-time friend and
producer of four of his previous Mexican films, Oscar Dancigers, as they

hatched a plan to have the production co-funded by United Artists and Dancigers.[9] The project was to be shot on a shoestring for a mere $40,000 (de la Colina and Pérez Turrent, 1986, p. 88).[10]

Unlike his subsequent non-Spanish language co-productions, for instance, there were, in fact, two versions shot of *Robinson Crusoe*. Ferrán Alberich, who has closely analysed the two versions, contends from his close examination that sequences from the Spanish-language version appear to have been shot after the English-language shoot.[11] The English-language version was presumed to be potentially marketable as it imitated the established Hollywood prestige genre of movie adaptations of canonical English novels. With the collaboration of Butler – whose Hollywood screenwriting credits, in addition to *Young Tom Edison* (1940) and *Lassie Come Home* (1943), included the script for Jean Renoir's *The Southerner* (1945) – *Robinson Crusoe* was designed as an intentional mix of popular film and Hollywood's version of auteurist *cinéma de qualité*.

But beneath such a veneer of conformity to mainstream genres there are signs of an effort to subvert the very conventions within which the film proposes to function. While critical attention has been focused understandably on the powerful Buñuelian imagery, it is really the conceptualisation of sound – perhaps for the first time more fully developed than images – that informs the development of *Robinson Crusoe*. The location shooting on Mexico's Pacific coast, the director's first English-language production and the plot of the hero's extended solitude all combine to underscore the element that Buñuel would later call the 'auditory imagination' that illuminates the nature of the cultural hybridity at the core of the co-production.

Marsha Kinder makes a persuasive argument for the centrality of the sound-track in Buñuel's cinema, observing the experimental nature of sound both in his first three films and his subsequent Mexican and Spanish productions. It was in these latter contexts, in which he made most of his films, 'where sound technology was technically inferior to Hollywood and where conceptual experimentation was therefore all the more essential' (1993, p. 294). She details the ways in which, in both his avant-garde and commercial films, Buñuel would employ sound in conceptual ways that run counter to the dominant patterns for naturalising narrative through the soundtrack, thus making sound itself an essential part of his experience of cinema. She notes, for instance, the insistent recourse in his films to distinctive ritualised sounds, as in the persistent drums of his native town of Calanda that he first uses in *L'Âge d'or* (1930). As well, in *L'Âge d'or*, his approach was to exaggerate elements of the soundtrack, 'where interior monologues obstruct the physical consummation of the lovers and where disjunctive animal sounds – a tinkling cowbell and a barking dog – bathetically rekindle the heroine's animal love' (Kinder, 1993, p. 298).[12]

Buñuel had more than a passive involvement in sound technology, as Kinder reminds us. He was employed in American dubbing facilities in France (1933–4), and later supervised dubbing operations at the Museum of Modern Art in New York between 1939 and 1943. In *Él* (1952), made shortly after *Robinson Crusoe*, Kinder notes a number of ingenious deployments of sound–image synchronisation. Some of these are consistent with his previous film work in France and Spain and frequently relate to a subversion of the desires of his empowered bourgeois protagonists.

Robinson Crusoe is completely consistent with Kinder's characterisation of Buñuel's conceptual approach to sound in his films and yet differs from his other productions in two important ways: first, in *Robinson Crusoe* sound is made a central and sustained focus of narrative action; second, for the first time, Buñuel's elaboration of sound is rooted in both geopolitical as well as individual psychological contexts, thereby setting the stage for a cluster of themes and treatments that will re-emerge in his mature films of the 1970s.

In a slip zone between cultures

Robinson Crusoe was part of a cycle of on-location jungle shoots in which Buñuel was engaged during this decade. Preceded a year earlier by *Subida al cielo* (1951), then followed by *El río y la muerte* (1954) and the three remaining foreign-language Mexican co-productions – *La Mort en ce jardin* (1956), *La Fièvre monte à El Pao* (1959) and *The Young One* (1960) – these productions contrast markedly with his studio shoots that focused on urban locales, films like *Los olvidados* and *La ilusión viaja en tranvía* (1953). The jungle setting and, more specifically, the treatment of tropical spaces as islands in the co-productions consistently debunk the idealisation of nature by setting it up for the invasion by Europeans. That paradigm, the very essence of the plot of *Robinson Crusoe*, introduces another distinctive feature of spatial thematics not seen in other Buñuel films of the period: an often menacing American space intruding upon the mindset of characters like Robinson, shaping their actions and, in a sense, determining their reactions. It is only in the later *El ángel exterminador* (1962), originally scripted under the title, *Los náufragos de la calle Providencia* (The Shipwrecked of Providence Street), that *mise en scène* so powerfully determines character action in this way.

The formulation of American space in *Robinson Crusoe*, reinforced through the plotline of the displaced traveller trapped on the tropical island, helps bring the geopolitical theme into focus. For Buñuel, travel clearly is used as a potentially subversive trope, disruptive of the illusion of an enclosed community, and Defoe's Robinson is the quintessential traveller. Particularly in his Mexican films, travellers are continually depicted as shattering social equilibrium, putting in doubt the self-sufficiency of the illusion of the unified community. There is a striking moment in *Ensayo de un crimen* (1955) that best exemplifies this disruptive quality. It is a scene in which the space of a typical Mexican *fonda* is invaded by a group of American tourists one of whom engages the hero, Archi, in a conversation in English. Later on the group shows up at the protagonist's house and thwarts his plan to kill the heroine, Lavinia. Not merely disrupting the plot in a comic gag, their very presence challenges the cinematic illusion of Mexican space itself precisely through the eruption of the foreign language. At moments like these, as Bakhtin would have argued, the sense of self-sufficiency of the home culture is breached: 'This verbal–ideological decentring will occur only when a national culture loses its sealed-off and self-sufficient character, when it becomes conscious of itself as only one among *other* cultures and languages' (1981, p. 370). These on-screen tourists symbolically highlight the commercial commodity status conferred on the periphery by the agents of the political and cultural centre. The recurrence of Bakhtinian dialogism suggests an embedded narrative motif within which Buñuel formulates both a social history and an economic analysis of the world evoked for the characters and spectators of the film. In the figures of displaced travellers in the Mexican co-productions – a plot staple of all four international co-productions – we may begin to discern the underlying logic of subversive travel: these are commercial plunderers, terrorists, fortune hunters, sexual poachers, in short, characters who, by virtue of the plotting of these films, are brought to the same essential site of primitive tropical space that leads in each work to an implicit critique – often more visual than verbal – of the presumed superiority of civilisation over the culture of the periphery.

As international co-productions designed to travel between cultures, these films often have recourse to an elusive form of self-reference. They designate the position of cinema within what in later decades would be called the world 'system' of commodity production. Importantly, these are not movies about movies, yet by undermining certain narrative clichés, they lead us to reflect on the status of cinema. In their conscious destabilisation of the local/global interface suggested by their plots, they mirror the commodity culture that shaped their very production, and thus gradually break down the borders and frames that have defined the asymmetrical relations of cultural and economic globalisation.

Acoustic imagination

As Buñuel's first English-language film and his first international co-production, *Robinson Crusoe* places special emphasis on the soundtrack in general and on spoken language in particular. On the occasion of the film's US release, *Life Magazine*, for instance, entitled a four-page story on the film 'Semisilent "Crusoe"

Exciting New Film Has Only 800 words' (23 August 1954). Though a slight exaggeration, the paucity of spoken dialogue, a logical consequence of the reduction of the cast to a single character for more than half of the film's eighty-four-minute running time, does make sound in *Robinson Crusoe* a self-conscious element. Buñuel noted the importance of sound in the film's construction:

> Pero la banda sonora era fácil. Un número de rollos de un solo personaje, más el ruido del mar, de la selva, de los pájaros, y luego unos rollos más con lo que dicen Friday y los personajes que llegan al final de la historia. Es una película con pocos diálogos.
>
> [The soundtrack was easy. A number of reels with only one character, then the sounds of the sea, of the jungle, of the birds, and then a few more reels with Friday and the characters who show up at the end of the story. It's a film with very little dialogue.]
>
> de la Colina and Pérez Turrent, 1986, p. 86

Ostensibly using Defoe's plotline, the script Buñuel rewrote from Hugo Butler's original treatment developed a basic connection between Robinson's plight on the tropical island and what the director would later call, in the context of *Ensayo de un crimen*, 'auditory obsessions' (de la Colina and Pérez Turrent, 1986, p. 108). In the latter film these were obsessions linked to fetishised objects as in the case of the music box that shapes Archi's obsessions. As Buñuel reasoned, this type of obsession is part of a process within which 'the auditory speaks more to the imagination than does the visual' (ibid.).

In *Robinson Crusoe* such acoustic obsessions, in fact, work more centrally than do images to open up the film's geopolitical theme. Robinson's status as a representative of mercantile commerce, displaced from his customary milieu, forces him to confront the natural world. His sense of superiority is shattered by the *mise en scène* as he finds himself driven by a series of fears and obsessions tied to the acoustic – what he can hear but not see. Inevitably, this tension between the auditory and the visual becomes a meta-cinematic theme as the persistent power of the off-screen world brings spectators to a potentially heightened awareness of the sound–image synchronisation of the cinematic story.

Mary Ann Doane describes Hollywood sound films as operating 'within an oscillation between two poles of realism: that of the psychological (or interior) and that of the visible (or the exterior)' (1986a, p. 59). In Buñuel's conceptualisation of Crusoe's story, the two poles are joined. The sounds and voices that populate the island form the constant drama and tension of Robinson's story. In this tropical environment he feels himself continually threatened by the menace of off-screen natural sounds disembodied from images; his response to his fear and loneliness is similarly acoustic. When he speaks within the diegetic space, for instance, it is invariably to fill the void of his solitude. In Buñuel's original script, one scene called for Robinson to have a bizarre dialogue-argument with his own echo. He is walking near a circular rock formation on the beach when a wasp stings him. He shouts '¡Ay, traidora!' ['Traitor!'] with the words echoing from the rocks. He responds to the echo with the word '¡Idiota!' ['Idiot!'] directed now to his own echo. Finally, in exasperation, he retorts to his auditory double '¡Odio tu voz!' ['I hate your voice!']. The sequence seems to have been the inspiration for the scene in the final version of the film in which Robinson visits the valley of echoes where he shouts the words of the Twenty-Third Psalm to assuage his desire for the sound of another human voice.

It has been argued that the function of synchronous sound in classical Hollywood narrative cinema serves to 'mask' the material heterogeneity of the cinematic illusion, its constructedness (Doane, 1986b, p. 340). The auditory obsessions that structure Crusoe's story, however, serve to counter that strategy, making the film's audience increasingly aware of the artificiality of this presumed realism. In keeping with that self-referential treatment of sound, Siegfried Kracauer identified the echo sequence in *Robinson Crusoe* 'as an instance of "sound phenomena" which affect the moviegoer through their physical qualities' (1985, p. 132). He describes these sound phenomena as a 'shift of emphasis from the meaning of speech to its material qualities' (ibid., pp. 132–3). In this way, sound ceases to serve its conventional purpose as it does in Hollywood cinema, that of background in order to naturalise narrative processes, and becomes, in effect, one of the elements of the story.

Disembodied sounds, absented bodies

Buñuel incorporates a series of seemingly minor details that might seem merely to embellish the story, but in fact, cumulatively construct a message that is in opposition to the original text: not an affirmation of the myth of mercantile capitalism – the self-made man – but its refutation.[13] The process of that textual transformation is intimately connected to the elaboration of Crusoe's acoustic imagination. Following the cue from Defoe's first-person narration, the script uses a conventional voice-over narration, that of Robinson, as he recounts the story of his shipwreck. The credit shot shows a gold-bound edition of the Defoe novel to signify its status as a classic. The credits are superimposed over this image in gothic letters. At the end of the credits, the shadow of Robinson appears over the book. We never see his body, only his shadow cast upon the book. As he opens the book the narration begins. Rooted in the clichés of the classic novel-into-film adaptations, the enunciative strategy of the narrator's disembodied voice affirms the Eurocentric cultural-economic position that relegates the New

World experience to an object status. Tellingly, Buñuel's construction of the sequence portrays Robinson as both the author and the reader of his own story, a conflation of the subjective and objective positions that prefigures the eventual transfer of the protagonist's auditory imagination to his audience.

Almost immediately after the credit set-up, the image dissolves into the storm and shipwreck, and the narrative illusion of the hero's power and control is shattered by the American space. This initial rupture is conveyed in a visual and auditory dissolve as the dramatised space of the formal enunciation – a book, a reader – gives way to the violent eruption of nature. Ironically, Robinson's textual authority as a disembodied voice gives way to the story he relays in which his first experiences on the island are ordered by his fears precisely of disembodied sounds, movement and animal noises from the brush. The pattern intensifies to include the sound of the crashing noise of his boat as it dislodges from the rocks and sinks, a sound that symbolically marks Robinson's imprisonment on the island.

Robinson is shown gradually learning to manipulate the most precious sound for him – the human voice – as a way of assuaging the burden of his confining solitude. The valley of echoes sequence, earlier commented upon, reveals his strategy of ventriloquism to deceive his own sense of solitude. The inadequacy of ventriloquism, however, is made apparent in later scenes in which we see him conversing with his parrot, Poll, whom he has taught to say a few words, words which, like the echo of the psalm, merely replicate Robinson's own voice in order to fill the void.

A later example of Robinson's acoustic ventriloquism occurs when, in a state of delirious fever, he imagines a dialogue with his father, with O'Herlihy playing both roles in a series of cross-cuts. What is significant about this latter instance of voice displacement is that it brings the audience to an awareness of the dissociative quality of sound used within the cinematic narrative, a point that will serve as a bridge to the eventual transformation of the hero's acoustic obsessions into a creative acoustic imagination.

The first signal of that transformation as it implicates the spectator derives from the deployment of a standard sound–image editing practice known as 'sound advance', which is, as Rick Altman describes it, 'the practice of introducing a sound before the image with which it is associated' (1992, p. 251). Altman identifies sound advance as one of the clichéd conventions of certain cinematic genres such as suspense and adventure films. In *Robinson Crusoe* the device first occurs in a sequence within which we see Robinson mastering a variety of domestic activities on his island, such as herding wild goats into a pen he has constructed. In the next scene we see a tree in the jungle and hear the sound of a gunshot, after which a bird falls from the tree. The very next shot is of

Robinson, apparently standing off-screen, having just fired his rifle. This use of off-screen space seems to create an acoustic equivalent of a *trompe l'oeil* as it positions spectators in a place roughly analogous to that of Robinson in earlier scenes when he was disconcerted by disembodied sounds.

It is important to note that the dichotomy between on- and off-screen spaces is not a feature of Robinson's world, but rather a self-conscious effect of the cinematic construction of the narrative. Buñuel's use of the disembodied sounds that highlight these off-screen spaces, however, makes the audience aware of their own engagement in and commitment to the 'ideology of the visible' as constructed by sound cinema. That awareness of the limits of the visible in turn parallels the hero's growing consciousness of his confinement within his own credo of empiricism as he confronts the natural world on the island that consists of much more than the eye alone can see.

Buñuel's strategy is to juxtapose the liberating power of acoustic imagination against Crusoe's entrapment within the regime of the visible. Perhaps the most subtle characterisation of that entrapment is to be found in the narrative alignment of Robinson's solitude with his mercantile mindset. He will only be free, according to Buñuel's version, when he learns to liberate himself from obsessive materialism fixed within the film precisely around the fetishism of the look. Control for Robinson initially means scopic control. Seeing, for him, is being: a spyglass, a self-placement in a high-angle position on a hilltop. His empiricist logic, however, only leads him to construct a prison of his own design. We see him gain increasing visual control of the natural world by reconstructing the world he left behind in England and enclosing that world into his own private earthly paradise.

Against the prison-house of the empirical world, the film juxtaposes the liberating acoustic imagination through the motif of absented bodies. Initially, the body is defined in sexual terms and seems to breathe psychological life into the original stoic Defoe character. The figure of the absented sexual body gradually becomes a leitmotif that punctuates Robinson's days and years on his island. He ponders the mystery of how the cat he saved from the ship produced a litter when he saw no other cats on the island. When he sets up a scarecrow for his wheat field, he places a woman's dress to cover the twigs. When the breeze blows he pauses in pain, obviously reminded of the absented female body.

The only solace from his loneliness comes from his faithful dog Rex and his parrot Poll, whom he teaches to repeat some phrases. Throughout the long section prior to the arrival of Friday, Robinson's brief dialogues with his pets constitute the only diegetic speech in the film. In this way the absented body is refigured as an auditory rather than simply a material symptom of the hero's loneliness.

The relationship with Friday

While following Defoe's narrative with relative fidelity to plot details, Buñuel has transformed the story into the struggle between the things Robinson can see and those he cannot, the latter gaining increasing dominance in his mind. He learns to embrace the incorporeal principally through his evolving relation with Friday. Out of an initial fear that Friday will kill him, despite having saved the islander from cannibals, Robinson tries to make Friday his slave, shackling his ankles. In keeping with his bourgeois dream of material achievement, he will later transform Friday into his domestic servant. Buñuel develops the relationship between the two men in such a way that Robinson's philosophical education, learning to see beyond the illusory nature of the merely visible, parallels his liberation from the mercantile obsession of seeing other human beings as mere chattel. We witness his gradual transformation as detailed in his extended contacts with Friday, through whom he learns to adjust to the tropical spaces and to master survival skills.

Conventionally, *Robinson Crusoe* is thought to be the story of the protagonist's triumph over adversity on his tropical island, with Friday usually relegated to the secondary status of a cliché in the Crusoe narrative. In Buñuel's version, however, Friday holds the key to Robinson's salvation. Together with Robinson, he embodies the film's humanistic theme of 'Man's re-encounter with Man'. In this sense, Buñuel's casting of Jaime Fernández, brother of the famed Mexican

Culture and imperialism in *Robinson Crusoe*

film auteur, Emilio Fernández, in the role of Friday is perhaps more than a coincidence. For this Friday serves as much as a refutation of the condescending European myth of the noble savage as a reminder of Emilio 'Indio' Fernández's marketing of exotic pseudo-indigenous characters like Dolores Del Río and María Félix as cinematic representations of Mexico to the world.

The turning point in Robinson's relation with Friday and one of the most commented-upon scenes in the film is Robinson's attempt to explain Christian theology to Friday, specifically the function of the Devil. The scene is set in Robinson's domestic space as the two men sit smoking their pipes. In the background we see Poll, seated on a perch. In an earlier scene we had witnessed Robinson teaching Friday to speak English in much the way that he had presumably taught Poll. In that first language lesson, Robinson taught Friday names: You Friday, Me master. Now, however, unlike his parrot, Friday is able to reason with Robinson, questioning why, if God wants man to be good, has he created the Devil who tempts man to do evil. Unable to explain, Robinson turns to the parrot and says: 'Poll, you understand, don't you? Poor Friday has a hard head.' The brief dialogue pointedly exposes the ventriloquism that has been masked as dialogue for Robinson throughout his sojourn on the island. Friday's question, in fact, begins to redress the asymmetry of the relation between the two men and of Robinson's relation to his New World environment.

It is telling that, with Robinson's bonding with Friday, the text inserts a new series of dissociative sound–image synchronisations that momentarily shatter the characters' equilibrium. In one such move, as the master and servant are working in the jungle, Robinson goes off to inspect a tree and a cannibal appears behind him about to shoot with a bow and arrow. At the exact instant that the arrow is about to leave the bow a gunshot is heard and the Indian falls dead. Framed from an off-screen space, the impression is again one of an aural *trompe l'oeil*. Decipherment of the meaning comes from beyond the frame. Friday has saved his master by shooting the cannibal. In a later scene when the cannibals are after the two men, Robinson shows Friday how to throw a heavy grenade or cannonball to explode among their adversaries. Robinson simulates a throw just as another off-screen gunshot is heard, this time announcing the arrival of the mutineers to the island.

These two moments of sound advance, similar to the acoustic dissociations of earlier scenes, are nonetheless staged with another purpose in mind. They emphasise the growing insufficiency of the edenic world that Robinson seems to have secured for himself with Friday. For the first time in the film, Robinson experiences the false synchronisations of sound and image within his own diegetic space, which reawaken him to the existence of a world beyond the frame and a meaning once again beyond the merely visible.

More than a textual 'trick', the knowledge of that off-screen space provides the diegetic mechanism for Robinson's deliverance as it initiates the final conceptual phase of Robinson's trajectory, his needed re-integration into society. He has already learned to harness his acoustic imagination and master appearances in the crucial final section of the film. We see this as he coaches Friday to lure the mutineers to the stockade with promises of gold, then ensnare them through the play of off-screen voices that suggest to them that they are surrounded by an army. With the arrival of the mutineers, he is now able to act upon his new-found understanding of hybrid culture. He defiantly challenges the exploitative Eurocentric mentality of the mutineers that sees American space as the object of possession, exploitation and destruction. His self-recognition of how much he has changed is dramatised in Robinson's final gesture before departing the island. Though more than thirty years have elapsed since he first arrived on the island, he looks into the mirror in his cave and sees the image of the young man who had been swept ashore in the storm. The contrast between the two images underscores the emotional as well as the physical change.

That sense of transformation is further emphasised acoustically in the film's final moments, Robinson's and Friday's departure from the island. As he is rowed to the ship that will take him to England, Robinson looks back and hears the barking of his dog, Rex, who had died some twelve years earlier. This is the precise moment in which the blazing words 'The End' are imposed over the image. The subversive move of the displaced bark of the dog effectively counters the rage for enclosure that characterised so much of Robinson's mindset during the early phases of his life on the island. The Robinson we now see with his man Friday is re-entering the modernity of the European world but with a perspective that clearly has broken from his former sense of control, closure and order. Instead of choosing Hollywood's conventional image of narrative closure, therefore, Buñuel inserts this open ending, one that leads the spectator to ponder the meaning of the previous story.

Co-producing culture

Positioned between the Mexican film industry and its international 'partners', *Robinson Crusoe* reflects Buñuel's effort to transform the hybrid mode of production within which he was engaged into an aesthetic and moral theme. As a work designed to travel, to transcend geographic borders in the name of commerce, *Robinson Crusoe* refigures the Defoe narrative through its conceptual deployment of sound. The cultural hybridity embodied in Robinson's relationship with Friday is more than a convenient narrative pairing of two dissimilar characters. It is a blurring of territorial identities that involves for each the continual rethinking of the hierarchy between centre and periphery. The formulation of that relationship is, as the previous discussion indicates, deeply rooted in Buñuel's notion of acoustic imagination.

The material practices related to his use of sound in *Robinson Crusoe* might well serve as a metaphor for the very transnational project of the film: the deployment of narrative and cinematic techniques aimed at awakening in audiences the desire to move beyond the closed limits of imposed personal and cultural experience. Seemingly confined by cinematic conventions, both of sound technology and film genres, Buñuel has invested into his own version of the Crusoe myth a liberating sense of global culture constructed upon the humanistic rebalancing of the commercial equation between the cultures of the core and those of the presumed periphery.

Notes

1. 'Tenemos obsesiones auditivas como tenemos obsesiones visuales. Creo, además, que lo auditivo habla más a la imaginación que lo visual.' This and all other translations of Buñuel quotations are my own.

2. In Victor Fuentes's authoritative *Buñuel en México* (1993), for instance, *Robinson Crusoe* and *The Young One* (1960) are treated as digressions from his Mexican work in a section marked 'Interlude' and entitled 'Su periplo en Estados Unidos: el cine norteamericano de Buñuel hecho en México' (His Wanderings in the USA: Buñuel's Hollywood Films Made in Mexico).

3. In this same context, some scholars see in *Robinson Crusoe* the hint of an allegory of Buñuel's own position at the interstices of cultures, aesthetic ideologies and film industries (de la Vega Hurtado, 1998, p. 237; Fuentes, 1993, p. 93).

4. The other three were *La Mort en ce jardin* (1956), *La Fièvre monte à El Pao* (1959), and *The Young One*. I purposely omit a third French-language film, *Cela s'appelle l'aurore* (1955), which was a French–Italian co-production, and, unlike the other four films, was shot outside Mexico, in Corsica.

5. Buñuel would later rework the allusion to *The Tempest* in *Le Charme discret de la bourgeoisie* (1972) in which Fernando Rey plays the corrupt ambassador of an imaginary Latin American republic, Miranda. The country, which is the source of much ridicule by the snobbish French characters in the film, carries the same name as Prospero's daughter in Shakespeare's play.

6. Victor Fuentes characterises the ambivalent nature of this and Buñuel's second American co-production of the period, *The Young One*, as the director's embrace of the 'transparencia estilística, la claridad y la economía expositiva' ['stylistic transparency, clarity, and economy of expression'] (1993, p. 92) of classical Hollywood narration precisely while weaving into that simulation of the Hollywood style 'la contestación buñueliana al clima inquisitorial de los Estados Unidos que le obligó a un segundo exilio, y al comercialismo y moralismo

archiconservador de Hollywood que le cerró sus puertas' ['the Buñuelian response to the inquisitorial climate of the United States that had forced his second exile, and to the commercialism and arch-conservatism of Hollywood which had closed its doors to him'] (1993, p. 92).

7. In a prominent 1954 interview with Tony Richardson in *Sight and Sound*, Buñuel acknowledged his own objective in *Robinson Crusoe*, contradicting the impression that this was an arbitrary choice for a film project:

> This was a film I really wanted to make … There's nothing Hollywood about it. I start with Crusoe on the island – no ship or wreck – I have him alone for seven reels, then with Friday for three, and then the pirates just at the end as it is in the book. I just watch Robinson build his house, make pots, grow wheat … yes. I made it about his struggle with nature … and about solitude … and despair.
>
> Richardson, 1978, p. 138

Review of the press material holdings of Buñuel's personal library at the Filmoteca Española in Madrid confirms the special regard the director had for this film. *Robinson Crusoe* and *Los olvidados* were the only two Mexican films for which he maintained his own personal scrapbook of US, British and French reviews.

8. Baxter writes:

> Buñuel's optimism about his career began to cool after *El bruto*. By the start of 1952, Mexico's film industry, its independence already cooling, was heading into the winter of all national cinemas which defy the Hollywood machine. Hoped-for overseas sales had not materialized, and local films, unpopular with Mexican audiences, were increasingly shelved in favour of those from the United States. Unions demanded more government investment and a limit on imports, aims they were ready, even eager to strike for. Unless he could break into the European or, better still, American market, he would find himself, after seven years in Mexico, back where he started.
>
> 1995, p. 218

9. As it turned out, the co-production scheme was in part a political 'front'. Working under the pseudonym Philip Roll, Butler prepared a script that Buñuel would rewrite before accepting the project to be co-produced by George Pepper, under the pseudonym of Henry F. Erlich. Beneath the surface of a Mexican-made film conceived for the US general audience, *Robinson Crusoe* contained a series of veiled and ironic references both to McCarthyism and the Hollywood blacklist, and even to Buñuel's own status as a political exile (Fuentes, 1993, p. 93).

10. Despite this modest budget, there were apparently efforts to transform this into a prestige production. Letters from the Buñuel Archives suggest that the project originally called for the acclaimed British actor Michael Redgrave to play the title role. The young Irish actor, Dan O'Herilihy, who eventually took the part, was

nominated for an Oscar in the best actor category, constituting Buñuel's first prestigious connection with Hollywood.

11. Notes from an unpublished catalogue of films for the Buñuel Centenary, Filmoteca Española (August 1999), np.

12. In an earlier appreciation of Buñuel's work, John Russell Taylor noted the impressive use of sound in *L'Âge d'or*:

> On the sound track alone practically every device known to the modern cinema – interior monologue, overlapping and distorted sound, recurrent aural leitmotifs, appropriate music intensifying what is happening on the screen and deliberately inappropriate music producing dissociation from it – is all to be found.
>
> Taylor, 1964, p. 86

13. John Russell Taylor describes the transformation of the Defoe novel by Buñuel this way:

> in filming it Buñuel neatly reverses practically all the points made in the book. Preserving carefully enough the outline of events, Buñuel has turned their significance inside out, and instead of Defoe's triumphant picture of reason ordering hostile nature he gives us instead a penetrating study of solitude breaking down a 'reasonable' man as he tried desperately to bolster his own progressively more shaky beliefs by hopeless and largely absurd adherence to the external forms of a way of life which has no relevance to his present situation.
>
> 1964, p. 99

References

Altman, R. (1992), 'A Baker's Dozen of New Terms for Sound Analysis', in R. Altman (ed.), *Sound Theory, Sound Practice*, New York and London: Routledge, pp. 249–53.

Bakhtin, M. M. (1981), *The Dialogic Imagination*, edited by Michael Holquist, Austin: University of Texas Press.

Baxter, J. (1995), *Buñuel*, London: Fourth Estate.

de la Colina, J. and T. Pérez Turrent (1986), *Luis Buñuel: prohibido asomarse al interior*, Mexico: Joaquín Mortiz/Planeta.

de la Vega Hurtado, M. (1998), 'The American Buñuel: *The Young One* and the Politics of Exile', *Nuevo Texto Crítico*, 21/22, pp. 237–48.

Doane, M. A. (1986a [1985]), 'Ideology and the Practice of Sound Editing and Mixing', in E. Weis and J. Belton (eds), *Film Sound: Theory and Practice*, New York: Columbia University Press, pp. 55–62.

—— (1986b), 'The Voice in Cinema: The Articulation of Body and Space', in P. Rosen (ed.), *Narrative, Apparatus, Ideology: A Film Theory Reader*, New York: Columbia University Press, pp. 335–48.

Evans, P. W. (1995), *The Films of Luis Buñuel: Subjectivity and Desire*, Oxford: Clarendon Press.

Fuentes, V. (1993), *Buñuel en México*, Teruel and Zaragoza: Instituto de Estudios Turolenses and Gobierno de Aragón.

García Canclini, N. (1995), *Hybrid Cultures: Strategies for Entering and Leaving Modernity*, Minneapolis and London: University of Minnesota Press.

García Riera, E. (1993), *Historia documental del cine mexicano*, VI, Guadalajara, Mexico: Universidad de Guadalajara, Consejo Nacional para la Cultura y las Artes, Instituto Mexicano de Cinematografía.

Kinder, M. (1993), *Blood Cinema: The Reconstruction of National Identity in Spain*, Berkeley and London: University of California Press.

Kracauer, S. (1985), 'Dialogue and Sound', in E. Weis and J. Belton (eds), pp. 126–42.

Richardson, T. (1978 [1954]), 'The Films of Luis Buñuel', in J. Mellen (ed.), *The World of Luis Buñuel: Essays in Criticism*, New York: Oxford University Press, pp. 125–38.

Taylor, J. R. (1964), *Cinema Eye, Cinema Ear: Some Key Film-Makers of the Sixties*, New York: Hill and Wang.

Vaughan, V. M. and A. T. Vaughan (1999), 'Introduction', in William Shakespeare, *The Tempest*, Third Arden Series edition, Walton-on-Thames: Thomas Nelson and Sons Ltd, pp. 1–138.

6

Domination and Appropriation in *The Young One*

Isabel Santaolalla

That's my noble master!

Ariel, The Tempest, I, II

The Young One (1960) remains one of Buñuel's most neglected films critically. The film is a US–Mexico co-production, resulting from Buñuel's collaboration with two victims of the McCarthy House on UnAmerican Activities hearings, who were resident, like him, in Mexico: scriptwriter Hugo Butler (credited as H. B. Addis) and producer George Pepper (under the pseudonym G. P. Werker). Buñuel had already worked with both men on *Robinson Crusoe* (1952), his only other film in English, much more successful in terms of box-office returns and distribution than the one under consideration here.[1]

The few pieces written on *The Young One* have tended to comment on a restricted number of topics – mostly its anti-racism and 'Lolitaism' – and to search for the Buñuelian signature in what is otherwise often classified as a stylistically conventional film.[2] In response to José de la Colina's comment that *The Young One* was his least personal film, perhaps a 'minor Buñuel', Buñuel himself remarked with typically mischievous contrariness: 'Really? I actually think it is one of my most personal films … There are many details: the corpse's feet, the spiders, the hens, the impartiality' (Pérez Turrent and de la Colina, 1993, p. 112).[3] He was also impatient with readings that simplified the film's treatment of race and sexuality, above all adolescent sexuality (Sánchez Vidal, 1984, p. 242). Taking its cue from Buñuel's disclaimers, this essay attempts to review the pivotal themes of race and sexuality through concentration on the role of space in the construction of characters and narrative – space here meaning not merely 'setting' but that which 'implies, contains and dissimulates social relationships' (Lefebvre, 2000, pp. 82–3).

The idea to make *The Young One* came from producer George Pepper, who saw in an adaptation of Peter Matthiessen's recently published 'Travelin Man' the potential for a film on the 'ever-increasing racial unrest in the USA at that time'

(Buñuel, J. L., 2000, p. 7). The story, which had won an O. Henry Award in 1957, follows the last four days in the life of Traver – the Travelin Man of the title – a black convict on the run who seeks refuge on an island off the Carolina coast, only to find that a white gamekeeper oversees it. After stalking each other for days, they come face to face, and Traver is outwitted by the white man and killed.

Hugo Butler was employed as a co-writer and, through his collaboration with Buñuel, produced a script that, while still reflecting 1950s' attitudes towards race in the United States, transcends immediate socio-political issues and becomes a parable about man's – and to a much lesser extent, woman's – quest for a psychological and physical habitat. In the process of adapting Matthiessen's story, Butler and Buñuel made numerous changes, the most significant of which was the addition of a major character, Evalyn (Key Meersman), the pubescent granddaughter of Pee Wee, late assistant to Miller (Zachary Scott), warden of the game-preserve island. In the film, Traver (Bernie Hamilton) loses part of his prominence in the original story – not least in the title – and forms the third side of the triangle created by his arrival on the island. In contrast to the short story, Traver is not an escaped convict, but a city jazz musician who flees from a white woman's false accusation of rape. The introduction of two other minor characters who briefly visit the island – Jackson (Graham Denton) and Reverend Fleetwood (Claudio Brook) – further complicates the dualistic pattern of the original story. By incorporating these, as well as, above all, the character of the young girl, Buñuel and Butler may have sought to avoid the potentially simplistic effect of the binary character pattern governing Matthiessen's story (Buñuel, L., 1982, p. 237).

One can only speculate about the decision by Butler and Buñuel to shift the emphasis of Matthiessen's race-conscious narrative, and, to some extent, sideline its black protagonist. Both scriptwriters would have sympathised and identified with Traver, a character on the run, like them persecuted by the advocates of a dominant ideology.[4] Even so, they rose to what must have seemed like the much more challenging task of exploring the psychology of the tormentor, rather than the victim's. In conversation with Pérez Turrent and de la Colina, Buñuel remarked: 'without trying to present a thesis, I wanted to understand – not to justify – the racist characters' (1993, p. 113). What, on his own admission (ibid., p. 99), interested Buñuel most in a character was its potential for change. Although most characters in *The Young One* evolve in one way or another during the course of the narrative, no one undergoes a greater transformation than Miller. He – and not the Travelin Man or the Young One foregrounded by the titles of the story and film respectively – is the narrative's main driving force. The choice of Zachary Scott, the actor audiences would have been most familiar with, seems to further support this case. Scott had an established career behind him, with titles that included *The Southerner* (1945),

Mildred Pierce (1945), *Flamingo Road* (1949) and *Appointment in Honduras* (1953), among others. Bernie Hamilton, by contrast, was virtually unknown: he had started his film career some ten years earlier, but had not yet managed to leave his mark on the industry, something that would only happen four years later, thanks to his role in the groundbreaking *One Potato, Two Potato* (1964). Even more significantly, the Young One, the heroine of the title, was played by a total unknown, with no previous experience in the cinema – or interest in it, according to Buñuel (Pérez Turrent and de la Colina, 1993, p. 113).

The island of the original story obviously remained an appropriate location for a narrative about characters placed under scrutiny. As if in a test tube, disparate agents are brought together in this isolated environment, and forced to interact. In this confined space (the camera never leaves the island), Miller, more than anybody else, comes under observation, not only in relation to his physical surroundings, but also to his female companion on the island, and the male stranger who appears from outside it. Miller's masculinity is thus put to the test both by internal – Evvie's developing femininity – and external threats – Traver's challenge to his status as the 'patriarch' of the island. Although Buñuel prided himself on the fact that his meticulous choice of exteriors and careful positioning of the camera had managed to create the illusion that *The Young One* had been shot in Carolina (despite the fact that it had been filmed in Mexico), a *mise en scène* laden with symbolism, the absence of names – unlike Matthiessen's original – and of temporal markers gives the film an abstract, somewhat transcendental quality. Interestingly, the film was exhibited in England under the title *Island of Shame*. The island itself, we learn early on in the narrative, is set for dramatic transformation: Miller's wild domain is soon to be developed into a modern hunting club. As if in communion with the natural space they inhabit, humans are also in a transitional stage: Pee Wee from life to death, Evvie from childhood to womanhood, Traver from alleged guilt to proven innocence, and Miller, perhaps above all, from a high-handed sexual and racial mindset to greater sensitivity and moral awareness.

Pee Wee's death just before the film's opening scene establishes Evvie and Miller as the only humans inhabiting a natural space overgrown with vegetation and populated by undomesticated animals. But the wilderness here is not romantically constructed as 'a symbol of earthly paradise, the place of before the fall where people lived in close harmony and deep sympathy with nature' (Short, 1991, p. 10). Like the Bosch-like jungle of equivocal delights in *La Mort en ce jardin* (1956), this is no Garden of Eden – at least not one without irony. In fact, the man, woman, apple and snake all reappear, but their part in the story modifies the Christian myth: neither does the snake whisper in the woman's ear (though it bites and kills her dog), nor is Evvie the defiant, seductive bearer of fruit personified by her namesake. When the girl, who has obediently tied her hair back and washed her face following Miller's order, offers him an apple, the camera delights in a shot that captures her softly lit, feminine features. Miller looks up at her, and a fast zoom-in captures the expression of a man who has suddenly discovered the woman in the girl. But even as this virginal Eve hands the apple to Miller, she remains innocent and ignorant of her sexual allure: insight and desire are associated exclusively with the film's culpable Adam, who will try to conceal his seduction of Evvie from the mainland intruders. But there is no hiding. Divine judgment eventually visits 'The Garden' in the shape of Reverend Fleetwood, who informs Miller: 'This is an abominable sin: the violation of an innocent.'

Significantly, Reverend Fleetwood's denunciation of Miller's sinful behaviour is simultaneous to his public defence of Traver's innocence. Through his influence, then, sin and guilt are transferred from the black man to the white man, a transition stressed by the circular structure of the film itself. Setting and musical score bring together beginning and end, creating a spiral whereby things are the same and yet different, where apparent opposites coincide.[5] The opening credit sequence had shown the black man landing on the island, throwing the weight of his exhausted body on the seashore, while a version of the famous 'Oh Sinner Man' song – sung by Leon Bibb, in a slightly altered version from the original 1958 recording – accompanies his moves, branding him as a sinner and prophesying his failure to find shelter or comfort there.

> Oh Sinner Man, where you gonna run to?
> Oh Sinner Man, where you gonna run to?
> Oh Sinner Man, where you gonna run to
>   all on that day?
> Run to the rock. Rock won't you hide me? …
> Lord says 'Sinner Man, rocks can see you hiding' …
> Run to the sea. Sea won't you hide me? …

Then, in a characteristically Buñuelian sound–image dissociation, the natural concert of maritime sounds and bird songs that had accompanied Traver's moves is interrupted by a woman's voice screaming 'Rape! Rape!' We soon realise this exists only in Traver's mind, a space immediately invaded by the camera, allowing us to share the black man's traumatic recollection of his flight from the city, while intentionally misleading us (by withholding the actual scene in the woman's bedroom) into accepting the song's definition of Traver as a sinner. But in the course of the narrative, spectators and characters alike discover that Traver is in fact innocent, whereas Miller is the morally objectionable character. It seems only just, therefore, that the last scene of the film should return us to the initial one, as if to 'rewrite' the script. Back on the seashore, the camera focuses on Reverend Fleetwood, Evvie and Jackson hopping on a boat in the distance, and then cuts to a close-up of Miller's face, looking directly at the camera, as the song 'Sinner Man' attaches itself to the soundtrack of natural sounds, and to Miller's plight. The song continues as Traver meets Miller on the seashore, gets help from him to push the boat to the water and speeds off. Camera and song, however, do not follow Traver this time, but remain instead with Miller. A long shot of him in the distance – framed by branches in the foreground – conveys the white man's isolation and smallness on this island, while the song plays on.

This is a morality play, bringing to light the blurred limits that separate guilt from innocence, and the film's construction of space creates just the right conditions for the enactment of such a drama. The island is a liminal space, connected to but separate from the world of the town on the mainland. Its amphibious nature – defined by water as well as by land – and its hybrid combination of untamed wilderness and civilising humanity gives it a dual quality. On the island, life-affirming forces coexist with destructive ones: clean, running water shares the ground with stagnant, treacherous swamps; honey-making bees with murderous racoons. The island's feral *mise en scène* is in line with the paradoxical meanings traditionally associated with the wilderness: on the one hand 'the classical perspective which sees the negative element of the wilderness experience, the view that wilderness quite literally bewilders', on the other, 'the wilderness as a place of spiritual regeneration' (Short, 1991, p. 21). The film's use of space and *mise en scène* encourage these parallel meanings: characters are certainly trapped by this isolated wilderness in various ways, but equally, it is here that the seeds of their material or spiritual freedom are planted.

The sense of entrapment pervades this as much as other Buñuel films – for example, *Robinson Crusoe* (1952), *La Fièvre monte à El Pao* (1959), *Viridiana* (1961), or *Simón del desierto* (1965), to mention only a few made around this same period. When Traver is at one point pursued by Miller, the camera pauses and registers the movements of the black man, miniscule in the distance, framed through a tangle of interwoven branches, effectively likening him to a small, defenceless insect imprisoned in a spider's web. Traver makes determined but unsuccessful attempts to leave the island in his boat, each seeming as futile and almost as inexplicable as those made by the guests in *El ángel exterminador* (1962), who are unable to leave their dinner-party hosts' house (a metaphorical island, as indicated by the original title of the film – *Los naúfragos de la calle Providencia*). At one point, Traver himself makes a new hole in his recently repaired boat by hurling the rifle carelessly inside it, as if unconsciously aiming to jeopardise his chances of escape – undoing, like some male Penelope, his own handiwork.

Evvie, for her part, has never left the island, having been bred, very much like the rest of the animals in this game preserve, in captivity. No wonder, then, that she should often be seen caressing the little deer that stands tied to a wooden pole outside the cabins, as if naturally drawn to a creature whose plight resembles her own. But the most conspicuous emblems of Evvie's entrapment are the two cabins that preside over the forest clearing. When early in the narrative Evvie rushes out of Miller's cabin, not fully understanding but still annoyed by his attempts to fondle and kiss her, she can only escape to the other cabin, where her grandfather's corpse lies unburied. Hovering between these two elementary forces of nature, Eros and Thanatos, escaping from the former and trapped by the latter, Evvie's reaction is to fit the dead man's boots on to his feet, and then to sit down and eat, seeking comfort in that most symbolic of foods: honey.

In this male-dominated environment, Evvie's identification with bees and honey – on three occasions she is seen handling or eating it – leads to a whole series of associations. Traditionally considered, like milk, the ideal, perfect source of nutrition, honey has often signified matriarchy and, because of the elaborate process necessary for its production, wisdom, spiritual endeavour and rebirth (Cirlot, 1982, p. 305). These links further strengthen the association between Evvie and the deer – a symbol of purity, morality and knowledge. Evvie is the island's Artemis, another goddess of the forest and the protector of deer. All these life-affirming qualities set Evvie in stark contrast to Miller, the keeper of the woods who, ironically, is responsible for preserving animal life only so that it can be preyed upon by recreational hunters. Miller, in fact, is no freer than the others, but this is something that he will only acknowledge towards the end, as his confession to Reverend Fleetwood ('You can't have a man cooped up on this stinking island!') and the closing shot of the film demonstrate. The wilderness' potential for discovering hidden depths contributes to Miller's heightened self-awareness. Prior to his transformation, though, Miller is an arrogant individual, convinced of his mastery over every living creature on the island, including Evvie. Traver's arrival threatens his status, and triggers the clash between those two representatives of different ends of the racial, social and economic spectrum. When Traver sets foot on the island, exhausted and injured, he looks up and sees a sign that defines it in unambiguous terms: 'Private game preserve'. This is a wild territory, of untamed fauna, flora and swamps, but even these are someone else's property. The close-up of the sign confronts the disadvantaged Traver with the extent of his destitution. Thus, already in this very first scene, the introspective theme carried by the score – 'Oh Sinner Man' – blends into the film's concerns with questions of social and economic (in)justice.

Traver's arrival provides a counterpoint to Miller's presence on the island. From the beginning, both men are defined through a series of contrasts. Miller

All about Evvie in *The Young One*

is a rural white Southerner who, though a hunter, actually leads a sedentary life on the island. Traver, a Northern black city-dweller, is in fact the one who leads a nomadic existence. Miller is earth-bound (he is on the island at the beginning and remains there at the end), while Traver is mostly identified with water (he arrives from the sea at the opening of the film and sets off by sea again at the end). When Miller is first glimpsed, he is shooting a rabbit, which he then dis-embowels in a scene that immediately follows one in which Traver munches through a live crab he has just caught in the sea.

Traver's intrusion on Miller's territory poses a threat to the system that governs it, and above all, to Miller's ownership. In the course of the narrative, Traver will be seen systematically trespassing Miller's wild as well as more domestic territories, and appropriating his possessions: honey, apples, shotguns, gas, nails, tar, a hammer, one of the cabins and – at least this is what Miller comes to fear – Evvie as well. The island with its various discrete but interconnected spaces reflects here the power struggle between humans, exemplifying Lefebvre's argument that '(social) space is not a thing among other things, nor a product among other products: rather it subsumes things produced, and encompasses their inter-relationships in their coexistence and simultaneity – their (relative) order and/or (relative) disorder' (2000, p. 73). A hint that the regime on the island has been unsettled comes when Miller's scornful apology to Traver for suggesting that

Evvie should sleep in his cabin rather than in the one to be occupied by the black man is met with even more refined irony from Traver: 'Not at all, man. Not at all. You just treat those cabins just like they were your own. Be my guest!'

Interestingly, Traver's acquisition of Miller's property is achieved not through violence, but mercantile transaction, either paying for whatever he takes or working for it. This emphasises the differences between the two men: 'The stress on the negro's offers to buy food and gas from Ewie [*sic*] makes him the representative of a trading, sophisticated, city code, in contrast to the game-warden's rural, almost Wild West atmosphere of property and guns, with its racial feudalism' (Durgnat, 1968, p. 117). As the story advances it becomes clear that Traver is less governed by the law of the wilderness than Miller. He is, in fact, much less aggressive, much more polite than the white man. An unfair, racist system alone explains the different positions they have come to occupy on the social, economic ladder.

While the moral conflict marking Miller's relationship to Evvie is conveyed through biblical imagery, the more secular issues of economic imbalance and unfair distribution of property are to a large extent expressed through evocations of fairy tale (especially 'Red Riding Hood', 'Goldilocks and the Three Bears' and 'The Pied Piper of Hamelin'), as well as of legendary and literary lore. Evvie and Traver's first encounter appropriately takes place in an archetypal setting: the forest. Here, the young girl is surprised by a big, dark, threatening creature that snatches the goods she carries in her hamper. Famished, Traver is nevertheless no wolf, and offers to pay for the apple he takes from Evvie's basket (a motif that recalls the earlier scene with Miller, and establishes another link between the two men, suggesting perhaps that he too might try to abuse Evvie's innocence). As before, Evvie remains mostly ignorant of the potential danger posed by the stranger, and allows him to accompany her to the cabins. Here, the folkloric associations proliferate. Traver is seen sitting comfortably on Miller's chair, at his table, sampling his goods. When he says '[t]his guy Miller might not like me eating his food, smoking his cigarette', the link with 'Goldilocks and the Three Bears' can hardly be missed. But although, as in the tale, we are confronted here with 'a stranger who invades privacy and takes property' (Bettelheim, 1988, p. 218), the original structure is clearly subverted. Here, the character with a 'Wee' in his name is not a baby bear, but a dead old man; and the trespasser is no charming little girl, but a strongly built, dark-skinned male, himself acutely aware of the fear he instils in others: 'You are cool' – he tells Evvie – 'I don't even frighten you.' Considering the brutish nature imposed on Traver by white society – a beastly rapist who must be hunted like an animal – he would seem closer to one of the bears of the tale rather than to the young, fair girl. And yet, Traver is, in fact, an innocent man. This is confirmed when, confronted with Evvie's unself-conscious half-nakedness as she leaves the shower and accompanies him into Miller's cabin, and although captivated, like Miller before, by her sensual body – portrayed through flattering light and emphatic camerawork – he forces himself to avert his gaze and offers Evvie something to cover herself with. His reticence here points to his innocence in the rape case, and reaffirms his role as a victim of racial prejudice, in much the same way as Evvie becomes the victim of sexual abuse. Innocence links Traver and Evvie, and suggests perhaps that they are two sides of the same coin, a double-sided Goldilocks, as together they seem to threaten Miller's painstakingly acquired possessions. In the end, the greatest divergence lies in this version's moral. Whereas the original story was 'a cautionary tale warning us to respect others' property and privacy' (ibid., p. 216), Buñuel's reformulation seems to suggest instead that private property, when the result of unfair distribution and an immoral social system, deserves to be taken away.

Miller certainly senses that his most valuable 'property', Evvie, is under threat by this man who has quasi-magical powers of allure. The Pied Piper of Hamelin's resort to music as a way of avenging the community's failure to give him what he feels is his due bears some resemblance to Traver's conduct. The first time he plays the clarinet, Evvie, who is lying in bed at night, dressed in her white nightgown, is instantly attracted by its music: she gets up and sits by the window, allowing her face to be swept by the breeze and the music drifting in from the seashore. Later, when Traver starts playing it outside one of the cabins, Evvie abandons Miller and approaches Traver, dancing happily to his tune. Fearing his 'possession' might be taken away from him, Miller interrupts the duo – 'Watch this!' – and throws a home-made grenade near the cabin, thus responding with primitive, sadistic violence to Traver's seductive art. Evvie will ask Traver to play again, and when he goes looking for his instrument, she starts to follow him, as if sleepwalking, until, corralled again by her 'lawful' owner, she is prevented from leaving the cabin.

Traver's music serves two purposes: it emphasises his sensitive, artistic temperament, linking him with the rhythms of nature, but it is also an instrument of seduction.[6] It proves irresistibly attractive to Miller's young ward, raising fears, initially, that this might lead her to a destiny no less uncertain than that of the children of Hamelin. In fact, the first shot of Evvie seen hypnotically listening to Traver's clarinet comes immediately after the disturbing scene in which a group of white hens is massacred in their own coop by a badger. The metonymic link here with the black outsider who has 'invaded' somebody else's territory and threatens to take possession of his property is unmistakable.[7]

Water, wind, music and seduction are, also, the defining features of the forest god Pan. A symbol of instincts and of the life-giving, fecundating power of nature in Greek mythology, he became, in the Roman version, the representative of pastoral, nomadic life. Traver has inherited both attributes of his mythical precursor, and one wonders at first whether his encounter with the young nymphette that inhabits this forest will condemn her to the same tragic fate that befell Echo, the nymph of the classical myth. After all, Traver's musical skills are linked, as in the myth (and also, as some have claimed, in the 'Pied Piper of Hamelin'), to sexual seduction: the phallic potency of Traver's clarinet is demonstrated in its effect on women – not just on Evvie, but also on the old lady who falls for Traver when she hears him play at the cabaret. More disturbingly, Traver's clarinet is, to a certain extent, responsible for Evvie's rape: even though from the very beginning Miller is aroused by Evvie's budding femininity, it is only as he listens to Traver's clarinet that he takes advantage of her sexually. Interestingly, then, though Traver is surrounded by an aura of sexual predatoriness, he is, in fact, no more than a catalyst for it in others.

This deviation from stereotype is in line with the film's generally off-centre portrayal of black masculinity and sexuality. Bernie Hamilton's plump, slightly overweight body, his fleshy cherubic cheeks, curly hair, and bright eyes give him a child-like air, something emphasised by his quizzical remarks and his natural, strange affinity with young Evvie. The camera avoids any shots that might seem to construct him as an oversexualised male, and, in fact, often flinches from exhibiting his body in a state of undress. Nowhere is this more obvious than in the scene where he is washing himself outside the cabins, in front of Miller and Evvie, without removing his shirt. The unmistakable coyness of the camera here is more unexpected precisely because Zachary Scott had also been seen washing in an earlier scene, in which, unlike here, the spectator is allowed to gaze at his bare torso, as he languorously, almost narcissistically, dries his body on the cabin porch. It would seem, then, that the film purposely avoids the specularisation of the black man's body, perhaps refusing to expand the list of racialist representations of the black male through emphasis on physical prowess and sexual potency. What the film does acknowledge, however, is that the material oppression of the black male inevitably leaves its mark on the body. Already on his first appearance, Traver's body bears such scars: his head is bandaged, and his dirty, sweaty body weakened through lack of food and rest. Later, he is shot at by Miller, has his ankle torn by one of Miller's traps, and ends up lame, walking towards freedom, but carrying on his body the marks of his subjugation. Like Tristana's, his physical mortification points to social and psychological damage.

In a psychoanalytically focused discussion of melodrama, Peter Brooks claims that it is in the logic of melodramatic 'acting out' that 'the body itself must pay the stakes of the drama' (1994, p. 19). He refers to the 'aesthetics of embodiment' as the way in which the most important meanings have to be inscribed on and with the body (ibid., p. 17). *The Young One*, although not straightforwardly a melodrama – not even a civil-rights melodrama of the kind, say, of *The Defiant Ones* (1958), a film with which it does, however, have strong links – was nevertheless made by film-makers committed to racial justice and to the denunciation of tyranny. The repeated metaphorical mutilation of Traver's body links him with Evvie. Traver, like Evvie, will have to struggle to keep his physical integrity in a society that sees them as subordinate to others, as someone else's property.[8]

In *The Young One*, Buñuel allows Evvie and Traver to survive their respective ordeals. The film's relatively upbeat – though clearly open and ambiguous – ending radically alters the closure of Matthiessen's short story, where Traver, despite his own proud sense of natural might – 'You doan know who you foolin with, white trash, you foolin with a man what's mule and gator all wrap into one!' (1990, p. 55) – ends up dead on the seashore (ibid., p. 56). In the film, Traver's amphibious nature – in this he resembles his literary predecessor – is conveyed through actions as well as symbols. A carefully developed correlation between Traver and water throughout the film turns him into a sort of semi-mythical aquatic being: he manages to cross the swamp (while Miller dares not), and when shot by Miller at the lake, appears to have fallen, dead, into the water, only, after a while, to re-emerge alive. The film, in fact, hysterically accumulates images of water: the sea, the lake, the swamps, the river, Evvie's shower, Miller's and Traver's ablutions, a storm, a baptism scene, a water jug on the table as Reverend Fleetwood reads the biblical passage about the Samaritan and the 'living water' (St John, 4, 11–14), Jackson's subsequent offer of water to Traver, and the final escape of all characters but one by sea. Water is the essence of all possibilities, and Traver's identification with this natural symbol of life and renewal goes hand in hand with the fact that it is precisely his presence on the island that instigates Miller's process of moral regeneration. It is also metaphorically connected with the constructive nature of the activities he performs – above all the eternal repairing of his boat. This is another point of contact with Evvie, indirectly established by the film in a variety of ways. Clever editing blends, at one point, Traver's and Evvie's respective chores: a shot of Traver's body bending over the boat in order to attach a piece of wood is smoothly taken over by one of Evvie's, in the same position, leaning over the honeycomb from which she is scraping the honey. By comparison, in an earlier scene, Traver's and Miller's efforts had been contrasted through juxtaposition of another pair of stylistically similar shots – Miller's hands filling a grenade with powder, and Traver's hands, in the same position, repairing the boat – thus inviting reflection on the conflicting implications of their respective activities.

But, as always with Buñuel, character construction is marked by ambivalence.

The equivocal spatial patterns of *The Young One* are mirrored by the riven nature of its leading characters. So, Miller, for instance, though mostly defined as an unsophisticated, primitive man, displays occasional signs of sensitivity (Buñuel in Ballabriga Pina, 1993, p. 181). When Evvie flees from his cabin and sexual advances, he doesn't follow her but, instead, takes his guitar and sings a melancholy love song – 'I wish I were a red rosy bush' – unconsciously expressing, perhaps, his yearning for change. As the narrative advances, the initially stark contrast established between Traver and Miller becomes progressively blurred, coming close to disappearing. The turning point occurs when Miller approaches Traver as the latter is – as always – repairing his boat. The two men are kept at a distance, divided by the boat, as well as by the film's editing, which keeps them in separate frames, via a shot/counter-shot exchange. In spite of this, surprising similarities between the men are revealed here: both served in the army in Italy, both are equally unsettled by offensive language, reacting angrily when called 'white trash' and 'nigger' respectively – in a scene highly reminiscent of the verbal exchange in *The Defiant Ones* where Sidney Poitier and Tony Curtis voice their respective loathing for the words 'boy' and 'thank you' – and, most significant of all, both suckled at a black woman's breast:

> *Miller*: You know. When I was a baby I was kind of puny. Needed special feed. Got
>   my milk from an old black mammy.
> *Traver (sarcastically)*: No kidding? So did I.

Through contact with Traver, Miller discovers the 'other' within.[9] Confined to the wilderness, that 'environmental metaphor for the dark side of the psyche' (Short, 1991, p. 9), Miller is confronted with – in Jungian terms – his shadow. What initially seemed totally alien turns out to be an integral part of him, a discovery that exposes the entrenched paradoxes of his psyche, and which will ultimately challenge his status from within.

In this, Miller is very much like the Buñuelian Robinson, that other representative of patriarchal authority stranded on an island, facing the collapse of his 'ego' through the encounter with both the 'other' from within (nightmares, daydreaming, fear, carnal desire) and the 'other' from without (an alien land, and a racially alien human being). The tension between socially acquired hierarchical racist thinking and instinctive human alliance is made explicit in both films. At one point, Traver automatically reaches for wood when asked for some by Miller, but suddenly realising that complying with the demand would put him in the position of a servant to the white man, he stops and answers back with a command – 'Give me some whiskey!' – that Miller, amused by this refusal of racial servility, obeys. This foregrounding of the ambiguities in the master–slave dynamics recalls the scene between Robinson and Friday, in the earlier film, where Dan O'Herlihy briefly kneels in front of Jaime Fernández to remove his shackles, before rapidly modifying a pose that is identified with submission. The visual impact of this tableau, however, lingers on. Buñuel seems to be reprising that scene where, in *The Young One*, Reverend Fleetwood goes down on his knees to tie a bandage around Traver's injured ankle. This temporary reversal of roles, as the humble and the exalted momentarily exchange places, recalls the Maundy Thursday scene in *Él* (1952), where the priest washes the feet of the acolytes, which in turn gestures to Christ's washing of the Apostles' feet in the New Testament.

There are more than merely incidental similarities between *The Young One* and *Robinson Crusoe*. Defoe's novel lends itself to subversive readings since, according to Diana Brydon and Helen Tiffin, it shares with a few other canonical texts of English literature commentary on 'what English society regarded as unsuitable alliances, and ... with the threat of the outsider, the Other, who is discovered or adopted, or suddenly arrives to disrupt an English domesticity' (1993, p. 109). Save for the national idiosyncrasies, the same could be said of *The Young One*. In this film, too, 'the unwitting enabler of ... reform is ... the outsider, ... the Other, who ... can offer a timely reminder to civilised (European) man of his darker and savage origins, traces of which still lurk in the human (i.e. European/English) heart' (ibid.). It is through contact with this contemporary version of the subaltern that the darker corners of the master's psyche come under scrutiny.

All this, plus the island setting, the presence of the young girl as a companion to the older man, and of another marginalised, alienated male, links *The Young One* to another key text on patriarchal control, subordination and restitution, and one that has also been subject to 'decolonising' readings: *The Tempest*. Like Prospero, Miller is a figure of authority, positioned between contrasted characters: the much younger girl whom he instructs and grooms, and the 'inferior' male in the margins whom he despises and mistreats. Prospero's decision to provide Miranda with the knowledge appropriate to her age – '... thee, my daughter, who art ignorant of what thou art ... 'Tis time I should inform thee farther' (Shakespeare, 1979, p. 2) – is echoed in Miller's insistence on Evvie's introduction to the world of the symbolic – 'There is som'in you gotta learn, baby. You gotta learn, you know? Not all men are like your granpa. Not all men are like old Hap either. I mean, you gotta learn to be careful of yourself over in town.' Like Prospero, Miller fears Evvie is in danger of being seduced by what he views as a racially inferior creature, and reacts violently to any approach the latter makes towards her. Traver, for his part, resents Miller's control over all things on the island, and his presence challenges the white man's status, and highlights the unfairness of the individual's material exploitation and colonisation, in ways that recall Caliban's own grievances – 'This island's mine ... which thou tak'st from me' (Shakespeare, 1979, p. 6).

Even here Buñuel's refusal to rely on dualistic paradigms is clear. All the characters are marked by contradiction and complication. Evvie, in particular, now a Miranda now an Ariel, plays an important role in destabilising the master–slave relationships of the film. Traver actually compares Evvie to an airy spirit, calling her at one point his 'angel of mercy'. And indeed Evvie, like Ariel, hovers between the two men, sometimes getting closer – physically as well as metaphorically – to Miller, at other times to Traver. Although racially identified with the victimiser (which perhaps explains the somewhat uncanny scene in which she gratuitously kills a black spider – Traver? – that inoffensively crawls on the ground, as well as those occasions on which she betrays Traver's whereabouts, thus exposing him to Miller and Jackson's racist persecution), Evvie is also, and perhaps above all, a victim.[10] Interestingly, the Buñuelian reworking of *The Tempest* liberates Caliban but keeps Prospero trapped on the island. However, like his literary predecessor, Miller comes to realise that he has to relinquish some of his power, and have a fresh start, redefining his relationship both to human beings and surroundings.

The concern with place and displacement, or as Ashcroft, Griffiths and Tiffin put it, with 'the development or recovery of an effective identifying relationship between self and place' (1989, p. 9), features largely in post-colonial debates, as it also does in Buñuel. His exilic condition made him acutely aware of the precariousness of territorial allegiances. Even the contradictory statements he made about the nationality of *The Young One* reflect his relentless struggle to escape geographical boundaries: while sometimes affirming the film was purely North American – 'All the actors – save Claudio Brook – are from North America, as is Hugo Butler, and the producer, even though we filmed on location in Mexico. And of course, the theme is North American' (in Pérez Turrent and de la Colina, 1993, p. 113) – at other times he insisted on its undeniable Mexicanness:

> It was filmed entirely in Mexico, in Mexican studios and locations; all the technical crew is Mexican, the director of photography is Gabriel Figueroa; the production company (Olmeca Films) is Mexican, and I myself am Mexican. Thus the nationality of the film needs no discussion.
>
> In Ballabriga Pina, 1993, p. 180

In the end, this film – like its island setting – belongs nowhere and everywhere. Its formal texture, *mise en scène*, and character construction make it transcend the barriers of national inscription, drawing on but subverting almost every code and narrative it touches, exemplifying Brydon and Tiffin's point that '[w]hen Caliban, Ariel, Miranda and Friday "talk back", a new configuration emerges' (1993, p. 89). Whether gesturing to Christian and classical myths, European folk and literary lore, or giving expression to contemporary issues, *The Young One* tirelessly examines their creative well-springs, allowing space for the expression of other views and voices.

Notes

1. For fuller details of the conditions of production and distribution of *The Young One* see the article by Randall Conrad (1993).
2. Among the few that have widened discussion of the film is Victor Fuentes's chapter in *Buñuel en México* (1993, pp. 85–100).
3. All translations of non-English texts are my own.
4. Various critics have made the connection between Traver and Buñuel and his team of exiles. Jean Gili elaborates on this, claiming that this film is 'a drama about an artist who is forced to set aside' – like Buñuel – 'his art while he concentrates on the struggle for survival in a hostile environment' (1963, p. 198).
5. Victor Fuentes identifies the 'coincidentia oppositorum' principle as the one governing many of Buñuel's Mexican films, including *The Young One* (1993, pp. 63–81).
6. Peter Evans points out that for Buñuel, as for García Lorca, 'the black is the American gypsy, who through music – jazz – remains in touch with the harmonies of nature' (forthcoming).
7. I depart here from interpretations that link the badger scene with Miller's sexual assault on Evvie (e.g. Pérez Turrent and de la Colina, 1993, p. 114; Fuentes, 1993, p. 99). Despite what has become a widespread claim, this scene (in the twenty-seventh minute) does not closely precede Miller's rape of Evvie (which does not take place until the fifty-third minute), but is inserted in between scenes that connect Traver and Evvie.
8. In a discussion of contemporary practices of violating black bodies, George P. Cunningham discusses the triangles that position black men and white men as adversaries in the contest over the body of women, claiming that '[f]ocusing on a triangulation as a configurative site of the relationship of racial and gendered bodies to each other provides a way of thinking and talking about the simultaneity of race and gender that traditional logics do not afford' (1996, p. 135). Cunningham relates this to Freud's Oedipal triangle and Eve Sedgwick's (1985) triangle of homosocial desire (i.e. a man's interest in a rival's wife or sexual partner is often really motivated as much by admiration or envy of the rival as by sexual desire). Limitations of space prevent me from expanding on this aspect, but its relevance should be noted. Even if Traver is not actively intent on stealing

Evvie – or anything else, for that matter – from Miller, this does not prevent the latter from treating his presence as a threat to his whole situation.

9. Victor Fuentes elaborates on the question of the 'splitting ... between the black and white characters', concluding that they end up together in a 'common root of human solidarity' (1990, p. 81). Although in agreement with the first point, my interpretation of this split clearly differs from his. The film, one might argue, suggests that Miller's decision to let Evvie and Traver leave is mostly prompted by his fear that Reverend Fleetwood could harm his status on the island – 'You report this, it will mean my job' – rather than by human compassion and solidarity.

10. I disagree with Buache's – and others' – claims that 'in fact, Ewie [sic] fully consented to make love, and as a result the film does not ... centre on rape but on an act of love' (1973, p. 114). The fact that Buñuel chose not to show the two scenes of sexual abuse does not invalidate the fact that Miller is actually imposing himself on a sexually ingenuous girl. As Buñuel himself comments, '... there is no doubt about his intentions towards Evvie, and so it has not been necessary to provide explicit scenes' (in Ballabriga Pina, 1993, p. 181). Evvie is, indeed, a victim. But one who, like others in Buñuel's films – for example, *Los olvidados* (1950), *Él*, *Viridiana* and *Nazarín* (1958) – is not unambiguously benign, but is an agent, at times, of somebody else's oppression.

References

Ashcroft, B., G. Griffiths and H. Tiffin (1989), *The Empire Writes Back. Theory and Practice in Post-Colonial Literatures*, London and New York: Routledge.

Ballabriga Pina, L. (ed.) (1993), *El cine de Luis Buñuel según Luis Buñuel*, Zaragoza: Festival de Cine de Huesca.

Bettelheim, B. (1988 [1978]), *The Uses of Enchantment. The Meaning and Importance of Fairy Tales*, London: Penguin.

Brooks, P. (1994), 'Melodrama, Body, Revolution', in Jacky Bratton, Jim Cook and Christine Gledhill (eds), *Melodrama, Stage, Picture, Screen*, London: BFI, pp. 11–24.

Brydon, D. and H. Tiffin (1993), *Decolonising Fictions*, Sydney, Australia and Muldelstrup, Denmark: Dangaroo Press.

Buache, F. (1973 [1970]), *The Cinema of Luis Buñuel*, London and New York: Tantivy Press and A. S. Barnes.

Buñuel, J. L. (2000), '1960. La joven', in Luis Buñuel, *La joven. The Young One*, Teruel and Zaragoza: Instituto de Estudios Turolenses and Gobierno de Aragón, pp. 7–17.

Buñuel, L. (1982), *Mon dernier soupir*, Paris: Éditions Robert Laffont.

Cirlot, J. E. (1982), *Diccionario de símbolos*, Barcelona: Labor.

Conrad, R. (1993), 'No Blacks or Whites: The Making of Luis Buñuel's *The Young One*', *Cineaste*, XX, 3, pp. 28–31 (also accessible at <www.lib.berkeley.edu/MRC/youngone.html>).

Cunningham, G. P. (1996), 'Body Politics. Race, Gender, and the Captive Body', in Marcellus Blount and George P. Cunningham (eds), *Representing Black Men*, New York and London: Routledge, pp. 131–54.

Durgnat, R. (1968 [1967]), *Luis Buñuel*, London: Studio Vista.

Evans, P. W. (forthcoming), 'Buñuel's Outsiders', in Diana Holmes and Stephanie Dennison (eds), *World Cinemas*.

Fuentes, V. (1990), 'Buñuel, un posible director del cine (otro) norteamericano', *España contemporánea*, III, I, pp. 71–86.

—— (1993), *Buñuel en México*, Teruel and Zaragoza: Instituto de Estudios Turolenses and Gobierno de Aragón.

Gili, J. (1963), '*La Jeune Fille* et le problème du racisme', *Études cinématographiques. Luis Buñuel 2*, no. 22–3, pp. 193–8.

Lefebvre, H. (2000 [1974]), *The Production of Space*, Oxford and Cambridge: Blackwell.

Matthiessen, P. (1990 [1957]), 'Travelin Man', in *On the River Styx*, London: Collins Harvill, pp. 37–56.

Pérez Turrent, T. and J. de la Colina (1993), *Buñuel por Buñuel*, Madrid: Plot.

Sánchez Vidal, A. (1984), *Luis Buñuel. Obra cinematográfica*, Madrid: Ediciones J.C.

Sedgwick, E. K. (1985), *Between Men: English Literature and Male Homosocial Desire*, New York: Columbia University Press.

Shakespeare, W. (1979), *The Tempest*, in *The Complete Works of Shakespeare*, London and Glasgow: Collins, pp. 1–26.

Short, J. R. (1991), *Imagined Country. Society, Culture and Environment*, London and New York: Routledge.

PART THREE

LATE BUÑUEL

7

Of Boxes, Peepholes and Other Perverse Objects. A Psychoanalytic Look at Luis Buñuel's *Belle de jour*

Andrea Sabbadini

> It could be said that perversion, like beauty, is in the eye of the beholder. There is little doubt that the leading 'erotogenic zone' is located in the mind!
>
> Joyce McDougall (1991, p. 178)

Let us begin at the beginning – or at the end.

Perhaps the horse-drawn landau coach, with its disturbingly reassuring jingling bells, stands for sexuality and death – the twin pillars of the Gothic component of Romantic tradition, as well as (classically disguised as Eros and Thanatos) of the psychoanalytic edifice itself. Or does its journey through the countryside indicate an uncanny shift away from conscious reality and into a dream-world of unconscious desires? This would be a twilight space dominated by that same Primary Process mental functioning – disrespectful of the laws of logic and temporality ruling our conscious existence – that also dominates life in the unconscious, in dreaming, and in moments of creativity and madness. Towards the end of *Belle de jour* (1966) Séverine (Catherine Deneuve) – who so often throughout the film looks dissociated and almost lost in a world of her own – tells her husband Pierre (Jean Sorel): 'I don't dream any more.'

By 1967, when *Belle de jour* was released to much critical acclaim and a hypocritical sense of scandalised disbelief, Luis Buñuel had already directed some twenty-six films, including many much-maligned Mexican melodramas (but see Evans, 1995) as well as masterpieces like *Un chien andalou* (1928), *L'Âge d'or* (1930), *Los olvidados* (1950), *Viridiana* (1961) and *El ángel exterminador* (1962).

However, well-known as he was among film aficionados, it was not until *Belle de jour* that the dubious tide of international mass popularity turned in his favour.[1] But, partly because of the explicit (for those days, at least) nature of its subject – a shy and beautiful woman's perverse sexual activities hidden under her bourgeois elegance and discreet respectability – and because of the censorial interferences that the film had to endure – not unlike, and for analogous reasons, Bertolucci's own *Last Tango in Paris* five years later – *Belle de jour* turned its nearly septuagenarian auteur into a household name.[2]

'It was my biggest commercial success,' writes Buñuel in his autobiographical *My Last Breath*, to then add with a hint of false modesty, 'which I attribute more to the marvellous whores than to my direction' (1994, p. 243). The theme of prostitution, of course, has been much exploited in the cinema: suffice to mention Federico Fellini's *Le notti di Cabiria* (1957), Billy Wilder's *Irma la Douce* (1963), John Schlesinger's *Midnight Cowboy* (1969), Chantal Akermann's *Jeanne Dielman* (1975) and Neil Jordan's *Mona Lisa* (1986). But we must guess that it is not the 'sex-for-money' aspect of the oldest profession or, *pace* Buñuel, the marvellous bodies of its practitioners, that makes *Belle de jour* so unlike anything we have ever seen before, or since.

'I don't dream any more.' Was Séverine's story then, we could ask, just a dream? Was it all a fantasy? We shall never know, any more than we could find out the contents of the magic box with which its Asian owner provokes the curiosity (fear? excitement?) of the girls in the brothel, while Buñuel uses that same box to provoke our own interest – a tactic akin to that used by patients in psychoanalysis, who hint at having just had an interesting fantasy, without however being willing to disclose it to their therapist. Maybe the box, with its intriguing buzzing-bees noise, represents the illusion that there is mystery in life – till one discovers, usually too late, that there was nothing to be discovered. Indeed, were we to have asked Buñuel himself about it, we would have become one of the countless people ('particularly women', he specifies, with a touch of forgivable Latin misogyny) to address him that 'senseless' question, to which – as he puts it – 'since I myself have no idea, I usually reply, "Whatever you want there to be"' (1994, p. 243). The Emperor is naked. The box is empty.[3]

Back to Séverine, we are left intrigued by the issue – already touched upon by Buñuel in the first scene of *Él* (1952) and in *Le Journal d'une femme de chambre* (1964) – of fetishism, perhaps the most subtly perverse of all sexual perversions. The classical psychoanalytic interpretation – from Freud's own daring, original and, in the end, surprisingly convincing speculations on this phenomenon – derives from the observation that the little boy cannot quite accept that female human beings, above all his mother, could be anatomically different from him, as this would evoke in him intolerable castration anxieties. Our boy, therefore, when faced with the reality of the female genitals, reacts by denying or, more precisely, by *disavowing* his perception of this obscure object of his desire and by replacing it with a sort of hallucination of what he unconsciously wants to believe, that is that his mother, after all, must have a penis as he does himself. Interestingly, that same boy would probably use a different defence mechanism, that of *rationalisation*, to explain to himself the lack of a penis he may have noticed in his little sister: 'She doesn't have one now because she is still too young, but of course she will grow one later.' Either way, the intriguing creation in the boy's mind of this imaginary female phallus is likely to cause him problems in adjusting to reality and, as a grown-up, in his erotic relationships. A possible solution (statistically infrequent, it must be said, at least in its pathological form of a fully fledged sexual perversion) consists in his 'replacing' this maternal penis with a fetishistic object of his peculiar choice – often another part of the body, a shoe, an item of lingerie – which might have, for whatever personal circum-stances, been originally associated in his mind with it. The fetish, then, says Freud in an oft-quoted essay on the subject, is a compromise, a penis turned into some-thing else, 'a token of triumph over the threat of castration and a protection against it' (1961b, p. 154). What happens, in the end, is that 'the pervert puts an impersonal object between his desire and his accomplice' (Khan, 1989, p. 9).

Two facts are of special interest to us here. The first is that, in this famous scene of *Belle de jour*, the fetishistic object happens to be a container (often the rep-resentation of the female genitals), as well as its mysterious content (symbolically,

Obscure objects of desire in *Belle de jour*

perhaps, a baby in the womb). The second is that such a box, and the perverse fantasy that goes with it, belongs to an Oriental man. In the article already referred to, Freud uses as an example of the mixed feelings of affection and hostility, regularly present in the fetish, 'the Chinese custom of mutilating the female foot and then revering it' (1961b, p. 157).

'Lasciate ogni speranza, o voi che entrate' ['Lay down your hope once you enter this place'] was the warning on the gateway to Dante's Inferno.

After an initial resistance to cross the threshold to the brothel, as if she believed that there could be no return from it, Séverine makes her mind up. Her reasons for attending Madame Anaïs's *maison*, however, remain complex and overdetermined. We would not even dream, of course, to expect a straightforward explanation of them by such a film-maker as Luis Buñuel, and we must also rule out without hesitation the suggestion he puts in the mouth of the impeccably unscrupulous Monsieur Husson (Michel Piccoli) that his friend Séverine does it, like everyone else, just for the money.

Her reasons, instead, probably relate to her need to disappear into this different space – a life of inner imagination populated by perverse, and therefore repressed, fantasies of degradation – which ironically may feel safer to her than the depressive normality of her social environment. Or to a deep-seated, unprocessed antagonism against the bourgeois system into which, at the same time, she fits only too well – as in the flashback scene where, as a child, she rebelled against the priest's expectation that she would take Communion. Or maybe we might come to the conclusion that she is discovering in the course of her journey through sexual desires – a sort of odyssey with a dubious Ithaca at the end of it – that she does not want men to worship her in the way her husband does, and that therefore she attends the *modisterie* as a distraction from her boringly chaste marital life. Or, again, that her unconventional behaviour may be dictated by a sense of insecurity about her feminine identity, which would then need constant confirmation through the variety of erotic activities she is allowed (indeed, expected) to perform in her 'free' afternoons. This would be consistent with the view that perversions 'are as much pathologies of gender-role identity as pathologies of sexuality' (Kaplan, 1991, p. 128), insofar as 'what makes a perversion a perversion is a mental strategy that employs some social gender stereotypes of masculinity and femininity in a manner that deceives the onlooker about the unconscious meanings of the behaviours she or he is observing' (ibid., p. 130). It should be stressed here that uncertainties in the area of *gender identity* (in this case, whether Séverine feels like a woman) are different from, though not altogether indifferent to, uncertainties in the area of *sexual orientation* (in this case, whether she feels an attraction to other women). In line with the psychoanalytic belief in a universal bisexual disposition in human beings, Séverine's behaviour suggests a conflictual attitude in this respect, exemplified by her attempt to kiss a reluctant Madame Anaïs (a mother figure) when leaving her workplace for the last time, in contrast with what had happened on her first day there when she had been the one to turn her face away from Madame's lips. It would be meaningless, of course, to interpret any sort of heterosexual behaviours, in brothels or anywhere else, as a defence against homoerotic anxieties; nevertheless, when heterosexuality takes on a compulsive quality (as in, say, Don Juan) one begins to wonder what latent desires the manifest behaviour may be concealing.

But perhaps Séverine's ultimate reason for becoming a prostitute (if only a part-time one) is simply that she cannot help it. 'I am lost …' she tells Pierre, 'I can't resist'. Indeed, it is a mixture of seduction and repulsion that prostitution may hold for any woman in Séverine's position. Catherine Deneuve, only twenty-two years old at the time, hides both reactions behind her magically frosty expression, thus forcing us, the viewers, into the uncomfortable position of having to explore our own fantasies and draw our own moral conclusions.

After her first encounter in Madame Anaïs's *maison*, where she looks and behaves more like a virginal Barbie doll than a real person, Séverine takes a cathartic shower and burns her underwear in the fireplace – though she clumsily moves one of her garments to the side of the fireplace, parapraxically leaving behind the evidence of her sexual activities. These will soon include a taste of all sorts of perversions, among them incestuous necrophilia with the Duke who, twenty years ahead of the camcorder revolution, places a movie camera in front of his carefully staged erotic scenario – and in front of Buñuel's own camera. And, crucially, voyeurism: Séverine, who can only let herself visit the brothel wearing dark glasses (the same ones that Pierre, injured in his eyes like an Oedipus who should not see his own murderous and incestuous crimes, will wear after the shooting) and who is constantly concerned about being seen, will look through a peephole in the wall at the gynaecologist's sado-masochistic tragicomedy – with Buñuel and, of course, with us.

Insofar as, in a general sense, all of us cinemagoers – or, more appropriately, film-lovers – could legitimately be described as 'voyeurs', a brief *excursus* into scopophilia will not be inappropriate at this point. Christian Metz, answering his own question about where we can locate a film spectator's point of view, states in his seminal essay that all the viewer can do is identify with the camera which has looked before him. But of course there is no camera in the movie theatre, only its 'representative consisting of another apparatus, called precisely a "projector"' (1982, p. 49). Thus, we have here a perverse situation whereby, while 'the actor was present when the spectator was not [during the shooting of the film], the spectator is present when the actor is no longer [during its projection]: a failure to meet of the voyeur and the exhibitionist' (ibid., p. 63).

We can identify two contrasting and complementary kinds of voyeurism. I shall call the first one *penetrative voyeurism*; it is a narcissistic form of aggression, directly related to Primal Scene fantasies, and it involves gratification through the furtive watching of objects unaware of being watched (for instance, a man hiding in a girls' changing room). The second one, *reflective voyeurism*, involves instead the experience of pleasure through the watching of objects who are aware that they are being watched (for instance, strippers in nightclubs); this is a more advanced form of perversion because it implies some recognition that others are not just extensions of one's own self, but real persons responding to the voyeuristic activities of the subject and possibly getting themselves exhibitionistic satisfaction from being looked at.

Let us now return to our film-lovers. When the movie we watch happens to be about voyeurism itself – such as Alfred Hitchcock's *Rear Window* (1954), Michael Powell's *Peeping Tom* (1960) or Krzysztof Kieślowski's *A Short Film about Love* (1988) – or at least contains explicit scenes of it, such as the one in *Belle de jour*, we find ourselves faced with an intriguing situation, because

> we are no longer just indulging in the scopophilic activity of watching a film, with all the wishes, anticipation, pleasure or disappointments that such an activity involves. What we are watching now is other voyeurs like ourselves. In other words, our identifications on the one hand, and our visual excitement on the other, have as their objects not only the film itself, but also the subjects and objects of the voyeuristic activities projected on the screen – a silver surface which thus turns into the disturbing, distorting mirror of our own suppressed desires.
>
> Sabbadini, 2000a, p. 810

What about the nature of the object of Séverine's voyeuristic activity, that 'sado-masochistic tragi-comedy' to which, unlike her more experienced colleague, she is herself unable to contribute other than from behind a hole in the wall as an unseen passive spectator? While the scene that we, those other passive spectators, are allowed to watch in identification with Séverine is explicit in all its grotesque physicality, one is reminded of a joke that emphasises instead the more subtle, and paradoxical, nature that emotional cruelty can take in such perverse relationships. Being begged by a masochist to *please, please* really hurt him, a dominatrix looks long and hard at her partner, smiles at him with satisfied contempt and then, triumphantly, replies with a simple 'No'. On the surface, of course, the essence of sado-masochistic relationships is power; not only, as is more obvious, on the part of the sadist who can get away with causing pain and, even more importantly, humiliation on a consenting partner, but also on the part of the masochist who has the mutually agreed, and consistently respected, authority of putting an end to the game at any time. It is, in other words, the masochist (the gynaecologist in *Belle de jour*) who turns passivity into activity by calling the shots. His mistress, who appears to give the orders, in effect just receives them.

According to Otto Kernberg,

> sexual excitement incorporates aggression in the service of love [while] perversity is the recruitment of love in the service of aggression, the consequence of a predominance of hatred over love; its essential expression is the breakdown of boundaries that normally protect the love relationship.
>
> 1991, pp. 153–4

However, if we care to look below the surface, we discover that the fascination in such perverse relationships is not so much in the physical or even in the emotional pain which is being caused, or suffered, through this 'predominance of hatred over love', but in the artificiality, in the theatricality itself of the scenario being played out. Or, better perhaps, in the tension between the unconscious script and its external manifestation, between the fantasies in the minds of its participants and their realisation in the external world. Some contemporary psychoanalysts would describe the complex ways in which perverse fantasies interact with their enactments, and impinge on one another, as 'adaptive and defensive compromise formations that may serve multiple functions' (Fogel, 1991, p. 2). Others, however, question the very notion of a 'perverse fantasy' on the grounds that there can only be perverse behaviour, since all fantasy, by definition, is about the objectionable and the unobtainable (McDougall, 1991).

It could be argued, of course, that the tension between fantasies and their actualisation, referred to above, applies to all sexual relationships, or even to all relationships *tout court*. However, it is precisely the emphasis on the more theatrical aspects of the sado-masochistic play – to the point of almost requiring for its successful accomplishment an imaginary, if not a real, 'third' as a spectator – that distinguishes it (and, indeed, other such perverse games) from other intimate rapports, that connotes its extremely limited, almost claustrophobic nature, whereby the experiential range of feelings and sensations is reduced to the compulsive repetition *ad libitum* of an almost identical pattern of stimuli followed by an almost identical pattern of responses. This, which from behind Madame Anaïs's peephole can look like an exciting erotic comedy, from the participants' viewpoints can ultimately only feel like a depressing tragedy.[4]

We may wonder whether Freud's original 'seduction theory', according to which adult neurotic symptoms are caused by childhood sexual abuse, may also, or even better, apply to perversions inasmuch as these are, in his own words, the 'negative of neurosis' (1953, p. 165). Indeed, modern psychoanalysis tends to locate the psychogenesis of perversions in early traumatic experiences. For instance, Glasser (1986) has identified what he calls a 'core complex', characterised by a tension between dread and fascination for a sort of 'black hole' associated with a powerful pulling back towards the mother's body.[5] According to Cooper, 'the core trauma ... is the experience of terrifying passivity in relation to the preOedipal mother perceived as dangerously malignant ... The development of a perversion is a miscarried repair of this injury, basically through dehumanization of the body' (1991, p. 23).

Now: Séverine's flashback memory of sexual molestation when she was a young girl – a story paralleled in the present by the brothel chambermaid's daughter who seems doomed, after finishing her studies, to become herself a whore – is exorcised by being replayed again and again *chez* Madame Anaïs. Relevant in this respect are also the view that 'perversion, the erotic form of hatred ... serves to convert childhood trauma to adult triumph' (Stoller, quoted in Fogel and Myers, 1991, p. 36); and Chasseguet-Smirgel's (1983) theory that perversions result from a confusion, taking place in the early years of development and often encouraged by adults, between the genders and between the generations; so that, for instance, a girl may be expected to fantasise that her own sexual body includes the male genitals, or to behave towards her father as if she were his wife.

Returning to *Belle de jour*, I would like to suggest that if there is a schizoid split between the bourgeois order of Séverine's marital relationship (or lack of it), skiing holidays, games at the tennis club and dinner parties on the one hand, and the deviant, perverse, disruptive sexual depravity of her afternoons in the brothel on the other, at the same time there is a striking continuity between these two apparently contrasting worlds. Séverine's (and Deneuve's) austere elegance – mirrored in the formal coolness of Buñuel's *mise en scène* and of Sacha Vierny's photography – fits as easily in the sordid ambience of Madame Anaïs's establishment since corruption and hypocrisy also belong to her middle-class existence.

We could speculate that the house of prostitution, as the metaphorical antithesis of marriage, has the unconscious function of keeping the latter alive and, with it, the normality it symbolises. After all, as McDougall points out, 'most sexual perversions ... are attempts to achieve and maintain a heterosexual relationship' (1991, p. 190). The link, the *trait d'union*, the go-between is Monsieur Husson. Belonging, more than Séverine does, to both worlds almost by nature, he quite concretely crosses the boundaries by coming into the brothel, by contemptuously leaving her, as payment, some money to buy chocolates for Pierre, and by finally revealing to him what his wife is up to every afternoon between two and five o'clock.

A reference perhaps, this last one, to Shakespeare's Mrs Alice Ford's free hour for Falstaff's visit 'between ten and eleven' (or, in Arrigo Boito's libretto for Verdi's opera, *'dalle due alle tre'*). As in ancient Rome, where 'Semel in anno licet insanire' [Once a year (that is only once a year, for Carnival), going crazy is allowed], such a temporal restriction, and indeed the whole mostly unspoken set of rules regulating life in the house of prostitution, provides a containment to the dangers represented by sexual deviancy. In other words, it is the presence of such boundaries that allows socially disruptive behaviour to occur without spilling over into madness or tragedy – which is of course what happens when Marcel forcibly trespasses those boundaries. Indeed, Séverine's emotional involvement with Marcel is more threatening by far to her psychological equilibrium and fragile marriage to Pierre than either her asexual behaviour as Séverine in the marital bedroom, or her sexual one as 'Belle de jour' in the brothel.

Let us end at the end – or at the beginning.

Perhaps the landau horse-drawn coach, with its disturbingly reassuring jingling bells, indicates that everything we have seen projected on the screen was but a dream all along; that fantasy and reality, like desire and its fulfilment, draw their *raison d'être* from each other and always merge. And that works of art – a good film for instance – have the function of reminding us that they are ultimately indistinguishable.

Notes
1. Bernardo Bertolucci once remarked to me how he saw Buñuel become so anxious when this film was presented at the Venice Festival (where it won the Golden Lion) that he had to leave the cinema halfway through.
2. The next films he directed before his death in 1983, five in all – including *Tristana* (1970, also with Catherine Deneuve), *Le Charme discret de la bourgeoisie* (1972) and *Cet obscur objet du désir* (1977) – confirmed his popularity and his status as a leading European film-maker.
3. Unlike another famous and rather larger box to be spotted on the silver screen: the content of which the Coen brothers – who could be counted among Buñuel's own many adoptive sons – also do not share with the viewers of *Barton Fink* (1991). In this case, however, their box looks quite heavy and is about the same size as the one in the final scene of David Fincher's *Se7en* (1995) – which, in that instance, we do know contained a severed head.

4. There has been a kind of U-turn in the psychoanalytic conceptualisation of sado-masochism after Freud's controversial 'discovery' that, beyond the Pleasure Principle, there would be a *Todestrieb*, a Death Drive pulling all organic matter (*homo sapiens* included) back to its inorganic sources (Freud, 1955). Our existence, then, would be but the titanic, and finally doomed, struggle of Eros (the life forces) to contain Thanatos. A consequence of such a grandly pessimistic view of our human condition is that what was originally considered as a 'derivative' of anger or aggressive behaviour, now begins to be seen as 'primary'. To put it simply, and in the context that concerns us here, masochism is no longer explained as sadism turned against the self; it is rather the sadistic behaviour to be considered as a form of masochism turned against the 'other'. In the end, however, sado-masochism, as the double-sided coin of the same perverse scenario, is accounted for on the basis of the fusion and de-fusion of the two classes of drives 'so that we never have to deal with pure life instincts or pure death instincts but only with mixtures of them in different amounts' (Freud, 1961a, p. 164).

5. I have argued elsewhere that these psychodynamics are also fundamental to the personality and behaviour of such film characters as Scottie (James Stewart), the protagonist of Alfred Hitchcock's *Vertigo* (1958), dominated as they are by an internal conflict consisting of a magnetic pull towards a deadly trap:

> The perverse activity is understood as a solution to the dilemma faced by those individuals who feel a tragic attraction for regressive dependence towards an engulfing, both protective and destructive, object – from which they cannot separate, nor let themselves be swallowed, while trying to achieve both things at the same time.
>
> Sabbadini, 2000b, p. 509

References

Buñuel, L. (1994 [1982]), *My Last Breath*, London: Vintage.

Chasseguet-Smirgel, J. (1983), 'Perversion and the Universal Law', *International Review of Psycho-Analysis*, 10, pp. 293–302.

Cooper, A. (1991), 'The Unconscious Core of Perversion', in G. Fogel and W. Myers (eds), *Perversions and Near-Perversions in Clinical Practice*, New Haven and London: Yale University Press, pp. 17–35.

Evans, P. W. (1995), *The Films of Luis Buñuel: Subjectivity and Desire*, Oxford: Clarendon Press.

Fogel, G. (1991), 'Perversity and Perverse: Updating a Psychoanalytic Paradigm', in G. Fogel and W. Myers (eds), *Perversions and Near-Perversions in Clinical Practice*, New Haven and London: Yale University Press, pp. 1–13.

Fogel, G. and W. Myers (eds) (1991), *Perversions and Near-Perversions in Clinical Practice*, New Haven and London: Yale University Press.

Freud, S. (1953 [1905]), 'Three Essays on the Theory of Sexuality', in *Standard Edition, Vol. 7*, London: Hogarth Press, pp. 123–243.

—— (1957 [1915]), 'Instincts and their Vicissitudes', in *Standard Edition, Vol. 14*, London: Hogarth Press, pp. 109–40.

—— (1955 [1920]), 'Beyond the Pleasure Principle', in *Standard Edition, Vol. 18*, London: Hogarth Press, pp. 1–64.

—— (1961a [1924]), 'The Economic Problem of Masochism', in *Standard Edition, Vol. 19*, London: Hogarth Press, pp. 155–70.

—— (1961b [1927]), 'Fetishism', in *Standard Edition*, *Vol. 21*, London: Hogarth Press, pp. 147–57.

Glasser, M. (1986), 'Identification and its Vicissitudes as Observed in the Perversions', *International Journal of Psychoanalysis*, 67, pp. 9–16.

Kaplan, L. (1991), 'Women Masquerading as Women', in Fogel and Myers (eds), pp. 127–52.

Kernberg, O. (1991), 'Aggression and Love in the Relationship of the Couple', in Fogel and Myers (eds), pp. 153–75.

Khan, M. (1989 [1979]), *Alienation in Perversion*, London: Maresfield Library.

McDougall, J. (1991), 'Perversions and Deviations in the Psychoanalytic Attitude', in Fogel and Myers (eds), pp. 176–203.

Metz, C. (1982 [1974]), *The Imaginary Signifier. Psychoanalysis and the Cinema*, Bloomington: Indiana University Press.

Sabbadini A. (2000a), 'Watching Voyeurs: Michael Powell's *Peeping Tom* (1960)', *The International Journal of Psychoanalysis*, 81, pp. 809–13.

—— (2000b), 'The Attraction of Fear: Some Psychoanalytic Observations on Alfred Hitchcock's *Vertigo*', *British Journal of Psychotherapy*, 16, pp. 507–11.

Stoller, R. (1991), *Perversion*, New York: Pantheon.

8

Buñuel Against 'Buñuel': Reading the Landscape of Fanaticism in *La Voie lactée*

Ian Christie

> 'You have touched on a subject, Sir Canon,' said the Priest at this, 'which wakes in me an old grudge I bear against the plays they act today. It is as great as my grudge against books of chivalry. For although Drama, according to Tully, should be a mirror to human life, a pattern of manners, and an image of truth, the plays that are performed nowadays are mirrors of absurdity, patterns of foolishness, and images of lewdness.
>
> *Don Quixote* (Cervantes, 1950, p. 428)

There is a teasing passage in Buñuel's memoir, *My Last Breath*, in the chapter entitled 'Surrealism' (1984, p. 125). After evoking the early Surrealist Group of the 1920s in Paris and declaring how his three years as a member 'changed my life', he moves to a memory of forty years later, in May 1968. Many of the slogans of that tumultuous time came directly from the history of Surrealism, such as 'All power to the imagination' and 'It is forbidden to forbid', while the thrust of protest was eerily reminiscent of the earlier movement's call to revolt against authority, and banality. Yet amid all the debate and planning, few knew how to act – fortunately in Buñuel's view: 'as Breton would have said, action had become just about as impossible as scandal' (ibid., p. 125). Buñuel's image of himself at this time – 'alone in Paris, like a curious but uneasy tourist [who] didn't know what to do with myself' (ibid.) – might imply an elderly disaffection. Yet the film that had been temporarily interrupted by the strikes and demonstrations, *La Voie lactée* (1969), and which would appear in the following year when the tide of revolt had subsided, is precisely about epiphany and Utopia, and violence in the service of ideals, although on a much broader scale. But rather than reduce this curiously neglected work to the status of an oblique comment on the doctrinal frenzy of May 1968 – in the way that Godard's *Week-end* (1967) is now often termed 'prophetic' – I want to consider how the issue of its interpretation can illuminate sharply contrasting attitudes towards Buñuel. Like Barthes's famous 'zero degree' of writing, Buñuel's film marks a point of interrogation of narrative, ideology and representation itself: a text that implicates us fully in its interpretation and our relationship to it. A valedictory summing-up, perhaps, even though he would, unexpectedly, continue making films.

Elsewhere in *My Last Breath*, Buñuel recorded with evident satisfaction how the film immediately divided opinion – echoing its last lines, when Christ says that he has come, not to bring peace but a sword, setting everyone against each other. Was it a destructive attack on Christian values, or anodyne enough to have been funded by the Vatican? Buñuel remembered Carlos Fuentes taking the former and Julio Cortázar the latter view, although his own gloss rejects such simplistic alignments: it simply represents 'a journey through fanaticism' of any kind (Buñuel, 1984, p. 245). However, the film's pragmatic travellers, who are nominally following the ancient pilgrims' route to Santiago de Compostela in the present, encounter a veritable encyclopaedia of emblematic religious figures and heretics along the way, interspersed with miracles, prophecies and revelations. *La Voie lactée* is, at the very least, a film composed of religious imagery and discourse; and even if it contains a number of moments likely to shock the devout, it can hardly be considered 'blasphemous' in the way that *Viridiana* (1961) was. Indeed its scrupulously traditional portrayal of Christ, Mary and the disciples in the style of Raphael and Poussin seemed disconcerting to many just five years after the earthy monochrome of Pasolini's naturalistic *Il Vangelo Secondo Matteo* (Gospel According to St Matthew) (1964).[1]

Looking back at the film's initial reception, there is a clear split between French admiration and a puzzlement, shading into irritation, among British and American critics. For the latter, Buñuel's most recent film on a religious theme, *Simón del desierto* (1965), had been easily assimilated as, in essence, another study of pathological obsession from the director of *Él* (1952) and *Ensayo de un crimen* (1955), richly comic in its portrayal of the crowd-conscious hermit and his delusions of diabolical temptation. In the following year *Belle de jour* (1966) conspicuously broadened Buñuel's reputation, beyond those who had become accustomed to his familiar litany of themes and motifs. Here was a triumphant instance of the old surrealist successfully modernising his familiar motifs and themes with the help of the strikingly contemporary figures of Catherine Deneuve and Pierre Clementi, and even converging with the narrative ambiguities then fashionable in the wake of *L'Année dernière à Marienbad* (1961) and in the same year as Robbe-Grillet's *Trans-Europ-Express*. By comparison, *La Voie lactée* seemed almost defiantly old-fashioned. For the influential modernist critic Richard Roud, it was a manifestation of 'the most tiresome aspect of Buñuel … his Village Atheist manner', despite the 'unanimous praise' it had already won in France (1969, p. 12). Another English reviewer was disconcerted by the 'flimsy picaresque structure', in contrast to the enigmatic elegance of *Belle de jour* (Tarratt, 1969, p. 56). And for the combative American critic John Simon it was 'a mere trifle wrapped in a triple cloak of befuddling obscurantism' (Walker, 2000, p. 537). Across most reviews, there was a strong sense of recognition – Buñuel and his famous 'obsessions': 'for the Buñuel devotee there are the familiar key images' (Robinson, 1969, p. 22); 'Buñuel at his mischievous best, sending up religion' (Hibbin, 1969, p. 6). We are in the realm of the favourite Buñuel tag-line, 'Thank God, I'm still an atheist', rhyming closely with 'still a surrealist'.

Certainly there are traces of distancing even in the overwhelmingly favourable French press reviews. As an example, Jean de Baroncelli (1969, p. 10) ended his review by predicting that it will 'disconcert some and fascinate others … only Luis Buñuel could have made *La Voie lactée*' (ibid.). But more intriguing is a group of three articles on the film in one 1969 issue of *Cahiers du cinéma* (Oudart, Pierre and Narboni) that constitute a radical debate on critical method, anticipating the journal's 'collective readings' that would begin in the following year.[2] In the first of these, Jean-Pierre Oudart identified three 'registers' of narrative – scenes from the life of Christ, from Christian life through the ages and from the present day – episodes of which 'enter into a double relation of opposition and association' (1969, p. 35).[3] This formal structure, he suggested, has indeed been created by Buñuel just so that it can be violated, but not merely to shock or amuse; rather to test how far he can go within a structure that positively invites transgression. Oudart went on to distinguish 'vertical collisions' between different historical periods and 'horizontal confrontations' (which can also be inverted), before suggesting that all the pieces which make up this 'score' have as their sole common denominator 'the imagination'. He then proposed 'an equalisation of all the imaginations (of the film's shooting, of the editing of its 'story' [histoire] and of history itself, of myth) on the basis of their common location, the film (ibid.).

Oudart's elegant semiotic-formalist account of *La Voie lactée* as a matrix of almost infinite possibilities leads to the suggestion that it accommodates the spectator's desires without demanding any specific allegiance, although by encouraging 'the imagining of transgressions' it may 'trap us in our desires'. The film's originality, he claims, consists in inaugurating a cinema 'which is nothing other than the imaginary space of a series of possible readings, texts and meanings, of which none is right, since each contradicts the others' (ibid.). The end result is a process of reflection on the nature of myth and imagination, and on cinema's utopian, self-contradictory project.

If Oudart was content to insulate *La Voie lactée* from either a biographical Buñuel or the mere intention to scandalise, both Sylvie Pierre and Jean Narboni took up the challenge of defending a position that insisted on the intrinsic self-referentiality of films, while admitting that they have 'content' and indeed authors. That *La Voie lactée* contains or 'speaks' scandal is undeniable, but is this what it is 'about'? Both found in it exemplary issues of reading (*lecture*) and representation. Pierre discusses the opening encounter between the pilgrims and the commanding figure of Alain Cuny. We suspect, she suggests, that he might be God. Then a dwarf appears beside him, followed by a dove, and we realise retrospectively that this represents the Trinity, with the Son portrayed blasphemously as a dwarf – although this is only apparent if we already have a 'correct' representation of this central mystery. For Narboni, the film's web of contradictory discourses evoked Buñuel's own history of misinterpretation, and its play of reverent and irreverent portrayals of Christ and the Virgin Mary raises the problem of hypostasis – how ideas become attached to (representations of) figures. For all three, the film offered an exemplary instance of textual structure articulating its own subject, whether this is contradiction, incarnation or myth. Only a naive critic, Oudart observed, would consider it an exercise in demystification.

There are, of course, major underlying differences between Catholic and Protestant cultures, and 1969–70 marked the beginning of an intensive development of textual theory in France which would eventually influence the creation of academic film studies in Britain and America. But these contrasting

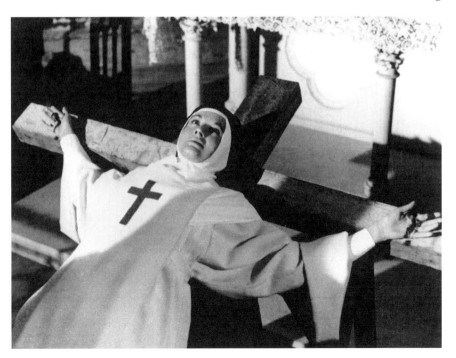

The landscape of fantacism in *La Voie lactée*

responses do point to a fundamental issue in Buñuel criticism (and not only in Buñuel) that was addressed by a member of the *Cahiers* board, Jean-André Fieschi, in an article specially commissioned for an English-language readership (Fieschi, 1980).[4] The core of this problem amounts to a 'Buñuel' defined as a 'catalogue of references and "obsessions"', which Fieschi suggests can either produce the reassuring sense of 'belonging to a circle of initiates', or irritation at an apparently constant resifting of 'repetitive symptoms' and the 'convenient refuge' of black humour. He summarises the well-tried reference points – Spain, Aragonese childhood, Surrealism, religion, psychoanalysis – admitting that they cannot be ignored, but insisting that they have long served to distract from a reading of the films themselves:

> These landmarks act as a bulwark against critical commentary; they mark out the
> area incessantly revisited (but not explored) in an attempt at taming Buñuel
> through biography and a twofold reduction: of the author to his origins, and of the
> oeuvre to the individual who created it.
>
> Ibid., p. 167

The major issue raised here by Fieschi is that which surrounds all auteurist-structural exegesis: to what extent the individual reading serves the structure, or the structure supports the reading. Whether, in this case, each film's instantiation of the 'landmarks', buttresses an already overdetermined 'Buñuel'; or whether a new film might be seen to enlarge the familiar terrain, to disturb the existing pattern of themes. His provisional conclusion is that, while there appear to be two conflicting approaches to Buñuel's 'oeuvre of extreme legibility' – surrealist-anarchist and Catholic-liberal – these are in fact two sides of the same coin, since both argue in terms of capital letter concepts and are both 'mired in metaphysics and morals' (ibid.). Even the required tools of Marxism and psychoanalysis are, in Fieschi's view, often invoked as 'terms of incantation, as answers to questions that are never asked' (ibid.). More precisely, they are fetish terms, here applied to an oeuvre which itself 'relentlessly exposes the fetish inherent in any act of interpretation' (ibid.). Following the already noted *Cahiers* line, Fieschi offers a number of corrective readings of key films, showing how they call into question spectators' attitudes in relation to a film text organised not in terms of narrative, nor even of covert meanings, but of a far-reaching 'displacement of signs' which will dislodge our certainties as spectators and destabilise any settled perception of Buñuel as a Spanish ex-Catholic and surrealist.

In Britain and America, where Surrealism was rarely more than an exotic import, Buñuel had long served as its sole authentic exemplar in cinema (like his one-time collaborator, Salvador Dalí, in painting). But the characteristic

Anglo-American complaints about *La Voie lactée* posit two problems: specialist subject matter and narrative insufficiency. Apparently lacking the sophisticated, enigmatic or comedic qualities of Buñuel's earlier and later films, it has come to be treated with either wary respect – 'one for those knowledgeable about religious dogma' (Andrew, 1997, p. 880); 'requiring special knowledge for full appreciation' (Walker, 2000, p. 537) – or marked down as minor Buñuel because its 'obsessions' outweigh its novelty.

Fieschi's warning seems timely: narrative summary of Buñuel rarely illuminates and often misleads by suggesting a merely moralistic or psychological interpretation. But this does not mean that the subject matter and the form are simply arbitrary, as *Cahiers* might appear to imply in the semiotic idiom of the 1970s. Nor is the implication that the film deals in esoteric matters entirely wrong. As I shall argue, there are good grounds for seeing it, less as an idiosyncratic return to the crude anti-clericalism of Breton and his followers, and more as a purposeful return to the roots of both Surrealism and fictional narrative.

We could begin by taking seriously what Buñuel and his co-writer Carrière said about the sources and genesis of the film. From their various statements, there were initially two key ideas, heresy and the picaresque, and it is from the elaboration and interconnection of these that this journey through the landscape of fanaticism emerged. Buñuel dated his interest in heresy back as far as his arrival in Mexico in the late 1940s, citing as his initial inspiration a classic work by the Spanish scholar and academic, Marcelino Menendez y Pelayo, *Heterodoxos españoles* (1880), which deals with the history of Spanish heretics from the fourth to the nineteenth centuries.

> Its accounts of martyred heretics fascinated me – these men who were as convinced of their truths as the orthodox Christians were of theirs. In fact, what's always intrigued me about the behaviour of heretics is not only their strange inventiveness, but their certainty that they possess the absolute truth.
>
> Buñuel, 1984, p. 244

When Buñuel eventually started work on the script in 1967 with Jean-Claude Carrière, they used a variety of documentary sources, including Abbé Pluquet's eighteenth-century *Dictionary of Heresies*. According to Carrière, they realised that heresy was always the product of mystery (Cohn, 1969b, p. 18). Whenever the early Church had sought to resolve a doctrinal dispute through formulating dogma – in such matters as the godhead, the eucharist or the immaculate conception – the result was often to produce alternative interpretations or resolutions of these mysteries, stigmatised by the Church as heresies. Heresy, then, records a struggle to penetrate mystery, and in so doing produces its own mysteries, as well as the exclusivity conferred by persecution. Buñuel invokes Breton's suggestion that the surrealists had 'certain points of contact' with heretics, and this may have been influenced by a discussion of parallels between Gnosticism and Surrealism proposed by the sociologist Jules Monnerot, an early associate of Roger Callois and Georges Bataille, in 1945:

> The Alexandrian epoch and ours are both syncretic times, and Gnosticism and sur-
> realism are typical products of this kind of period. Just as the Naassenes, the
> Peratae and the Sethians mingled Babylonian, Phyrigian, Phoenician and Greek
> myths with biblical stories interpreted allegorically and neoplatonic philosophical
> speculation, so the surrealists claimed inspiration from both Gérard de Nerval and
> Marx, from the Marquis de Sade and medieval courtly love, from Feurbach and
> Huysmans, Robespierre and clairvoyants, from dreams and psychoanalysis … from
> Lenin and pulp literature.
>
> Monnerot, 1945, p. 95[5]

The Marquis does indeed appear in *La Voie lactée*, played in a brief cameo by Michel Piccoli; and this might encourage us to see the pattern of inscriptions which make up the substance of the film – from Jesus and Mary to the Gnostic bishop Priscillian, de Sade and the Devil – as a 'forest of symbols', in which what is at issue is less any one doctrine than the *principle of opposition* that is enshrined in the tortuous dialectic of heresy/orthodoxy. More precisely, however, what scandalised the early Church and led to the violent repression of Gnostic sects was the persistent rumour of sexual scandal at the heart of this heresy. Common to most Gnostics was a distinction between the spiritual and the material, with the souls of mankind belonging to the former realm, although temporarily imprisoned in material bodies. Two resulting practices were asceticism, which denied the material, and promiscuity, which had a wide variety of theological justifications, ranging from the sacramental (emulating God's original love that created man, or gathering up the scattered fragments of divine 'seed'), to the apocalyptic (seeking to increase evil in order to hasten the Last Judgment). While asceticism would be more associated with the Cathars of the eleventh and twelfth centuries, early accounts of Gnostic sects, all compiled by their oppo-nents, tended to stress sexual immorality. A typical account is that of Epiphanius, the future Bishop of Salamis, who recounted his experiences as a young man drawn into a Gnostic cult in Egypt around 335 (quoted in Filoramo, 1990, pp. 183–4). Such lurid accounts of orgiastic sex ensured that Gnosticism's theology received less attention than its alleged immorality, and the challenge that its clandestine converts posed to both Church and State.

There is an obvious parallel to be drawn with attempts to censor the upsurge of what were known collectively and euphemistically as 'philosophical books' in the eighteenth century. As Robert Darnton and others have shown, the now better-known works of de Sade were preceded by some thirty years of energetic activity under the *ancien régime* on the part of authors both respectable and unknown, aided by a network of clandestine publishers and booksellers (Darnton, 1996). Typical works of this movement, such as *Thérèse philosophe*, combined frankly pornographic writing with philosophical discussion of equally controversial issues affecting the Church and the court. *Thérèse* and Diderot, one of its possible authors, Darnton suggests, 'belonged to the same world – the bawdy, naughty, cheeky world of the early Enlightenment, where everything was held up to question and nothing was sacred' (1996, p. 190). The surrealists in turn played a vital part in resurrecting the reputation of de Sade, stressing his political aspect as a prophet of 'revolt' against all forms of authority, and also reviving the Enlightenment fusion of sexuality and subversion in their commit-ment to eroticism. Buñuel recorded the impact of reading de Sade at the age of twenty-five, with his 'recipe for cultural revolution' (Buñuel, 1984, p. 219); and one of his unrealised personal projects, conceived between *Le Journal d'une femme de chambre* (1964) and *Belle de jour*, was to adapt an English novel that shares the Sadean climate of sexual and spiritual transgression. M. G. Lewis's *The Monk*, dating from 1796, was greatly admired by the surrealists, especially in a translation by one of their number, Antonin Artaud.

Set in Spain, *The Monk* chronicles the debauchery of a devout Capuchin by a girl who has entered his monastery disguised as a novice, and is also the model for his adored portrait of the Virgin Mary. After his initiation, he preys on other women, believing himself under the protection of the Devil, and so destroys his own sister and mother, before discovering that his seductress was a satanic emis-sary and facing final damnation. Had Buñuel succeeded in making this film, it might have produced an earlier confrontation between Surrealism's 'heretical' canonisation and English literature's traditionally low regard for such Gothic material. We might recall that the pioneering comparative critical study of 'extreme' Romanticism, Mario Praz's *The Romantic Agony*, first published in Italy in 1930, and soon translated into English, did not become widely known or influential until its reappearance in paperback in 1970. Introducing this edition, the influential critic Frank Kermode noted approvingly Praz's distinc-tion between de Sade's undoubted influence, in large part due to his promotion by the surrealists, and any attempt to justify his dubious qualities as a writer. Buñuel of course drew no such distinction in paying tribute to de Sade, follow-ing the surrealist imperatives of anti-bourgeois attitude and capacity to scandalise. When his and Carrière's script of *The Monk* was later filmed by the surrealist critic and occasional film-maker Ado Kyrou in 1972, Anglo-American responses were generally dismissive. One of the few dissenting verdicts was from David Pirie, who would soon afterwards publish a polemical defence of Hammer horror films as Britain's 'lost', or at least despised, Gothic cinema (Pirie, 1973). The film's failure may be attributed mainly to Kyrou's inexperience, but it might also be interpreted as a reflection of the difference between a self-consciously 'surrealist' approach to one of the movement's fetish texts, and whatever Buñuel would have made of it.

His commitment to maintaining a Sadean element in cinema was in fact long-standing. The film he made immediately after *La Voie lactée*, *Tristana* (1970), was based on a novel by Galdós, for whom he had a high regard ('often as remarkable as Dostoevsky': Buñuel, 1984, p. 222), but this did not prevent him from taking considerable liberties in the adaptation, as he had already done in his first Galdós film, *Nazarín* (1958), where the changes included a scene transposed directly from de Sade, in which 'a dying woman cries out for her lover and rejects God' (ibid., p. 205). Earlier in his career, as he recalled ruefully, a long-planned version of another novel cherished by the surrealists, *Wuthering Heights (Abismos de pasión*, 1953) was compromised by the dictates of Mexican casting. Buñuel's solution, or retaliation, was to include a passage from the disputed Solomonic text, *Book of Wisdom*,[6] effectively a call to sensual abandon in the face of mortality, the impact of which he remembered as 'like reading one of the more sublime pages in de Sade' (Buñuel, 1984, p. 206). Even in his adaptation of Defoe's *Robinson Crusoe* (1952), as Raymond Durgnat noted, Buñuel could not resist giving Friday an argument in favour of atheism by de Sade, which Crusoe cannot answer (Durgnat, 1967, p. 82).

What these allusions suggest is a number of senses of heresy, ranging from the claims of Monnerot that Surrealism itself should be seen as heretical in relation to both Marxism and psychoanalysis, appropriating their revolutionary and therapeutic aims, to a level of textual subversion as practised by Buñuel in his treatment of classic works. If de Sade functions as the heretical 'other' of the Enlightenment, undermining belief, morality, even rationality; then his interpolation across Buñuel's work may be taken as the main signifier of a systematically heretical enterprise, which is nothing less than undermining the progressive rationality of the 'Enlightenment project'. To this end, the structure of *La Voie lactée* is neither as arbitrary or predictable as was assumed by many English-language reviewers. On the contrary, it marked a major break with the narrative conventions that had largely contained Buñuel's vision since his arrival in Mexico. Almost all of his films from 1947 to 1965, whether commercial or personal, had presented an internally coherent, fictional world. This might include subjective elements, such as dreams or hallucinations, and it might be distorted by unexplained patterns, such as the mysterious stasis visited on the guests in *El ángel exterminador* (1962). But these do not significantly disturb the underlying narrative structure. With *Simón del desierto* and *Belle de jour*, a new pattern began to emerge, marked by rupture and, technically speaking, multiple diegesis. Thus the hermit Simón is abruptly transported from his fourth-century vigil to modern New York, although this is 'explained' (motivated) by the theme of diabolic temptation, and is finally reducible to the traditional form of the Faust story. Likewise, in *Belle de jour*, Severine inhabits three distinct worlds, two of which appear to be contemporary (her home life and the brothel) and the third is presumably a subjective fantasy world; thus all three can be related as reality/compensation–rebellion/motivation. But in *La Voie lactée*, there seem to be up to four narrative levels which have some thematic, but no clear diegetic, connection. The two tramps claiming to be pilgrims traverse a landscape that is at least locally 'real', and some of the film's other characters appear to inhabit this same world, however bizarrely; but others – some of whom are historical and others allegorical – seem to exist in different fictive worlds, while a series of episodes from the life of Christ, both canonic and invented (heretical), appear as if in apposition to the main direction of the pilgrimage narrative.

Pilgrimage occupies a privileged place in the English history of narrative thanks to the centrality of Chaucer's *The Canterbury Tales* (c. 1387) and Bunyan's *The Pilgrim's Progress* (1678–84), but in continental Europe the Spanish form of the picaresque played an equally generative role. For Buñuel this was an instinctive cultural reference: he introduced *My Last Breath* as 'a semiautobiography where I often wander from the subject like the wayfarer in a picaresque novel seduced by the charm of the unexpected intrusion, the unforeseen story' (1984, pp. 5–6).

Carrière testified that the narrative model for *La Voie lactée* from the start was the picaresque fiction that had originated in Spain in the sixteenth century, with *Lazarillo de Tormes*, inaugurating the tradition of popular novels which traced the opportunistic careers of young adventurers. Elements of the picaresque mingle with parody of chivalric romance in *Don Quixote*, and the term was brought into English use during the nineteenth century for many kinds of episodic narrative. But if *La Voie lactée* is picaresque in external form, as a series of encounters, it is far from the traditional pattern of adventures befalling a single protagonist. Rather, it is we, the spectators, who are embarked on a fantastic journey through ideology and contradiction, ignoring historical propriety. What are we to make of such a departure from the normal pattern of a Buñuel film? One line of speculation would point to the growing number of such fractured or multi-diegetic works throughout the 1960s, starting with the conspicuous exercises in 'new narrative' by Alain Resnais, *Hiroshima mon amour* (1959) and *L'Année dernière à Marienbad*, written by the leading exponents of the *nouveau roman* Marguerite Duras and Alain Robbe-Grillet respectively. But these remain essentially re-ordered or problematised diegeses, as did Resnais' later *Je t'aime, je t'aime* (1969). More relevant to *La Voie lactée* are two striking filmed versions of the picaresque: Wojciech Has's *Rekopis Znaleziony w Saragossie* (*The Saragossa Manuscript*, 1964) and Godard's *Week-end*.

Buñuel insisted on the first of these as one of his favourite films, having seen it 'a record-breaking three times' (1984, p. 224) and persuaded his producer to buy it for Mexican distribution; and it would not be difficult to see it as a likely influence on the elaborate neo-picaresque structure of *La Voie lactée*. The bewildered protagonist is a Walloon officer travelling through seventeenth-century Spain, who becomes enmeshed in an increasingly elaborate series of stories-within-stories, with interlocking characters, many of which turn on sorcery or erotic adventures. Its author, Jan Potocki, was a Polish count writing at the beginning of the nineteenth century, who left no definitive version at the time of his suicide in 1815. Potocki apparently conceived it in the spirit of a Gothic novel, with all the mystery and horror associated with that genre, but its multiplicity of tales also invites comparison with the tradition of Chaucer and Boccaccio (Maclean, 1995, pp. xi–xx). Working at a time of relative freedom in state-run Polish cinema, Has succeeded admirably in finding a form to convey the novel's peculiar blend of mischievous pedantry and dark fantasy, helping to define a new idiom of 'period irreverence' that would embrace other such literary adaptations as *Tom Jones* (Richardson, 1963), Fellini's *Satyricon* (1969) and *The Devils* (Russell, 1971). *The Saragossa Manuscript*'s cabalistic underpinning also chimed well with a growing interest in forms of exotic mysticism, such as the *I Ching* and the Tarot. Simultaneously, its play with narrative form, plunging the viewer into a Chinese box succession of 'nesting' tales, appealed to a growing interest in narrative form, stimulated by translations of Russian Formalist texts from the 1920s and by the contemporary polemics surrounding the *nouveau roman*, in the wake of Robbe-Grillet's controversial ventures into cinema (Christie, 2002).

In view of its fantastic world of intrigue, erotic adventure and mystery, *The Saragossa Manuscript* had an irresistible attraction for latterday surrealists. The leading surrealist critic Robert Benayoun hailed it in *Positif* as 'fantastic and pagan, with a fine sense of humour', identifying as the reason for its success the combination of the writer's sense of humour with a 'distant' objective tone established by the director (Benayoun, 1965, p. 36). By contrast, *Positif*'s rival, *Cahiers du cinéma*, saw the film's 'elegant and ironic detachment' as one of its failings, together with 'an even distance from its material' and a literalism in its structure (Daney, 1967). For Serge Daney, these qualities combined to create an arbitrary 'experimental' world where, since anything can happen, no development, however fantastic, has any human or artistic significance. Surrealists, however, had made a cult of such closed worlds, from the castles and convents of depravity in de Sade and other Gothic writers, to the dream logic of Lewis Carroll and the obsession of *amour fou* in their own writings. From this perspective, Has's cool and witty *Saragossa Manuscript* would provide an excellent model for initiation into overlapping worlds of mystery and exoticism, and also, on a formal level, for the abrupt 'horizontal–vertical' cuts between diegeses that characterise *La Voie lactée*.

The other, more immediate, model for such ahistorical structuring was Godard's *Week-end*, another film that Buñuel admired (Cohn, 1969a, p. 12). Godard, of course, had experimented with narrative form from the start of his career, often alternating 'real-time' episodes with elaborate forms of ellipsis governed by voice-over narration. Compared with the anti-naturalism of much of his previous work, *Week-end* was notably realist for much of its duration, following a bourgeois couple on their journey out of Paris to visit the woman's mother, with a notorious ten-minute, continuous tracking shot along a traffic-jam. But after the brutal murder of the mother, the pair enter a dislocated world of 'revolution', centred on their kidnapping by a home-grown 'liberation front', in which the comic-strip violence of eating a captured Englishman is juxtaposed with the surreal presence of such historical and literary figures as Emily Brontë, Saint-Just and Lewis Carroll. This may be the closest precursor to the emblematic landscape of *La Voie lactée*, populated by similarly embodied quotations, but both films could also be considered part of a tendency in the late 1960s and early 1970s to hybridise the picaresque and the fantastic, producing such ambitious and problematic works as *2001: A Space Odyssey* (Kubrick, 1968), *El Topo* (Jodorowsky, 1971), *O Lucky Man!* (Anderson, 1973) and *Celine et Julie vont en bateau* (Rivette, 1974).

Other contemporary parallels could be multiplied – the strange worlds of Borowczyk's *Goto, l'île d'amour* (1968) and *Blanche* (1971), Pasolini's mysterious *Porcile* (1969) (its first part originally intended to accompany Buñuel's *Simón del desierto*), Fellini's science-fiction of the past in *Satyricon* – to show that *La Voie lactée* was in many ways characteristic of its time. But while it may be important to rescue the film from being seen exclusively in terms of 'Buñuel', we must also address its specificity and its devastating simplicity. What proves most disconcerting is not the time-travelling slippage of epochs, which has long been a stock part of cinema's dramaturgy, but the absence of either reverence or mockery in the portrayal of the Gospel characters. Again, Buñuel provided a straightforward explanation: 'I wanted to show [Christ] as an ordinary man, laughing, running, mistaking his way, preparing to shave – to show in other words, all those aspects so completely alien to our traditional iconography' (1984, p. 245).

Bernard Verley's Christ is thus 'orthodox', speaking predominantly biblical lines; 'human' in his everyday life, yet conscious of his (pre-?)ordained destiny. In his final scene, which is also the end of the film, he declares, 'I have come not to bring peace but a sword'; and as he strides off briskly with the disciples, two blind men stumble behind him. Fieschi suggests that 'the endings of the films bring the meaning full circle, or suspend it on a laconic sign ... The variation implies neither optimism nor pessimism ... simply an exact statement of relative forces' (1980, p. 178). If we accept this view of Buñuel as a kind of ideological realist, then we can certainly interpret the thrust of the scene as taking us back, 'full circle', to the beginning of Christianity's onward march as the dominant ideology of the last two millennia – an interpretation confirmed by the curious end caption which insists that 'everything in this film concerning the Catholic religion and the heresies which it has caused is rigorously exact'. So on one level, we have seen that dogma will produce heresy, as surely as thesis leads to antithesis; and that a synthesis, or compromise, will be resisted in the interest of maintaining the Church's authority, as happens in the Inquisition scene when a young monk asks if it is necessary to burn heretics, before submitting to his superior. All of this may amount to 'an exact statement of relative forces' (Fieschi, 1980, p. 178), but it also requires sophisticated forms of reading and interpretation by an informed spectator. And it leaves open how we read the final image of the scene and the film, as the blind men who have come to be healed by Christ, stumble forward, only to stop at a ditch. In a film whose semiotic economy appears to have weighed every image and its relation to dogma or heresy, there is an undeniable pull towards an allegorical reading of this hesitation. Human weakness? The gap between ideology and 'the concrete attitudes and stances adopted by men' (Louis Althusser, quoted by Fieschi, 1980, p. 177)? And/or an image from the fetishistic series of feet that have recurred through Buñuel's work from *L'Âge d'or* onwards?

There cannot of course, be any bar or end to interpretation. We are free to bring whatever knowledge we have to Buñuel's meticulous yet ultimately mysterious fictions. The value of the *Cahiers* debate of 1969 is as a call to order, to resist the constant threat of a sceptical or sentimental Anglo-American recuperation, collapsing Buñuel into a familiar 'Buñuel'. But if *La Voie lactée* stands today, somewhat neglected, outside the charmed circle of 'late Buñuel', this is surely because it bears witness to a lifetime deeply marked by both Catholicism and Surrealism. As an impersonal *apologia pro vita sua*, it is animated by the dialectic of these apparently opposed, yet interrelated, value systems; and, *pace* Fieschi, it invites us to steer a course of interpretation which respects the biographical and cultural, as well as the conjunctural, while not reducing the film to any of these. If it also invites a scrupulous decoding of image and text, this may argue for including Buñuel in the tradition in which Borges placed Léon Bloy: 'a continuer of the cabbalists, a secret brother of Swedenborg and Blake: heresiarchs' (Borges, 1966, p. 134).

Notes

1. Raphael (1483–1520) established the traditional iconography and palette of the Gospel narrative in his paintings and frescos, later refined by the French painter Nicolas Poussin (1594–1665) who spent much of his life in Rome.
2. The most famous of the 'collective readings' is that of John Ford's *Young Mr Lincoln*, published in July 1970 (de Baecque 1991, vol. 2, p. 218).
3. All translations from French are my own.
4. Roud's *Critical Dictionary* was published in 1980, but most of its articles are known to have been written in the early 1970s; and *Tristana* (1970) is the latest film mentioned by Fieschi.
5. I owe this suggestion to Paul Hammond, peerless font of surrealist advice; and am grateful to Michael Richardson for providing access to a copy.
6. The 'deutero-canonic' *Book of Wisdom*, traditionally ascribed to Solomon, is included in versions of the Catholic Bible (Vulgate and Douay), but not in the Protestant Bible, having been rejected as heretical.

References

Andrew, Geoff (1997), '*La Voie lactée*' entry, in J. Pym (ed.), *Time Out Film Guide*, fifth edition, London: Penguin, p. 880.

Benayoun, Robert (1965), 'Des zakouskis de résistance', *Positif*, no. 71, pp. 25–36.

Borges, Jorge Luis (1966), 'The Mirror of the Enigmas', in *Other Inquisitions 1937–1952*, New York: Washington Square Press, pp. 131–4.

Buñuel, Luis (1984), *My Last Breath*, London: Fontana.

Cervantes, M. de (1950 [1605]), *Don Quixote*, translated by J. M. Cohen, Harmondsworth: Penguin.

Christie, Ian (2002), 'A Garden of Forking Paths: The Western Reception of Has's *Saragossa Manuscript*', in E. S. Shaffer (ed.), *Comparative Criticism*, 24, Cambridge: Cambridge University Press, pp. 217–37.

Cohn, Bernard (1969a), 'Les aventures théologiques de Don Luis de Calanda', *Positif* no. 103, pp. 4–16.

—— (1969b), 'Jean-Claude Carrière scénariste de Luis Buñuel', *Positif*, no. 103, pp. 17–18.

Daney, Serge (1967), 'La fin de l'éternité', *Cahiers du cinéma*, no. 187, pp. 69–70.

Darnton, Robert (1996), *The Forbidden Best-Sellers of Pre-Revolutionary France*, London: HarperCollins.

de Baecque, Antoine (1991), *Les Cahiers du cinéma: Histoire d'un revue*, 2 vols, Paris: Cahiers du cinéma.

de Baroncelli, Jean (1969), '*La Voie lactée*', review in *Le Monde*, Paris, 29 April, p. 10.

Durgnat, Raymond (1967), *Luis Buñuel*, London: Studio Vista.

Fieschi, Jean-André (1980), 'Buñuel', in Richard Roud (ed.), *Cinema: A Critical Dictionary*, London: Secker and Warburg, pp. 166–80.

Filoramo, Giovanni (1990), *A History of Gnosticism* (*L'attesa della fine: Storia della gnosis*), translated by Anthony Alcock, Oxford: Basil Blackwell.

Hibbin, Nina (1969), 'Film review', *Morning Star*, 25 October, p. 6.

Maclean, Ian (1995), 'Introduction', in Jan Potocki, *The Manuscript Found in Saragossa*, London: Viking, pp. xi–xx.

Monnerot, Jules (1945), *La Poésie moderne et le sacré*, Paris: Gallimard.

Narboni, Jean (1969), 'Le nom', *Cahiers du cinéma*, no. 212, pp. 40–2.

Oudart, Jean-Pierre (1969), 'Le mythe et l'utopie', *Cahiers du cinéma*, no. 212, p. 35.

Pierre, Sylvie (1969), 'Les deux colonnes', *Cahiers du cinéma*, no. 212, pp. 37–40.

Pirie, David (1973), *A Heritage of Horror: the English Gothic Cinema 1946–1972*, London: Avon.

Pluquet, Abbé (1768), *Memoires pour servir à l'histoire des égarements humains, ou dictionnaire des hérésies, des erreurs et des schisms,* Paris: Barrois.

Robinson, David (1969), 'Pilgrims' Progress', *The Times,* 25 October, p. 22.

Roud, Richard (1969), 'The Milky Way to Heresy', *Guardian*, 6 April, p. 12.

Tarratt, Margaret (1969), 'Review of *The Milky Way*', *Films and Filming*, vol. 16 no. 3, pp. 55–6

Walker, John (ed.) (2000), *Halliwell's Film and Video Guide 2001*, London: HarperCollins.

9

The Indiscreet Charms of the *Bourgeoises* and Other Women

Peter William Evans

Buñuel claimed he only understood male desire. His films contradict him. Many either have women protagonists (for example, *Susana* [1950], *Tristana* [1970], *Viridiana* [1961], or *Belle de jour* [1966]), or else allow generous space for the free expression of women-related topics. In these films women are unavoidably to some extent the projections of male fantasy. But they are clearly also, like any great film-maker's, characters whose authenticity emerges from the imperatives of artistic objectivity. For every meek Viridiana (Silvia Pinal) there is an Amazonian Inés (María Félix in *La Fièvre monte à El Pao* [1959]), or a defiant Djin (Simone Signoret in *La Mort en ce jardin* [1956]), and the strong women match the submissive ones in number. Undeniably, though, the assertive females often end up defeated, victims of the film's rhetoric or narrative demands: Inés and Djin are punished with death, Susana (Rosita Quintana), returned to the reformatory, while Tristana (Catherine Deneuve) lives on with bitterness, her treatment of Don Lope (Fernando Rey) casting her forever as the ghastly spectre of male castration anxiety. And yet, Inés and Djin are played by two of the cinema's most assured and vibrant female stars, in their dynamic presence here validating Foucault's claim that where there is power there is also resistance (1984, pp. 92–102).

María Félix made forty-seven films, and was the incarnation of the femme fatale in Mexican cinema. Married several times, her intense beauty and aura of power made her even more formidable in a country dominated by the ideology of machismo. Off-screen she belonged to circles that included Diego Rivera and Frida Kahlo, sharing a house at one point with them (inviting rumours about the more than Platonic relations between the two women); on-screen she was immortalised in endless *mujer devoradora* (vamp) roles, such as *La diosa arrodillada* (Gavaldón, 1947*), La devoradora* (De Fuentes, 1946) and, most famous of all, *Doña Bárbara* (De Fuentes, 1943). As Terenci Moix puts it, her off-screen appearances added to her projection of female power:

Los vestidos de terciopelo negro, las pieles como símbolo de poder, los abrigos y chaquetones con enormes solapas, acaso imaginados para esconder parcialmente un rostro culpable, son elementos que contribuyen a realzar la ilusión de una mujer que todo lo puede y a quien ha de cuadrar como a nadie el mote que le dio el pueblo: La Doña.

[The black velvet dress, the furs as symbols of power, the coats and three-quarter length jackets with huge lapels, perhaps designed to conceal, partially, a guilty demeanour, are elements that help reinforce the illusion of a capable woman, some-one most suited to the nickname given to her by the public: La Doña.]

Moix, 2002, p. 84

The aura of power and of sexual guilt finds its Gallic equivalent in Simone Signoret, both women bringing to their roles in Buñuel films attributes that resist the prejudices of gender endemic to their cultural environment. Before making *La Mort en ce jardin*, Simone Signoret had already starred in major French films: *La Ronde* (Ophuls, 1950), *Casque d'Or* (Becker, 1952), *Thérèse Raquin* (Carné, 1953) and *Les Diaboliques* (Clouzot, 1954). All of these, like María Félix's films, feature her in roles of strength and determination. Simone Signoret's sexuality differs from 'La Doña's' haughty glamour in its more feline, proletarian quali-ties. Her sleepy eyes, the softer contours of a buxom frame, bear no resemblance to María Félix's more masculine look of the merciless dominatrix. A killer in *Thérèse Raquin* and *Les Diaboliques*, she is no stranger to violence and treachery. In *La Mort en ce jardin* these features of a predatory self serve her well in a role that demands selling anyone who threatens her own security down the river. From one point of view, she is the misogynist's *bête noire*, awaiting punishment, which duly arrives in the form of slaps and hair tugs from Shark (Jean Marais), and subsequently through a fatal bullet despatched by her former lover (Charles Vanel). For all that, despite her victimisation, she emerges as a life force. Every gesture, every knowing, smiling glance, every line delivered, oozes with self-conscious mockery and resistance, an impression awarded its most appropriate setting in the scene where the lost secular pilgrims in this fallen jungle paradise come across the crashed aeroplane and its spilled contents. As some of the group search for victuals, as Castin's daughter and others look for sensible clothing to replace their ragged garments, Djin – her finery justifying her baptism after an exotic bird – recovers her Parisian fashion sense by slipping on an elegant, body-hugging black-lace gown, further nuancing this display of narcissistic pageantry by wearing pendulous earrings and a diamond necklace. The specularisation of the self here goes beyond passive acquiescence in cinematic vampish stereotype. Faced with the certainty of death, Djin makes a statement about life, gesturing colourfully and defiantly against the fate that awaits all.

As Djin and Inés, these stars portray the struggle by women against both local and more universal prejudices and injustices. Their deaths are readable in this light as the failure by determined women to alter the premises of the social order. Nevertheless, despite their almost predictable fate – Buñuel's wry comment on the limits of French and Mexican feminism in the late 1950s – the achievement of Djin and Inés, the former a virago, the latter an eventually politicised rebel – point to the future. Their gestures of defiance remain in the memory, their tragedy of frustrated opportunity sufficiently moving to undermine the artificiality of each film's closure. These resistances to stereotype characterise the nature of Buñuel's heroines even in comedy, a prime example of which is *Le Charme discret de la bourgeoisie*.

Like the three Graces or Charities of Greek mythology, the three main women characters of *Le Charme discret de la bourgeoisie* stroll through life inspiring awe and reverence among the various male characters who intrude on their lives. In common with their mythical forebears, these secular divinities exemplify contemporary Parisian ideals of beauty and, as such, earn the devotion of various males, ranging from callow young men compelled to treat them as alternative models of authority to whom to confess their disturbing dreams or memories, to more mature admirers drawn to their powerful aura of self-conscious sexuality.

Set in Paris, with mainly French characters, *Le Charme discret* conceals beneath the thin veneer of its Gallic elegance the familiar obsessions of Buñuel's Hispanic background. What he brings to this film is above all both an amused contempt for European ignorance of Latin America – as is repeatedly demonstrated through the insults hurled at the fictitious Latin American republic of Miranda – and, in keeping with his lifelong socialist tendencies, admiration for the radical activists who struggle against the tyrannical regimes from which the political life of the continent is seldom free. In a film that again belies the received wisdom about his insensitivity to such issues, Buñuel represents women in ways that are often identified with transgression against the dominant order. There is no sense here of women being imaged as deficient men, even though their adherence to bourgeois norms means their friendships and other relationships are more the reflection of their husbands' commitments and interests than their own.

Although the graceful threesome provide Buñuel's sharpest focus on these interrelated questions, the film's minor women characters add further significant dimensions. In common with other Buñuel films, *Le Charme discret de la bourgeoisie* offers a spectrum of females in which stereotypes abound, and while many of these images of femininity are Oedipal constructions, the text allows opportunities for the women characters to resist the processes of control and victimisation. In both the dream and non-dream sequences women seek release from conformism and illusion. Of those who only ever appear in dreams or reminiscences, one is an adulteress (in the young lieutenant's story), and another an incestuous mother/lover figure (in the sergeant's dream), the former challenging the system through betrayal of a caricature of an authoritarian husband, the latter seeming to ignore taboo by appearing as an ethereal sexual fantasy dreamt up by her tormented son/lover's unconscious. In keeping with contemporary trends, these two narratives within the frame narrative are also confessions, reflecting Buñuel's fondness for the device, as well as exemplifying Foucault's argument that we have progressed beyond pleasures derived from accounts of heroism or sainthood to those acquired from embarkation on inner journeys (Foucault, 1984, p. 59). *Cet obscur objet du désir* is the film that takes this interest to its furthest extreme. There Mathieu/Mateo (Fernando Rey), as here the young lieutenant and the soldier, seems as if under some sort of compulsion to narrate, or 'confess', as he and other characters, weighed down by guilt, apparently in need of understanding and of being shriven, tell their strange stories. Buñuel seemingly acknowledges in these instances his own Freud-inspired conviction that through narrative comes diagnosis and understanding not only of individual but also of wider social causes of disturbance.

In neither case, however, is transgression ultimately rewarded: the lieutenant's mother's indiscretion leads to her own and her lover's death; the soldier's mother lives only in her son's entropic unconscious. In yet another dream sequence, the complicated dream-within-a-dream, in which Henri Thévenot dreams that Henri Sénéchal is dreaming, another woman character (the colonel's wife), with no existence beyond the world of Thévenot's troubled unconscious, acts out a less positively transgressive role. This dream is predominantly about wish fulfilment, the desire of Thévenot for Don Raphael's final humiliation and possible death. In an almost classically Freudian formulation the dream expresses the cuckolded husband's wish for his rival's annihilation through a characteristic pattern of transference and displacement motivated by the ego's need for self-protection (Freud, 1982). Thévenot's dream, in which Sénéchal dreams the dinner date at the colonel's house in what turns out to be a nightmarish appearance on stage in a production of Zorrilla's Romantic play, *Don Juan Tenorio* (1844), establishes the connexion between Don Raphael and the iconic rake, but in a way that allows the dreamer to avoid the full, direct blow of confrontation with the reality of his betrayal by a friend (Babington and Evans, 1985, pp. 14–18; Evans, 1995, pp. 13–35).

In the second part of the dream the oneiric *mise en scène* transfers to the colonel's house and to the soirée where in an earlier scene – not a dream – the colonel, on the night of the army manoeuvres, had invited the group of friends. Here we meet the colonel's wife, but as neither we nor Thévenot have previously seen her – nor do we set eyes on her ever again – we must assume she is a construct of Thévenot's dreaming mind. His own wife, like Sénéchal's, also appears in this dream – significantly seated, in the *Don Juan Tenorio* dinner scene, next to his secretly loathed rival Don Raphael. As by now Thévenot has found good cause for reflecting on his life as a drug-smuggling, well-to-do bourgeois whose lifestyle has done precious little to bring him either lasting personal happiness or marital fidelity, it seems reasonable to assume that his fantasy version of the colonel's wife could well represent a screen projection of all that he now finds unsatisfactory in Mme Thévenot.

The colonel's wife, then, is the nightmare double of the female bourgeois ideal, the dark side (she is a brunette) to his blonde wife Simone (Delphine Seyrig), the pale and faithless neo-Gothic beauty. The colonel's wife's raucous voice, insincere greetings, hollow conversation and mannered gestures and movements, so self-obsessed she offers port to guests whose glasses are already filled, together form a caricature of bourgeois etiquette prompted by what must be – despite appearances to the contrary – growing but repressed frustration with Simone, his wife. In a further neat little detail twinning this hyperbole of bourgeois shallowness with the treachery committed by a despised and formerly trusted friend, Thévenot's dream arranges it for the colonel's wife to be the character who prevents Don Raphael from making an early exit when the discreet and not so discreet insults hurled through him against the Republic of Miranda finally become intolerable. The colonel's wife, whose interference ensures that Don Raphael will get his come-uppance at the soirée, is locked through this malicious act in a mutual gesture of wish fulfilment designed to expose in a fantasy, even if not in reality, the hypocrisies of a world where form is never compromised by content.

Yet even though here the female character is the creature of a disillusioned, avenging unconscious, elsewhere, not in dreams, women often take the lead in exposing or at least upsetting the mechanisms of bourgeois ideology. This is achieved through the actions both of the proletarian women and their bourgeois superiors. The former category includes the maid, the Mirandan revolutionary, and the peasant who leads the vengeful bishop to the dying gardener, all of whom decline opportunities to appease the male through the masquerade of femininity, preferring instead to adopt a strategy of direct womanly – as opposed to feminine – challenge to the patriarchal order, a policy that may be read as castratory (Lebeau, 2001, pp. 104–5). Where, in Joan Riviere's terms, the bourgeoises alternate between womanliness and femininity, now through womanly self-assertion assuming a phallic role, now through a masquerade of femininity seemingly accepting their submissive, castrated identities (Riviere, 1986), the proletarian women are governed by no such ambivalence. Through them, social, political and religious issues are directly addressed. The maid seems perversely to avoid colluding with her employers' deception when, in an early scene, she fails to prevent the Sénéchals' guests hurriedly leaving the house after they believe their hosts have been anticipating a police raid, not knowing that they are actually in the garden making love behind a bush. The Sénéchals rebuke the maid for her failure of initiative, for not reading their absence more plausibly. But, standing outside the bourgeoisie, she interprets sudden departures from a proletarian perspective. Through her failure to prevent the guests' departure the film exposes the relativism of experience and perception, above all when these are formulated in response to different social experiences. But beyond the general point, the maid's inability to explain her employers' absence in ways consistent with their own desires, distances her from the Sénéchals and, by extension, from the social thought processes and mindsets they represent.

If here it is primarily the gulf in social backgrounds that falls under the film's scrutiny through the agency of a recalcitrant female, elsewhere, through the Mirandan terrorist, the target is politics. Even though Don Raphael is traced over with seductive as well as disagreeable tendencies, his embodiment of political corruption earns the characteristic scorn of a director still outraged by the post-Civil War history of Spain. We may savour Raphael's sweetly venomous formulation of fascist sentiment, his elegantly patronising dismissal of idealistic revolutionary fervour, his easy Sadean charm and suave urbanity, all designed to confront us with our own secret prejudices, but there is no denying the reality of the peculiarly Latin American political corruption he plainly represents. At one level, through the verbal indignities aimed via Don Raphael at Miranda the film satirises European failure to distinguish between the distinctiveness of individual Latin American countries: a succession of characters ask him, for instance, about the Pampas or pyramids, not features, he struggles to explain, of the Mirandan landscape. Don Raphael is surrounded by insular Europeans, whose insults recall Barthes's comments on the bourgeois' fear of otherness:

> The petit-bourgeois is a man unable to imagine the Other. If he comes face to face with him, he blinds himself, ignores and denies him, or else transforms him into himself. In the petit-bourgeois universe, all experiences of confrontation are reverberating, any otherness is reduced to sameness. The spectacle of the tribunal, which are both places where the Other threatens to appear in full view, become mirrors. This is because the Other is a scandal which threatens his essence.
>
> Barthes, 1972, p. 151

But, at another level, Don Raphael's presence serves as a pretext for another of Buñuel's assaults on political corruption. Significantly, though, the revolutionary activist who seeks to assassinate the parody of tin-pot dictatorships is female.

The conflict between these two characters provides an opportunity for the staging of a contest on sexual/political as well as on purely political grounds. Though also to some extent an image of transgression, Don Raphael's Sadean politics lead him not to the overthrow of the system but to a smoother accommodation with it. No philanthropist, he swells his own bank account with narcotic profits, fills his belly with the succulent morsels of a bourgeois diet (accepting a second helping of Mme Sénéchal's *gigot*), and consoles himself with stolen libidinal pleasures, enjoying the favours of Thévenot's wife and reaching out indiscriminately, even though forlornly, for the erogenous zones of the young Mirandan revolutionary. Don Raphael, the archangel not of light but of darkness, appears perfectly cast as patriarchy's apologist; not for him either the utopianism of alternative political agendas nor the consciousness-raising politics of the women's movement.

In this, of course, he shares the unliberated attitudes of his clones – also played by Fernando Rey – Don Jaime (*Viridiana*), Don Lope (*Tristana*) and Don Mateo (*Cet obscur objet du désir*), none of whom seems prepared to respond to women beyond the confines of bed or board. And even when, as in *Le Charme discret de la bourgeoisie*, there is a side to the corrupt self-seeker that earns his creator's uncontrollable, instinctive approval, the rhetoric of scenes such as those involving the female revolutionary ultimately condemns his acquiescence in the ruthless victimisation of the very people he has been appointed to serve.

The key scene between the Latin American ex-patriots in Paris takes place when the activist appears at the Mirandan embassy intent on shooting the ambassador. Cleverly disarming her, Don Raphael takes an opportunity not only to grope her nubile form, but also to offer her a piece of his tradition-warped mind, urging her to surrender her physical charms not to the worthy ideals of a political cause but the carnal appetites of her country's heroes. Don Raphael's glib references to Mao and Freud reflect the impatience of the smug bourgeois with the demands of social injustice. But when he decants the contents of her bag, the discovery amid the groceries and lethal weapon of '*la clef des songes*', a witty surrealist conceit on the revelations of the unconscious, even this most hardened of sybarites is forced to acknowledge the nobler aspirations of the revolutionaries he either pities or scorns. Yet while for the Sadean terrorist '*la clef des songes*' unlocks primarily lubricious pleasures, for the political terrorists, who – as he elsewhere admits to his bourgeois cronies – must be swatted like flies, the dream is social justice unlocked by the key of political reform. The Latin American woman here abandons other familiar roles – the *mujer devoradora* of *El bruto* (1952), or the Oedipalised Chingada (violated mother) offering in a dream her love-starved son that piece of glistening raw meat that has all the appearance of a ripped vagina in *Los olvidados* (1950) – for that of the revolutionary, in her terrorist attacks on the Mirandan ambassador aiming at both the private and public corruption of Latin America.

The chic female Parisians never come into contact with the Mirandan revolutionary but the film deliberately sets up revealing indirect comparisons between the representatives of privilege and dispossession. While the rebellion of the Parisians is largely peripheral, the Mirandan strikes at the very heart of political power and influence. Her failure merely highlights the nature of the overwhelming forces opposed to social reform.

The social and political dissidence exemplified by the behaviour of the Sénéchals' maid and, above all, by the Mirandan activist perhaps finds clearest reflection in the fleeting appearance of the peasant woman (Muni), another of Buñuel's dispossessed souls, seeking a priest to comfort the dying gardener who long ago had murdered his cruel employers, the bishop's mother and father. Muni here wears her characteristic expression of the downtrodden woman in whom resistance has not been entirely stifled. Haggard, exhausted, impoverished, she still manages here to offer the bishop, as he prepares to give his parents' assassin extreme unction, a blasphemous parting shot. Her promise to explain her dislike of Jesus Christ is appropriately repressed by the realistic narrative, one of the film's clearest metaphors for the silencing of the unconscious, but in the passion of her eyes and the paralinguistic force of her abrupt and uncompromising words she expresses the film's conviction of the way in which Christianity has often proved for many to be not the elixir but the toxicant to emotional, social or spiritual fulfilment.

These vignettes of female resistance inescapably compromised by circumstances prepare the ground for the more leisurely treatment of the same issue in the portrayal of the film's unholy trinity of bourgeois women: Simone, Alice and Florence. Too comfortable or ideologised to risk radical alienation from their social milieu, they nevertheless flirt more than the men with transgression. Like the men, though, these wayward pilgrims seem to travel aimlessly along the same road leading nowhere, on a journey prompted perhaps by frustration with the failures of bourgeois decadence. And yet, as with the minor women characters, flickers of revolt occasionally illuminate their orderly existence, something nowhere more clearly expressed than in the early scene of the aborted dinner at the restaurant whose recently deceased owner's corpse, lying in a room adjacent to the dining hall, proves too unpalatable for even the hardiest appetites among the group of friends. Even so, while the men – true to the Rousseauesque definition of the bourgeois as someone primarily motivated by instincts of self-preservation – remain locked in conservative codes of etiquette, refusing to compromise civilised behaviour by investigating the wailing sounds emanating from a hidden corner of the restaurant, the women rise as a group, inquisitive to the point of unseemliness, intent on discovering the source of that terrible sobbing, ignoring the men's view that they will appear, as one of them significantly remarks, 'indiscrètes'.

For various reasons risking less than the men who, after all, in their world hold the reins of power, the women respond more eagerly to the clarion of revolt, each of them expressing their insubordination in idiosyncratic ways through language, codes of dress and behaviour, and treatment by the camera. All of these elements of form are characterised by ambiguity. In speech, these women mix banality with intelligence. Simone, for instance, of Gothic provenance (though not taken to the almost ghoulish extremes of the incestuous aunt in *Le Fantôme de la liberté* [1974]), her glacial blondeness, reminiscent of Séverine's (Wood, 2000), combining here with the hard-edged sophistication characteristic of her French New Wave roles (Haskell, 1987, pp. 354–5), makes surprisingly informed political comments. On one occasion, for instance, she refers to the scandal of marijuana-smoking US officers whose drug-confused brains drive them on a weekly basis to bomb their own soldiers in Vietnam. Florence, too, shows awareness of Latin America by remarking that Miranda belongs to the southern hemisphere, whose summer is Europe's winter, a comment that leads M. Thévenot, her brother-in-law, to declare the French a nation ignorant of geography. Simone's distance from her geographically challenged husband is more emphatically marked by adultery with Don Raphael, the deeper motivation for which seems to be an undeclared contempt for a husband insufficiently enlivened by sexual desire to abandon his single bed, and grown too wearisome through respect for the more trivial niceties of the bourgeois code. Her husband, after all, is the bore who seeks the cheap humiliation of Maurice, Don Raphael's chauffeur, in the scene where proletarian awareness of cocktail etiquette, *pace* Buñuel's own enslavement to these rituals, is wittily, but also somewhat tediously, put to the test. The extent of his wife's ultimate exasperation with her husband's stultification by such dubious sources of conviction and amusement perhaps explain part of the reason why, following his unscheduled visit to Don Raphael's apartment just at the point at which she is set to resume her affair with her middle-aged Latin lover, Simone emerges unsummoned from the bedroom, unnecessarily announcing her presence to her cuckolded husband. Since concealment of her rendezvous at Don Raphael's flat would have been perfectly possible, her sudden appearance seems designed as much to register her boredom with Don Raphael's passionate attentions as to take sadistic pleasure in tormenting the feelings of a husband too constrained by bourgeois protocol – where a working man might have at least punched his rival on the nose – to make a scene.

Costume, too, plays its part in not only conforming to the laws of realism but also in signalling identity and difference. Increasingly recognised as a key element of a film's agencies of meaning, costume in its latter function is in *Le Charme discret* drawn self-consciously to the audience's attention on more than one occasion: through the play in Thévenot's extended dream sequence with Napoleon's hat, the decision by Alice not to change out of her nightgown for the visit to the deceased owner's restaurant, and Florence's curiosity about the clothes worn by the Nazi fugitive in Miranda. The proletarian women dress austerely, while the three radiant bourgeois beauties are showcases for *haute couture*. And yet, beyond the requirements of verisimilitude, the austerity of the working-class women's clothes also reflects in a narrative of superficial lightness their darker mood (the maid's preoccupation with police raids, the peasant woman's with her contempt for the Saviour), while the ever-changing wardrobe of the bourgeoises seems like commentary on what Simone de Beauvoir might have referred to as their own 'focus of liberation' (Street, 2001, p. 3), each outfit – for instance those designed by Jean Patou for Delphine Seyrig – a declaration of individual creativity. Conspicuous consumption here seems less governed by male expressions of wealth and status than by the women's need to affirm their own identities. The fashion-conscious women's costumes are parallel signifiers of masquerading conformist femininity and resistance to the superficial blandness of bourgeois life.

The costumes range from the more predictable pastel shades of the older women, Alice and Simone – in the case of the former the diaphanous pale apricot-shaded satin dressing gown, or in the latter, the off-white suit worn at the second invitation to lunch *chez* the Sénéchals – to more emphatic, florid creations increasingly on display as the film progresses. Florence, on the other hand, is first seen in an ankle-length skirt, with paisley designs, and later with more colourful waistcoats and scarves, all denoting her more youthful, modern, slightly hippie 1970s' look, setting her at a little distance from the older pair. But all three women complement their more usual styles with contrasting fashions. Alice, normally seen in skirts or dresses, wears jeans in the garden to modify the more formal side of her glossy magazine persona; her skirts and dresses sometimes replace conservative tones and patterns with more vivid colours, denoting resistance to the grey conservatism of her social milieu. In the restaurant scene where they meet the young lieutenant, Alice's dress has a white and red floral pattern. In contrast, Florence's modern look is sometimes replaced by more chic styles, such as the light blue, easy-flowing dress, in a reverse pattern of youth's regression to conservatism, worn at the theatre. This pattern of ambiguity is reflected in the women's treatment by the camera. Though each has her own set of circumstances, the camera and framing patterns often link them or group them together. So, for instance, when the group (minus the Sénéchals and the bishop) visit the restaurant with the unburied corpse, the women are seated together in a row, the camera focusing on their reactions as a group to the wailing off-screen.

Elsewhere, close-ups of the women are used to significant effect: twice of Florence, in order not to glamorise but to provide ironic facial commentary on the relevant scene, and once of Alice. The close-up of Alice – whose face momentarily fills the frame – occurs as she announces to her diners, now joined by the French army on manoeuvres, that bunching up will be the only way everyone will fit around the table where, unavoidably now, the food portions will be small, almost a crisis for bourgeois epicureans accustomed to fuller menus. Alice, here, projects the domestic face of woman, fulfilling her designated role as housewife and hostess. The shot comes soon after a slightly less extreme close-up of Simone making her political comment about Vietnam. In juxtaposition, these shots belong to the film's many patterns of conceits about the entrapment and flight of women from conformist definitions of gender.

But Alice is no mere conformist. She too, as ambivalent as Simone and Florence about the seductions of the bourgeois life, is often motivated by a need to challenge the very codes to which she is otherwise content to remain faithful. These outrages range from the trivial flouting of etiquette when she allows the bishop, after all, to bring down to the dining table the inappropriate chairs, to more profound mockery of social form when she insists on satisfying her libido rather than greeting her dinner guests, or, even more so, when she joins in poking fun at the bishop as he is ludicrously forced to put on the hat Napoleon wore at Wagram. Since this latter incident takes place in Thévenot's dream, it suggests that even he – perhaps the most compromised bourgeois of the group – recognises Alice's potential for transgression. Stéphane Audran, as Alice, combines bourgeois glamour with enigmatic beauty. Her carved Aztec cheekbone features and large, clear eyes set her apart from her circle. The memory of her roles in key Chabrol films–such as *Les Biches* (1968) and *Le Boucher* (1969) – plays into *Le Charme discret de la bourgeoisie* and contributes towards the interrogation of the allure of bourgeois poise and sophistication. Unlike Simone, Alice seems at least to have found a playful, libidinal companion in her husband, her eagerness for sexual excitement much more natural and carefree than Simone's. John Simon goes as far as to say that 'if these solidly married bourgeois can still pant for each other so at high noon, all is not lost. Where the blood stirs, there is hope' (Simon, 1978, p. 364). Raymond Durgnat takes a similar view: 'The Sénéchals … represent the bourgeoisie at its most youthful, flexible and engaging' (Durgnat, 1978, p. 378). Whereas, through Simone, Buñuel paints a portrait of the bourgeoisie so sophisticated as to be beyond desire, creating an image of a woman whose narcissism nevertheless demands the attention of a lover, through Alice he creates an image of someone who remains alive to the thrills and rewards of desire. When both women are presented with an opportunity for risk-taking in the name of passion, Simone withdraws, leaving Don Raphael in cruel frustration, while Alice, though her guests are already assembled in the salon, prefers to slide down the drainpipe and to rush into the garden, in obedience to a priapic law more binding than the rules of hospitality. The transgressive Alice – locked in sexual embrace with Henri, laughing at the bishop's inadvertent impersonation of Napoleon, visiting the restaurant in her satin pyjamas – sits comfortably beside a more demure Alice. The latter is the visual epitome of *Vogue*-style elegance, the mouthpiece for the hollow formulaic words of the bourgeoisie, the victim of appearances (castigating the maid for admitting the bishop to the house when he appears dressed not in his Episcopal finery but in the soiled overalls of a gardener), gliding through the narrative at the leisurely pace of a woman clearly no stranger to luxury.

If in Alice these '*comme il faut*' forms of elegance finally eclipse other more eccentric qualities, the tension seems more equally balanced in Bulle Ogier's portrayal of Florence. Her earliest appearance in the narrative prepares the audience for her more radical exposure of the bourgeois ethos. Drinking to excess, vomiting out of Don Raphael's car window, making irrational remarks (such as her dislike of cellists), scoffing at psychoanalysis (claiming she suffers not from the Oedipus but from the Euclid complex), or discoursing on astrology, thus

Bourgeoises leading the way in *Le Charme discret de la bourgeoisie*

using a low-order item to ironise the higher bourgeois forms, she is a surrealist female *gracioso*, or allowed fool, unafraid to demystify through the perspectives of vulgarity the pretensions of her own social milieu. The camera approves of this critique most unambiguously when, in the film's first scene at the Sénéchals' house, it allows her to approach the lens in close-up, thus blocking out the other members of the group, in a gesture that unmistakably comments, through the muted semiotics of her bored, cynical expression, on the superficialities of the world of which she is contemptuous, but from which she has found – like the characters in *Huis Clos* – no final release.

For all their minor acts of subversion, the three principal European women in this film are ultimately compromised: closure sees them, after all, still part of the group condemned to walk that comfortless road, like some modern female clones of Palinurus. Often viewed through the Oedipal, patriarchalised perspectives of men who treat them as secular deities, they are characters whose confinement by ideology and culture the film is prepared to recognise. In that respect, like so many others in Buñuel's films, these women draw our attention – something not always acknowledged by his critics – to their creator's awareness of the struggle against prejudice and fixed categories of gender. No feminist, in the narrowest sense of the term, Buñuel looks through his female characters beyond the dumbshow of femininity at the authentic desires and experiences of women. When in *Le Journal d'une femme de chambre* (1964) Joseph informs Célestine, 'on ne connaît pas les gens du premier coup ... les femmes, surtout, c'est le diable à connaître ... mais, vous, maintenant, je vous connais bien' ['one doesn't know people at first ... women, especially are the devil to get to know ... but you, now, I know you well'], her reaction – a mixture of bewilderment and resentment – speaks for all women seeking release from the traps of control, preconception and stereotype.

References

Babington, B. and P. W. Evans (1985), 'The Life of the Interior: Dreams in the Films of Luis Buñuel', *Critical Quarterly*, vol. 27 no. 4, pp. 5–20.

Barthes, R. (1972), *Mythologies*, selected and translated by Annette Laver, London: Paladin.

Durgnat, R. (1978), '*The Discreet Charm of the Bourgeoisie*', in J. Mellen (ed.), *The World of Luis Buñuel: Essays in Criticism*, New York: Oxford University Press, pp. 373–96.

Evans, P. W. (1995), *The Films of Luis Buñuel: Subjectivity and Desire*, Oxford: Clarendon Press.

Foucault, M. (1984), *The History of Sexuality: An Introduction*, translated by Robert Hurley, Harmondsworth: Penguin.

Freud, S. (1982 [1900]), *The Interpretation of Dreams*, translated by James Strachey, Harmondsworth: Penguin.

Haskell, M. (1987 [1973]), *From Reverence to Rape: The Treatment of Women in the Movies*, second edition, Chicago: University of Chicago Press.

Lebeau, V. (2001), *Psychoanalysis and Cinema: The Play of Shadows*, London and New York: Wallflower.

Mellen, J. (ed.) (1978), *The World of Luis Buñuel: Essays in Criticism*, New York: Oxford University Press.

Moix, T. (2002), 'La Doña, El Charro Cantor y el Flaco de Oro', *El País Semanal*, 18 August, pp. 84–9.

Riviere, J. (1986), 'Womanliness and the Masquerade', in V. Burgin, J. Donald and C. Kaplan (eds), *Formations of Fantasy*, London: Routledge, pp. 35–44.

Simon, J. (1978), 'Why Is the Co-Eatus Always Interruptus?', in J. Mellen (ed.), pp. 363–73.

Street, S. (2001), *Costume and Cinema: Dress Codes in Popular Film*, London and New York: Wallflower.

Wood, M. (2000), *Belle de Jour*, London: BFI.

PART FOUR

THE BUÑUEL WORLD

10

The Constant of Exile in Buñuel

Victor Fuentes

With the renewed interest in exile and diaspora studies at the end of the twentieth and the beginning of the twenty-first centuries, Luis Buñuel's cinema offers new answers to those who approach its study from these perspectives. He inscribed on the screen, perhaps as no other film-maker in the past century, that sphere of 'extraterritorial' and transnational creation that has been so fruitful in the universal literature of exile and of the exiled. Buñuel made contradiction the key to his cinema and, therefore, exile, an insoluble contradiction, becomes also a main creative force in him.

Exile in both his life and cinema, save for a few exceptions, has been studied very little.[1] We have the incongruous, but not illogical, anomaly that in the institutional recuperation of Buñuel on the part of the Mexican and Spanish governments, in 1996, and on the occasion of the centenary of his birth (a recuperation captured in the monumental exhibition 'Buñuel! The Look of the Century') the word 'exile', one of the most significant voices and experiences of the century – a word lived in the flesh by Buñuel – is conspicuous by its absence; it has been exiled out of the voluminous official tome dedicated to him.[2]

Already, during the first stage of his Parisian life the theme of exile is present in Buñuel's work. In the French capital, he became one of *les méteques* – as foreigners living in Paris were disparagingly called – something he recalls in a section significantly titled 'Nosotros los metecos' from *Mi último suspiro* (*My Last Sigh*) (1982, p. 79). It is this very same condition that allowed him to offer his first fruits of a Spanish–French transnational art and cultural hybridity on the big screen.

His first screenplay, *Goya*, was written in 1926, centred on a famous exile: his fellow compatriot Goya. In it, he recreated a lively evocation of early-nineteenth-century Zaragoza and Madrid – done from Paris in the 1920s – with a trait so characteristic of exile: the fact of being in one place, but to have one's imagination focused elsewhere. The last section, which takes place in Bordeaux, opens with an original exilic image: the playwright Moratín seated on a bench on a deserted promenade on the outskirts of the city, with three or four 'friends, well advanced in years':

> In the gaps of their conversation they look lifelessly towards the ground. With the tip of his cane, Moratín traces a name on the soft earth. The others see the written name and turn their heads away sullenly. With a spark of rage in his eyes, Moratín bitterly says a few words. A close-up of the name written in the dirt 'ESPAÑ ...' and the tip of the cane erasing it nervously.
>
> (Buñuel, 1992, p. 99. As in other quotes translated from Spanish, the translation is mine, S. M. Bennett).

This scene foreshadows a situation that Buñuel would live out himself after the defeat of the Republican cause in 1939. We also find echoes of his 'Goya' in *Le Fantôme de la liberté* (1974), in which Buñuel, accompanied by another main figure of Spanish exile, José Bergamín, gets shot inside a filmic recreation of the painting *Los fusilamientos de la Moncloa* (*The Shootings of La Moncloa*).

Buñuel's own terrible experience of exile began in the United States in 1939. Like so many others in exile (some famous, most nameless) he found himself, during our age of exile, *aterrado* – in the original sense of the word, i.e. 'landless'[3] – and also unemployed. This state of being and of mind corresponds to the first stage of all those in exile, who, according to the exiled Polish Nobel Prize winner Czeslaw Milosz, live under three conditions that bring on desperation: the loss of one's name, the fear of failure and a moral anguish. Remembering his early times in the United States while unemployed, Buñuel declared: 'I could not work in the movies because I had bad grades from Hollywood. My previous experience, as you will remember, was not recommendable ... After all, and considering how our war had ended, very few things mattered to me' (de la Colina and Pérez Turrent, 1986, p. 45).

In New York, he associated with two different groups of exiles: the surrealists, mostly French, and the Spaniards.[4] His main aspiration during those years was to return to Spain. We find proof of this in a letter – already quoted many times by critics – to his friend Gustavo Pittaluga. Writing from Los Angeles, and while believing in his imminent debut as a cinematographic director in Hollywood, Buñuel informs Pittaluga that his experience will benefit him greatly upon his return to Spain (Sánchez Vidal, 1988, p. 306). His awaited break as a Hollywood director never took place, and he lived in the Mecca of cinema in complete anonymity, working on dubbings for Warner Bros. or unemployed: an experience of loneliness and of uprooting similar to that of the famous German exiles such as Brecht and Adorno, exiles with whom Buñuel shared the vision of Hollywood as a great Taylorised factory

(Brecht) and the criticism of the Americanisation of culture and of consumer society (Adorno). Much of his vision of Hollywood would have been captured in the film he planned with Man Ray, *Las cloacas de Los Ángeles* (*The Sewers of Los Angeles*), which remained unfinished, like so many of his important film projects.

Buñuel arrived in Mexico in 1946 on the way to France. He had a project, likewise unsuccessful, that was going to merge his name with that of his friend Federico García Lorca: the filming of *La casa de Bernarda Alba* (*The House of Bernarda Alba*), which, if made, would have represented a great success for Spanish culture in exile. In Mexico, he began making commercial films to survive, and reclaim a career that exile had brought to the point of ruin. Buñuel has commented on the lack of enthusiasm with which he made these films, in words that reflect a state of hopelessness, still deeply tied to the loss of the Civil War. Answering the question of what he thought about his first Mexican film, *Gran Casino* (*The Great Casino* [1946]), he answered: 'I thought it very bad, but I did not consider it to be of much importance. Years had passed, we had lost the war and I said to myself: "What the hell!"' (de la Colina and Pérez Turrent, 1986, p. 49).

Buñuel's film career in Mexico was filled with numerous planned and failed projects. His first Mexican film was a box-office failure. With that first film, Buñuel ran into the difficulties that most exiles face in any country: the resistance of the new medium in which they see themselves forced to work and also the lack of knowledge of this medium on their part. Clearly the situation in Mexico was more favourable than that in the United States, because of the similarity of language and culture and the existence of a large community of Spanish exiles, among whom were a few of Buñuel's most intimate friends. Nevertheless, during those early stages in Mexico, he continued to live in a situation of uprootedness, accentuated by the fact that the hopes and dreams – so firmly maintained by Spanish exiles – were destroyed after the end of World War II. Nor was Buñuel's entry into Mexican cinema completely resolved: 'Around here everything is going from bad to worse,' he wrote to his friend José Rubia Barcia, in a letter dated 3 August 1948, two years after his arrival, in which he also expressed his intention of leaving Mexico (Rubia Barcia, 1992, p. 39).

At a banquet celebrating the occasion of Buñuel's first great triumph as a film director in exile, *Los olvidados* (*The Forgotten Ones*, also translated as *The Young and the Damned*) in 1950, his good friend José Moreno Villa spoke of the desolation felt by Buñuel between 1947 and 1949, some ten years after his exile began, and the fact that he was at the point of being torn apart by the terrible experience of exile:

I cannot forget Buñuel's first years in exile. I watched him waste away physically, and seated on a couch for hours on end, facing the same wall, as if without any possible horizon. We then let out a cheer because the exile overcame anguish.

Moreno Villa, 1994, p. 96

As is known, and can now be documented by the letters written to José Rubia Barcia between 1947 and 1950, Buñuel in Mexico fought tirelessly on two fronts. On the first, to make a poetic, personal cinema: his earliest attempt down this path was the failed filming of the screenplay he wrote together with Juan Larrea, on one of Larrea's first sketches, *Ilegible, hijo de flauta* [*Illegible, the Son of a Flute*]. On the second front, to project his personal and cultural vision on the commercial cinema within which he was working. These two tendencies are synthesised in the great success of *Los olvidados*, a magnificent example of a dimension of counterpoint (the capacity of combining two cultures) that Edward Said highlights as one of the most positive qualities of the condition of exile (1990, p. 366).

From his early Mexican projects, we see how Buñuel attempted to infuse this counterpoint in the more prevailing genres of the Mexican film industry (melo-drama and comedy) by injecting into them works of already proven artistic value from the Spanish literary and theatrical tradition. One must remember that it was not only Buñuel, but a whole group of Spanish actors, screenplay writers, musicians and film-makers (generally exiles) who brought a Spanish infusion to the Mexican cinema of the 'Golden Age'. From very early on, Buñuel not only wanted to take *Nazarín* (Pérez Galdós, 1895) to the big screen, but also *Doña Perfecta* (Galdós, 1876), *La malquerida* (Jacinto Benavente, 1913) and *El último mono* (*The Lowest One on the Totem Pole*) (Carlos Arniches, 1927). It seemed that Buñuel tried to continue in Mexico the work he had began in Republican Spain at Filmófono Studios: to make a popular commercial cinema, but with cul-tural dignity. To this purpose, we can add a new peculiarity – so unique to the authors of exile – that will be present even in the least successful of Buñuel's commercial Mexican films, as well as in all of his subsequent films: the incorpo-ration of his own reminiscences and personal and cultural recollections, a form of overcoming the severing of roots (with the homeland and the past) that exile imposes. This may be understood as an answer to exile itself, a gesture that can also be found in the greatest works of international exile, such as in Joyce or Nabokov. In the light of the terrible experience of exile even the pleasure caused by Buñuelian humour – something that shines through all his films – is readable as an attempt to resist and to replace the painful effects so distinctive of exile.

The Spanish critics and authors of exile seemed to have done something that Paul Ricoeur would conceptualise later on: when a community experiences a fundamental crisis of existence, seeing itself threatened by external or internal destruction, it feels obliged to return to the roots of its identity – the mythic nucleus – that, in the end, solidifies and determines such a community (1995, p. 238). This would explain why the return to roots would be more evident in the authors of exile than in those considered 'nationalist' and 'traditionalist' inside Franco's Spain. Buñuel seemed to believe that the destiny of Hispanic culture was now being decided more in Mexico City or Buenos Aires than in Madrid or Barcelona. His contribution to the forging of such a destiny, the corpus of his Mexican films, was part of a larger narrative trajectory that touches on Galdós' 'contemporary novels' and goes back even further to Cervantes' *Novelas ejemplares*. What Cervantes expressed in his prologue to these novels could be applied to Buñuel's Mexican films:

> I have given these stories the title of Exemplary; and if you look closely, there is not one of them that does not afford a useful example. If it were not that I do not wish to expand upon this subject, I could show you the savoury and wholesome fruit that is to be had from each of them separately and from the collection as a whole.
>
> Cervantes, 1967, p. 707

The attempt to create a personal, poetic cinema in *Ilegible, hijo de flauta* appears closely tied to the desire to reconnect with the symbolic and mythic roots of Spanish identity. The aim was to create a project of great value, but of dubious implementation, since, more than in Mexico, where it was to be filmed, it was going to take place in that no man's land in which a part of exile existence is lived. Ultimately, the disagreement between Larrea and Buñuel impeded the making of this film, one which Buñuel so eagerly wanted to produce at different stages of his career, and for good reason: its central theme was freedom – or 'the phantom of liberty', to put it in Buñuelian terms. Freedom is one of the great themes of exile, as expressed by the poet José María Valente, another victim of exile: 'Could exile itself be a constant or necessary form of history itself, the negation of the spirit, to accept, whatever its forms may be, all non-freedoms in any form, that force or power would like to impose on the spirit?' (1995, p. 19).

The successful realisation of his second Mexican film seemed to reconcile the exiled Buñuel with his host country, as expressed in a letter to Rubia Barcia, dated 5 September 1949: 'I am already beginning to plant roots in this land of free reign, because where else am I going to go? I have spent a terrible year and a half but now everything is going smoothly' (1992, pp. 46–7). In the same letter, he also announced the upcoming production of a new film, *Los olvidados*, and informed his friend that he had become a Mexican citizen. In a letter dated

30 January 1950, even before he began filming *Los olvidados*, he announced to him what this film would represent for his career: 'it is like a mixture of *Tierra sin pan* and *L'Âge d'or*, but with elements evolved throughout these past fifteen years' (ibid., p. 50). It is important to underline that those fifteen years of evolution were those of war and exile, and a marginalisation through which Buñuel himself became more like the leading characters of his own film, *Los olvidados*. For Buñuel, that crossing of the desert, specific to the first phase of exile, teaches one of its greatest lessons: humility and, in his own case, solidarity with the 'nameless'. These two attitudes led to the creative force that exploded on the screen with *Los olvidados* and that reverberated in all his subsequent Mexican films, in which, working in conditions of almost complete anonymity, he achieved international success.

With *Los olvidados*, Buñuel's creative talent, now rooted in his new country, produced the fruit that once again brought his name to the forefront of world cinema. Moreno Villa's words highlight the key to the success of Buñuel's first great film in exile:

> the exile, consciously or unconsciously, knew how to tie the objective into his work, the Mexican and the universal, throwing himself with true inkling at the capital's periphery. And in this way, with bravery and self assurance, the exiled Buñuel identified himself with Mexico and made it possible for his movie to triumph in a far-off and demanding country.
>
> 1994, pp. 96–7

This last remark referred to the Cannes Film Festival Palme d'or awarded to *Los olvidados*. This was a great feat, even more so if we consider that it was made against the dominant trend of nationalistic exaltation of the so-called Golden Age of Mexican cinema. In spite of his success, Buñuel never completely ceased being an exile working within the Mexican cinematographic institution.

From then on he lived reconciled with his country of adoption: 'But I came to love Mexico when I got to know it … I have become a Mexican citizen and I plan to live here always. Now by means of advance payments and banks, I am building myself a house', he wrote to Rubia Barcia on 7 October 1952 (Rubia Barcia, 1992, p. 59); his words show that he appears to have found himself in a condition of a *trasterrado*, of an emigrant who, after much hard work, has achieved a peaceful and better life. This is a general peculiarity of the second phase of exile: when the exiled author begins to take into account what he has achieved in the new country. In Buñuel's case this is reflected in the array of films directed after *Los olvidados*. Between 1952 and 1955, some of these films won the Arieles prize; Carlos Fuentes described his achievements: 'And the great exile, Buñuel – *Él* (1952), *Los olvidados*, *Ensayo de un crimen* (1955) – is perhaps the first to penetrate, thanks to the negated Spanish tradition, the internal landscapes of our society' (1970, p. 247).

In spite of his success, by 1956, the doors to the Mexican film industry had already practically been closed on him. His last three great Mexican films, *Nazarín* (1958), *El ángel exterminador* (*The Exterminating Angel* [1962]) and *Simón del desierto* (*Simon of the Desert* [1965]) were made with independent producers. *Simón del desierto* – an allegory of Buñuel's own crossing through the desert and of his loneliness as an exile – remained incomplete through lack of funds. From much earlier on, he had searched for other outlets and horizons for his creativity. In 1952 he made the first of his two US–Mexican co-productions, *Robinson Crusoe*, and later, in 1960, *The Young One*. In both cases, the movies were made with a North American producer and a screenwriter exiled in Mexico, victims of the McCarthyist persecution of which Buñuel himself was an earlier target.[5]

In the 1950s, he also made two French–Mexican co-productions, *La Mort en ce jardin* (*Death in the Garden* [1956]) and *La Fièvre Monte à El Pao* (*The Ambitious Ones* [1959]). Significantly, there are many exilic characteristics of style in all these films, starting, in the US–Mexican films, with the director's own condition, but also the producer's and the screenwriter's, themselves casualties of the 'witch hunt' in Hollywood. When he announced the first of these two films to Rubia Barcia, Buñuel said that he had 'anti-Hollywood interests' (Rubia

A matter of life and death in *La Mort en ce jardin*

Barcia, 1992, p. 59) – and he could have also added 'exilic interests' – since it dealt with the filming of *Robinson Crusoe*, a paradigmatic work of exile.

Both films take place on an island, like the ending of *Ilegible, hijo de flauta*, a space of exile *par excellence*. Although these two films – especially the second – had very little success, Buñuel must have been pleased by the accolades he received from the most renowned new American film critics of the 1960s. Andrew Sarris included Buñuel in his book *The American Cinema. Directors and Directions 1929–1968* (1968) and Jonas Mekas in his *Movie Journal. The Rise of the New American Cinema 1959–1971* (1972), noting that there was more cinematographic value in the last scene of *The Young One* than in all the writings of the critics at the New York Festival, who ignored Buñuel's film (Mekas, 1972, p. 24).

But in spite of seeing himself consecrated once again as a film-maker – praised by prestigious critics both in the United States and France – in reality Buñuel continued living in this no man's land, unique to exile: unrecognised or claimed by any national cinematography. In his two French–Mexican co-productions, Buñuel was forced, contrary to his own instincts, to deal with a political theme in an explicit way, something that he himself disliked. However, he took advantage of the occasion to slip in scenes and situations that evoked exile, the Spanish Civil War and the figure of Franco, the dictator. The titles of his French films, *La Mort en ce jardin* and *La Fièvre monte à El Pao*, carried with them allegorical and symbolic allusions to the Spanish war and exile, as well as prophetic premonitions of the situation that so many Latin American countries would see themselves in during the second half of the twentieth century. In the first film, there are instances that evoke the 1934 miners' insurrection in Asturias, and the subsequent military repression that would lead to the military uprising of 1936. These events included the flight to France after the disaster of the Civil War, and being locked up in concentration camps, an entrapment that, literally, reappeared in the second film, on the penal colony of the island. The island also recalls the Franco-supporting Caribbean dictatorships of the time, such as Batista's Cuba and Trujillo's Dominican Republic, where so many leftist Spanish exiles were in a situation similar to that of Ramón Vázquez, the protagonist of *La Fièvre Monte à El Pao*. The film is a Buñuelesque contribution to the dictator narrative that has been so influential in Latin American literature in the last half of the twentieth century.

It was between 1958 and 1970, in the creative trajectory from *Nazarín* to *Tristana* (1970), that Buñuel's cinema reached what could be called the apotheosis of a cinema of exile redeemed. *Nazarín*, *Viridiana* (1961), *El ángel exterminador* and *Simón del desierto* belong to the main part of Buñuel's great Spanish–Mexican period. In *Los mundos de Buñuel* (Fuentes, 2000), I delve into the ways in which, interweaving the three main lines of his cinema – Surrealism, traditional Spanish realism and the theological approach – the exile Buñuel has made a distinctive cinematographic contribution of an art for 'after Auschwitz'. In the desolate and desolating world of *Nazarín*, *Viridiana*, *El ángel exterminador* and *Simón del desierto*, Buñuel offers unparalleled examples of the catastrophic backdrop to which our own world seems headed. We find only a tenuous and fleeting hope, almost eroded by failure flickering in the blank stares of Nazarín, Viridiana and Simón at the end of their respective movies, from whom the gesture of human (and divine?) loving expression, even in confusion and failure, does not fade away.

The creative apex of this moment is *Viridiana*, which marks Buñuel's return to film in his native land, in a co-production with a producer identified with the anti-Franco resistance. José Bergamín, talking about Buñuel's return to film in the native land, spoke of his *'anteísmo'*, comparing him to the mythic Antaeus who, upon touching his Mother Earth, recovered his enormous strength. *Viridiana* is a film of Mexican and Spanish hybridity and counterpoint, as so many other works of exile. Buñuel had seen the painting of Viridiana the Saint, paradigm of penitence, that gave name to the film in the National Museum of Mexico, painted by Echave (the elder), and he brought its pictorial *atrezzo* (the crown of thorns, the cross) to the screen in Spain, with a Mexican actress (Silvia Pinal).

Both critics and Buñuel himself underlined the scandal caused by the film, which showed that the Franco regime continued to be as recalcitrant as during its first stages. Clearly, those who with a bloody stroke had tried to erase the entire great heterodox tradition of what has been called the 'Silver Age' of Spanish culture were not going to permit what *Viridiana* (whose name, in its Latin etymology means to re-green, to relive) was bringing back home. In *Viridiana*, Buñuel combined external and internal exile, restoring Spanish artistic creativity, kidnapped by Franco for so long, to the forefront of world attention.

Neither the censors of the regime, nor Franco himself, could – or wanted to – see that with *Viridiana*, a figure of repentance, the great sin of fraternal hate would come to be purged and erased. The scene in which Viridiana washes the floor obsessively (because of her possible responsibility in the suicide of her uncle) can be understood as an allegory for the desire to purge the great sin of the Civil War and its consequences. Perhaps to some extent because of this, in a recent survey, seventy-seven representatives of Spanish art and culture chose *Viridiana* as Buñuel's best film (Cobos, 1998, p. 79).

With *Viridiana*, Buñuel comes to terms with his long enforced absence from the Spanish screen. Although the film was prohibited, and Buñuel did not return to direct in Spain until ten years later, the door remained ajar, thanks to his contacts with film directors and critics of the new generation. The scandal of *Viridiana* was a great incentive for young movie-makers who, in Spain as much as in Mexico and in other Latin American countries, were introducing, or had already launched, a 'New Cinema'.[6] There is also a transnational dimension in Buñuel's cinema of exile that goes beyond the Hispanic world: *Los olvidados* can be considered as a 'herald' of a cinema of marginalisation and of exile, cultivated by Latin American, Asian and African film directors in recent decades.

In the 1960s and 70s Buñuel moved into his final stage, working within the French cinema industry, but with another independent producer (Serge Silverman), anticipating what many directors from different European countries also aspire to achieve in our day: a new cinema of the European Union, based on European cultural hybridism (although Buñuel's cinema – as seen in the rude and ignorant ways in which various characters, during a fancy party, treat the 'Latin American' ambassador in *Le Charme discret de la bourgeoisie* [1972] – places us on guard against European ethnocentrism and xenophobia). He returned to European cinema with a narrative heritage that came from Spanish sources (the picaresque, Cervantes, Galdós and Goya, among others), to which he had added the drives of Latin American New Narrative and his US experience. Not surprisingly, Carlos Fuentes included Buñuel with Vargas Llosa, Carpentier, García Márquez and Cortázar in his book *La nueva novela hispanoamericana* (1969).

At the beginning of the 1960s, when a flood of Spanish workers and maids engulfed other European countries as emigrants, Buñuel returned to film in France. In fact, in his last film, *Cet obscur object du désir* (1977), he merged the theme of exile with that of economic migration, by using the case of Conchita (Carole Bouquet) and her mother (Angela Molina), pursued and, finally, forced out of France, by Immigration Services. The man carrying the sack, who fleetingly crosses the screen in his last film, is the emblematic figure, who, since the bandits in *L'Âge d'or* and the *hurdanos* in *Tierra sin pan* (1933), reappears in his cinema as an incarnation of the social outcast. In his first three films from this period – *Le Journal d'une femme de chambre* (1964), *Belle de jour* (1966) and *La Voie lactée* (1969) – the theme of exile, as part of the human condition, is prominent, and culminates with the fusion of pilgrimage and exile that takes place in *La Voie lactée*. In this film we can also find, in the figures of the two central characters – the wandering beggars – a celebration of the nomadism and freedom of exile. Throughout the film, Buñuel revisits the theme of exile *par excellence*: the return to the native land, a theme which also appeared in his last film *Cet obscur object du désir*, in which the projection of a 'touristic' Spain is redeemed by ironic exilic nostalgia.

Buñuel's return to filming in Europe has a touch of celebratory vengeance. On encountering the new Europe of the Common Market and consumer society, forgetful of its recent holocausts, he warns against the risk of an apocalyptic end in his last three films.[7] In his final phase, technology and terrorism represent two of the four riders of the Apocalypse.

To end this essay, I come back to the theme of Spanish exile. One could say that Buñuel's return to film-making in France was also an excuse to spend some time in Spain: a semi-return of the exiled, when the dictatorship was on the point of disappearing (*Tristana* contains ample allegory of the dictator's end). Still, Buñuel remained faithful to those words he wrote in 1952, 'I have become a Mexican citizen and I plan to live here always' (Rubia Barcia, 1992, p. 59). Although in the last phase of his life he relived his 'Spanish passion', it is certainly true to say that up to the end he lived in that perpetual exile, defined by Sánchez Vázquez as that condition whereby a person discovers 'that whether one returns or not, one will never stop being an exile' (1997, p. 47).

'I am fatally attracted to Spain,' Buñuel told Max Aub, who included the quote as an epigraph in *La gallina ciega* (*The Blind Hen* [1971, p. 16]). Buñuel and Max Aub are two iconic figures of never-ending exile. From the 1960s, they could have returned to live in Spain, but they did not; moreover, they only returned in an almost clandestine way (such as when we find them in the pages of the two Max Aub books, in spite of the attention they attract, strolling alone in the early morning or at nightfall through the places of the Madrid where they lived their revolutionary utopias in the 1920s and 30s), because that Spain, under the last repressive fluttering of the Franco regime, was not the one they left or dreamed of. On one of the pages of his projected book on Buñuel, Aub remembered a conversation with him, after one of his returns from a trip to Spain: Buñuel told him that he had witnessed, through the gates of the gardens of the Royal Palace, a pro-Franco demonstration of more than 50,000 people. Back at his house, Max Aub recreated the scene in verse, beginning with the following, 'El viejo está asomado en su balcón/ de la torre de Madrid …' ['The old man is out on his balcony/of the tower of Madrid'], and finished in this manner:

> He did not want to believe
> That which he is seeing:
> He is watching his past
> Parade on by.
> To have lived for this!
> There, down below,
> In the grey of winter,
> The 'Casa de Campo'.
>
> 1985, p. 146

Buñuel lived his 'fatal attraction for Spain', in his periodic stays during the 1960s and 70s, confined mainly to the twenty-seventh floor in the Torre de Madrid which was like his watchtower, with the ever-present shadow of Calderon's *La vida es sueño* (*Life Is a Dream* [1635]) hanging over him. During his stays in the capital, he descended from the heights of the tower to attend the *tertulias* with friends (so nostalgically evoked in *Tristana*) in the nearby Café Viena, or to take frequent walks down La Moncloa, perhaps repeating, facing the Sierra, that iconic poem by Antonio Machado – '¿Eres tú, Guadarrama, viejo amigo/la sierra gris y blanca,/la sierra de mis tardes madrileñas/que yo veía en el azul pintada?' ['Was it you, Guadarrama, old friend/the white and grey sierra/the sierra of my Madrid afternoons/that I saw in the painted blue?'] – that carries the *ritornello* of never-ending exile, and allows me to close – or re-open – this essay on a cinema of exile.

Translated by Scott M. Bennett

Notes

1. Burton, Gubern and Kinder are among the few authors who have studied Buñuel from this point of view. The latter tells us that 'Luis Buñuel is a nomadic subject with a unique experience of serialized exile' (1999, p. 12).
2. For more on such institutional recuperations, see Marvin D'Lugo (1999).
3. Adolfo Sánchez Vázquez, another famous Spanish exile, reminds us of this etymology: *aterrado* has, thus, a double meaning: frightened and landless (1997, p. 46).
4. In her book, *Surrealism in Exile and the Beginning of the New York School*, Martica Swain makes a few brief references to Buñuel. One of these is a quote from Anaïs Nin's diaries in which she talks about her re-encounter with the group of surrealists in New York and about her meetings with them in the 'Village', where she danced with Pierre Matisse and Luis Buñuel (1995, p. 185).
5. The producer of the films was George Pepper, who in 1945 was executive secretary of the Hollywood Democratic Committee and of the HICCASP (Hollywood Independent Citizens Committee of the Arts and Sciences Professions), the strongest coalition of liberals and radicals of post-war Hollywood. In the first film he used the name Henry F. Ehrlich and in the second one George P. Werker. The screenwriter of both films was the reputed Hugo Butler, who used the names Philip Roll and H. B. Addis, respectively.
6. Ernesto R. Acevedo-Muñoz finishes his doctoral thesis (1998) with a conclusion titled 'From Buñuel to "Nuevo Cine"', in which he highlights the exiled film director as the tie that brought together classical Mexican cinema with the *nuevo cine* that came about in the 1960s and that flourished in Mexico in the 1980s and 90s. In Spain, from the mid-1960s on, a cinema of exile began to be made. Marsha Kinder deals with this in her *Blood Cinema* (1993, pp. 280–6).

7. His last project not filmed, *Agón*, anticipates the terrible explosion of the Concorde that tragically took place just a few years ago: in the movie it is caused by a group of terrorists, a harbinger of the events of 11 September 2001.

References

Acevedo-Muñoz, E. R. (1998), *Deconstructing Nationalism: Luis Buñuel and the Crisis of Classical Mexican Cinema, 1946–1965*, unpublished PhD dissertation, University of Iowa.

Aub, M. (1971), *La gallina ciega*, Mexico: Joaquín Mortiz.

—— (1985), *Conversaciones con Buñuel. Seguidas de 45 entrevistas con familiares, amigos y colaboradores del cineasta aragonés*, Madrid: Aguilar.

Buñuel, L. (1982), *Mi último suspiro*, Barcelona: Plaza y Janés.

—— (1992), *Goya*, Teruel: Instituto de Estudios Turolenses.

Cervantes, M. (1967), 'Two Exemplary Novels. Prologue', in *The Portable Cervantes*, edited and translated by S. Putnan, New York: Penguin Books, pp. 705–8.

Cobos, J. (1998), 'Noventa y cuatro españoles eligen las seis mejores películas de Buñuel', *Nickelodeon*, 13 (Winter), pp. 78–87.

de la Colina, J. and T. Pérez Turrent (1986), *Luis Buñuel: prohibido asomarse al interior*, Mexico: Joaquín Mortiz/Planeta.

D'Lugo, M. (1999), 'Buñuel in the Cathedral of Culture: Reterritorializing the Film Auteur', in Kinder (ed.), *Luis Buñuel's* The Discreet Charm of the Bourgeoisie, Cambridge and New York: Cambridge University Press, pp. 101–10.

Fuentes, C. (1969), *La nueva novela hispanoamericana*, Mexico: Joaquín Mortiz.

—— (1970), *Casa con dos puertas*, Mexico: Joaquín Mortiz.

Fuentes, V. (2000), *Los mundos de Buñuel*, Madrid: Akal.

Kinder, M. (1993), *Blood Cinema. The Reconstruction of National Identity in Spain*, Berkeley: University of California Press.

Kinder, M. (ed.) (1999), *Luis Buñuel's* The Discreet Charm of the Bourgeoisie, Cambridge and New York: Cambridge University Press.

Mekas, J. (1972), *Movie Journal. The Rise of the New American Cinema, 1959–1971*, New York: Macmillan.

Moreno Villa, J. (1994), 'Escritos sobre Buñuel', *Boletín de la Fundación Federico García Lorca*, 12, pp. 84–102.

Ricoeur, P. (1995), 'Universality and the Power of Difference in Languages', in R. Kearney, *States of Mind. Dialogues with Contemporary Thinkers*, New York: University of New York Press, pp. 33–8.

Rubia Barcia, J. (1992), *Con Luis Buñuel en Hollywood y después*, Sada-La Coruña: Ediciones do Castro.

Said, E. (1999 [1990]), 'Reflections on Exile', in Robert Ferguson, Martha Gerer, Trinh T. Minh-ha and Cornel West (eds), *Out There: Marginalization and*

Contemporary Cultures, New York: The New Museum of Contemporary Art, pp. 357–66.

Sánchez Vázquez, A. (1997), *Recuerdos y reflexiones del exilio*, Barcelona: Gexel.

Sánchez Vidal, A. (1988), *Buñuel, Lorca, Dalí: el enigma sin fin*, Barcelona: Planeta.

Sarris, A. (1968), *The American Cinema. Directors and Directions 1929–1968*, New York: E. P. Dutton.

Swain, M. (1995), *Surrealism in Exile and the Beginning of the New York School*, Cambridge: MIT Press.

Valente, J. M. (1995), 'Poesía y exilio', in Rosa Corral, Arturo Souto Alabarce and James Valender (eds), *Poesía y exilio. Los poetas del exilio español en México*, Mexico: Colegio de México, pp. 17–26.

11

Scenes of Liturgy and Perversion in Buñuel

Vicente Sánchez Biosca

I

There is nothing new in saying that *L'Âge d'or* (1930) launches from the very heart of Christianity, namely, of Christ himself, a sacrilegious denunciation of Catholicism. The last section of the film projects Christian iconography upon the Sadean universe of *The 120 Days of Sodom*; the result is a devastating attack, ridiculing the fundamental principles of Christianity. However, any half-attentive viewer will notice two additional elements: first, that the religious emphasis at the centre of a surrealist attitude is characteristically Spanish, something familiar to those with Buñuel's background and education, but somewhat alien to those from other European countries less burdened with Catholicism (France, in particular); second, that the joke produces a comic effect in place of the intolerant seriousness of a frontal ideological attack without, of course, dispensing with it altogether. It is very likely that both elements are more interrelated than appears to be the case at first sight. I would like to concentrate on the comic implications.

Thirty years later, Buñuel made *Viridiana* (1961) as a Mexican–Spanish venture. This film established him as a director (his triumph at Cannes was much talked about, above all for the scandal it provoked).[1] Religious issues (chastity, charity, devotion) are also at the heart of this film, replete with the most varied perversions (fetishism, necrophilia, transvestism). The effect produced is also, at least in part, humorous.

There is one enormous difference, though, between these two examples: if Buñuel's position can be qualified as external to religion in *L'Âge d'or*, it is interior to it in *Viridiana*; that is, in order to develop the script and to create with a level of technical mastery seldom found in Buñuel, the world of objects – fetishes – the links of the religious world with that of the flesh, of the sacrificial with the nuptial bed and from here to the mortuary, of the sublime with the obscene, it was essential to live very close to the subject, to feel and enjoy its overlaps. This is only possible when one surrenders to evocations, to metaphors, to the rhythms of those worlds that no longer shock as logically they should, but instead intertwine, in the process clearly provoking short-circuits, but also pleasant slippages.

Religion in *Viridiana* is a condition of pleasure and for that reason it is a *conditio sine qua non* to live it from within, displaying it, but also, like the fetishist, detaining it in each of these displays, delaying the climax, noticing unexpected connections and exploring them with delight.

II

The Christian religion is far from being an accidental component in Buñuel's work. All his films show complex transactions with its referents, oscillating between the popular ingenuity with which the farce of original sin is staged in the pastoral *La ilusión viaja en tranvía* (1953),[2] the boundless and hyperbolic temptations and miracles of *Simón del desierto* (1965), and the systematic recreation of hierarchies of *La Voie lactée* (1969).

I shall concentrate on a specific area of religion: liturgy. This choice is neither accidental nor capricious, as liturgy is nothing other than 'the Church in prayer', that is to say, the Christian assembly performing ritual acts that strengthen the bonds between its faithful, linking them to their God. The precise distinctiveness of liturgy lies in the fact that manifested within it is the Christian imagination and its capacity for the codification of evocative scenes. According to a reputable essay:

> the majority of liturgical symbols are biblical symbols, the understanding of which is given by the Sacred Scripture that has formed and nourished the Christian imagination ... Through liturgical actions, when we make the gestures of prayer, when we act, we reproduce the gestures and actions of those who have preceded us in the faith since Abraham. Liturgy reproduces the images of the history of salvation that the Bible makes significant for us.
>
> Martimort, 1992, p. 199

A stronger reason recommends this choice: its high ritual value makes liturgy, with its repetition of participatory scenes, monotonous for the outside observer, but laden with performative power in the participants' eyes, the celebrant included, as demonstrated by the sacraments. So cinema would appear a suitable medium for turning these ritual scenes into representations of another sign (the perverse phantom, also repeated to the point of satiety, would be a good example to illustrate the Sadean source of Buñuel's work).

For several reasons the Mexican films are a particularly rich area for the study of liturgical representation, distortion and perversion: first, because of their strict generic codification that fixes stereotypes and follows them faithfully; second, because of their subjection to narrative criteria that forces the use of liturgical ritual in the story, in contrast to what happens in Buñuel's French films, which are freer and more given to the collage style; and third, as a result of the weight of Christian iconography in the Mexico of the 1940s and 50s.

I will look at three examples from Buñuel films. In the first of these, *Ensayo de un crimen* (1955), the liturgical reference is apparently a mere anecdote of no importance. However, close analysis reveals a strong link with the narrative and imagery of the film. In the second, *Él* (1952), a liturgical motif, the Maundy Thursday washing ceremony, initiates the narrative and remains crucially linked to it. The third, *Viridiana* (1961) – a real liturgical arsenal – presents the core of Marian devotion in a boldly sexual manner. In all three cases, woman – her virginity, innocence and purity – is represented erotically. Rather than a transgression of Marian chastity, an eroticisation of woman, through her coupling with liturgical codes that refer to the Virgin, is at play.

III

Ensayo de un crimen, a film inspired by fantastic more than by religious tales,[3] contains nevertheless two scenes that, between them, condense the liturgical contribution to the imagery of this fiction. Archibaldo (Ernesto Alonso) arrives at the house of Carlota Cervantes (Ariadna Welter) for the first time, and her mother asks Alejandro (Rodolfo Landa), Carlota's lover, to leave the mansion. At this stage, the plot is not yet clear, but the link between Carlota and Alejandro is easily deduced, as is the pretence that the Cervantes family makes of Carlota's purity and innocence in front of Archibaldo who is, after all, a good catch as a husband. Archibaldo is urged to enter a private chapel where he discovers Carlota in an attitude of prayer. The camera makes a highly complex gyratory movement while focusing on the mother who, dressed in black, *blocks* the vision of Alejandro, with whom she shares the secret of her daughter's pretence. This is one of those almost Hitchcockian subtle camera movements that are rarely found in the work of Buñuel, who never denied that his technique was limited, achieving in the best of cases an effective discretion. Meanwhile, Carlota's voice is heard off-screen reciting a Hail Mary. The scene concludes with a medium shot of Alejandro, once the mother has left the scene. It is at this point that we enter the chapel.

In close-up, we have Archibaldo; in the background, on her knees before an altar to the Virgin, Carlota concluding her prayers. The half-light lends serenity to this *sancta sanctorum* of the bourgeois home. Archibaldo brings Carlota a clay glass that he has made, and she places this as an offering to the Virgin. The protagonist, who a moment earlier had been troubled by terrible memories that brought to the fore his criminal instincts, is moved by the sacred atmosphere of the place. 'I am moved', he says, 'by this peaceful atmosphere you all live in' (Me conmueve este ambiente de paz en que viven ustedes). Tormented by his future, he opens up before Carlota:

> Usted es para mí un ideal. Sé que su pureza y su ingenuidad podrían salvarme. Pero no me atrevo a pedirle que se ligue demasiado a un destino que puede ser trágico. Estoy convencido de que no soy un hombre como otro cualquiera. Conozco mis aspiraciones y me dan miedo. ¿Me creería usted? A veces quisiera ser un gran santo; otras veces veo con gran certeza que puedo ser un gran criminal.
>
> [For me you are an ideal. I know that your purity and innocence could save me. But I do not dare to ask you to attach yourself too closely to a destiny that could be tragic … I am convinced that I am not a man like others. I know my aspirations and they frighten me. Would you believe me? Sometimes, I would like to be a great saint; at other times I know with certainty that I could be a great criminal.]

They are filmed now in medium shot, without the altar being visible, but the confession is interrupted by the mother. When this happens, the couple hide on either side of the statue of the Virgin. The altar again becomes visible.

The scene condenses the relationship between Carlota and Archibaldo. The incarnation of the pure and innocent woman in the eyes of her suitor, Carlota also represents the possibility of salvation, that is to say, of redemption from his terrible desires. However, Carlota presents herself before our eyes and ears in a state of purity thanks to the religious setting and the prayer she so devoutly recites directed, not coincidentally, to the Virgin. Despite everything, the girl's purity will soon be contradicted, and her falseness has, in reality, already been suggested. So, behind the apparent chastity of the redeeming woman hides a sinner. A fuller understanding of the meaning of this sequence requires analysis of the second scene in which the Hail Mary is recited by the same lips, as this contains another turn of the screw.

On the eve of the wedding that will, or so Archibaldo hopes, banish forever the spell of the musical box that unleashes the fulfilment of his destructive desires, a letter from Alejandro reveals the stark reality that Archibaldo has to contemplate while crouching outside a building: Carlota is not the pure and saintly woman that he had imagined. She is going to meet her former lover under cover of night. Destroyed by the revelation, and with all hope of salvation ruined, the box's music, distorted as it always is when his criminal impulses resurface, sounds in his ears, and Archibaldo fantasises about a murder plan for the wedding night. In the matrimonial chamber, Carlota, about to remove the crown and the veil of her white wedding gown before the mirror, is detained by

Archibaldo and subjected to a ceremony that must end in the crime. It is a perverse ritual that threatens the non-existent purity, and dramatises it through a
religious code as if death had to be prefaced by the representation of such purity.

> Quiero mirarte así, cubierta con esta corona y ese velo que simbolizan pureza. Tu
> cándida pureza, tan blanca y transparente, que permite contemplar, sin velos, tu
> alma de niña. Quisiera verte arrodillada, rezando, como te presentaste ante mí
> aquella mañana – ¿Te acuerdas? – en que te dije que quisiera ser un gran criminal
> o un gran santo … Te he visto tantas veces rezando en mi imaginación. Quisiera
> volverte a ver como aquel día.
>
> [I want to see you like this, covered with this crown and veil that symbolise
> purity. Your innocent purity, so white and transparent that it allows one to see your
> child-like soul unveiled. I would like to see you kneeling, praying, as you presented
> yourself to me that morning – remember? – when I told you I wanted to be a great
> criminal or a great saint … I have seen you praying so many times in my mind! I
> wanted to see you again as you were that day.]

This is strange conduct. After all, the moment to which Archibaldo refers here
was not their first meeting (although it is indeed the first time the spectator sees
them together). It is therefore surprising that it is precisely this moment that has
etched itself so deeply in his mind. It is essential to recapture the impact of this
moment of pretence (the impure woman feigning purity and praying to the
Virgin, the incarnation, after all, of supreme purity) as a scene prior to the
murder. Forced to do so, Carlota kneels, crosses her hands in a pious attitude
and begins to recite the Hail Mary aloud and deliberately. Of course, the choice
of prayer is spontaneous and nobody, neither the viewer nor the characters, asks
why this particular prayer, but it seems clear that the staging of sin and purity
require a prayer to the Virgin.

A new, surprisingly subtle camera movement accompanies the unchanging
soundtrack. Carlota progressively penetrates the imaginary, expiatory world of
the prayer she has been immersed in, emphasising her prayer with a heartfelt
supplication, or rather her convincingly feigned repentance, to the crowned
Virgin (this is the meaning of the Hail Mary). A low-angle shot emphasises the
penitential attitude of the prayer further still. The scene is extremely complex
within its simplicity: a woman dressed in her wedding gown in the intimacy of
her matrimonial chamber, about to give herself to her husband, recites a prayer
of penitence to the Virgin in the presence of someone who (although cheated
and now the author of this staged betrayal) enjoys – and, of course, also suffers
– the image of purity he knows to be feigned and fraudulent. An imaginary
scene, that is to say, a phantasm, of blemished purity and sexual potential,

unfolds by invoking the Virgin Mary herself: this is the ideal moment to perpetrate the crime on the body of the sinner, which, furthermore will be carried out on the bed, prepared for an act of sex that will not take place. The scene is, then, the premise for the execution of the crime, but now we find ourselves not merely witnessing a punishment carried out by a betrayed husband in the depths of despair, but the scenographic work of a pervert: that of Archibaldo, and perhaps above all, Buñuel.

IV

The Mercedes Pinto novel upon which *Él* is based is an autobiographical tale sandwiched between reputable discourses (legal and medical) at the beginning and end of the book, which offer scientific explanations, as well as practical ones, to the problems raised by the story.[4] In each scene, the book sketches the psychological symptoms of a paranoiac with great acuteness, if with a certain lack of concern for the narrative articulation and recreation of the plot's period. Mercedes Pinto places herself as a passive and suffering subject of horrific, delirious actions who contemplates them from outside. Buñuel, on the other hand, imposes a significant change: he postpones Gloria's (Delia Garcés) story until he has placed the plot and its imaginary settings at the margin of the feminist viewpoint, that is to say, at a position external to the psychotic outburst.

The symptoms of paranoia in *Él*

The narrative perspective of the woman is only established later on through a flashback designed to evoke the torments of married life between Francisco (Arturo de Córdova) and Gloria, already manifest on their wedding night. In short, Buñuel offers the viewer the delirious subject's unmediated point of view.

So, this use of the point of view occurs specifically in the initial sequence that takes place in the church. Here too the complete separation from Mercedes Pinto's novel is notable: there is not a trace of religion in the novel. In Buñuel, on the other hand, not only does religion play an orienting role in contextualising the characters' conventions and their bourgeois, well-to-do world (the hero's beliefs, familiarity with the Church and its representatives, Francisco's becoming a monk in the end), but the Church itself, as far as physical and ceremonial space is concerned, becomes the stage upon which the following three passions are displayed: initial fascination (first sequence), mutual though unequal captivation when Gloria and Francisco meet for the second time (just a few scenes later), and the outburst of madness expressed as auditory and visual hallucination (the penultimate sequence of the film). Neither will the destiny of the hero of Mercedes Pinto's novel be the religious withdrawal to the Colombian monastery in which we see him at the end of the film, but rather the clinical coldness of an asylum. The reasons for these changes are similar to those that led Buñuel to replace an enigmatic episode concerning the heroine's torture by means of ropes and other implements with one of the most disturbing scenes in the history of film, Francisco's frustrated attempt to sew up her genitals.

The strategic presence of the Church cannot therefore be dismissed as lightly as has frequently been the case. I propose to spend some time on the first sequence of the film, as Francisco's expression is anchored, explained and unleashed from a ritual deeply codified in Catholic liturgy: the washing of the feet.

Él starts off *in medias res*. The opening shot shows candlesticks with white wax candles, enveloped by the smoke and, presumably, the smell of incense. We are inside a church. Following some altar boys with a pan to the left, the camera films the altar where, probably halfway through the Maundy Thursday mass, the ritual of the washing of the feet will take place. The customary simplicity of the Buñuelian staging, its sobriety, opens the way for certain marked features that emphasise particular aspects of the ceremony. In effect, the structure of the scenes is subordinate to a more precise revelation of the accessories and acts of the ritual. The movements of the camera, the reaction shots and the close-ups are subject to this same end. The liturgical ceremonial is here much more than a set without personality.

The sequence runs entirely without dialogue, but the canticle of the hymn *Ubi caritas et amor*, a Benedictine antiphony, the singing of which is mandatory during the washing, creates an atmosphere of gravity. Two shots deserve special attention: the first of these ostentatiously isolates the kiss that the lips of the celebrant (later we will know that this is Father Velasco) deposit upon the naked and carefully washed foot of a clean-shaven youth. So emphatic is the gesture, so excessive even within the frame of the ceremony, that a reaction shot expresses the stupefaction, amazement, or perhaps the discomfort of the boy. The second track is by now constructed from a point of view internal to the narration, that of Francisco, and follows the priest's second kiss, no less emphasised, upon the naked foot of another child. Instinctively, Francisco, who has retained the detail, transports it to another place where feet, shod this time, are present in the act of worship. In the same way that the kissing of the feet – a symbol of humility and purity – is loaded with significance for the liturgical ceremony, it is also so, although in a different way, from the viewpoint of the fetishist observing them, and who, after running his eye over some worshippers' feet, returns to those of a woman wearing black shoes: the right foot – we must remember that it is precisely this one that should be kissed in the bathing ceremony – is more slightly forward, and both shoes have heels that highlight the instep. These, although not devoid of reverent discretion, display a feminine elegance absent in the feet of the other worshippers, where piety seems to have stifled any appearance of femininity. When the gaze rises up the legs, taking in the entire female body up to the face, the liturgical ritual will have become not yet the core of the scene, but rather a distant murmur that confers the enveloping atmosphere necessary for the beginning of a fascinated gaze irrevocably fixed on its object. The unknown woman will be aware of being beseeched by these proud and penetrating eyes, before which she will be capable of responding only with submission. The play between shot/counter-shot supporting this asymmetrical mixing of gazes, not really reciprocated, will thus become a telling and premonitory expression of the future relationship between the characters.

The importance of this sequence has not, of course, escaped the attention of the critics, though this has in general limited itself to retaining the fetishism without adequately considering the significance of the ritual staged at such a key moment of the film. It is hardly necessary to mention that, just as in the case in *Ensayo de un crimen*, the account of a meeting between a man and a woman is not only influenced, but also inspired by the sacred ceremony. Is this coincidental? Some attention to the ceremony's semantic roots seems necessary.

The washing of Maundy Thursday is a ritual deeply rooted in Catholic liturgy. Already appointed as such in the XVII Toledo Council (694), it evokes the act that the Gospel of Saint John (13, 4–9) attributes to Jesus during the Last Supper with his apostles. It is, then, a symbol of humility in which the celebrant, originally Jesus, washes the feet of twelve, preferably poor, men, and follows a very precise ritual (Martínez de Antoñana, 1957, p. 1006).

The ceremony relies on special utensils: one or several jugs of water, a wash-bowl, towels, an alms bag (in the event that these are required during the ceremony), a cross with a purple veil, candlesticks with white wax candles, the missal with its lectern, a carpet on the steps of the dais, with perhaps fragrant flowers and herbs scattered about.[5] Buñuel, whose library contained curious liturgical works, demonstrates knowledge not only of the technical details of the ritual, but also of their significance, so much so that he rewrites it in order to represent another scene within it: an erotic scene that differs from the well-established atmosphere of the former, but which through significant additions acquires a sacred dimension. This sacred character is precisely the point of departure for the description of a perverse diversion of the ritual in the direction of fetishism. The result is as follows: the erotic encounter is inseparable from a liturgical ritual; even more than that, it is metaphorically associated with it. Hardly, though, has the partial eroticisation been produced than it ends up becoming fascination, which causes the fetishistic characteristics to vanish momentarily in the interests of passion. In this way Buñuel inscribes the birth of desire in a ritual that, by its nature and significance, denies it. It is no accident that we are looking at a purification ritual, where the foot's nakedness is rigorously desexualised. Thus, the purifying operation is inverted: only because there is a purification ritual – the washing of the sinful that recalls Jesus' humble gesture during the Last Supper – can there be a harnessing of desire. Or, put another way, this latter is born from its supposed prohibition. Desire is born, therefore, from the pleasure taken in besmirching the ideal.

The idea that guides this behaviour is not strange to Buñuel: without the sensation of sin there is no intensity in desire, or more precisely, the latter emerges from the oppression imposed by the moral demands of Catholicism. If desire is always a pursuit for an object, neither reached nor possessed, Buñuel's peculiarity consists in this inaccessibility being interwoven with the fixed and codified ceremonial of religious ritual (the liturgy). To recapitulate: within the religious ritual of purification – Jesus' last act before the sacrament of the Eucharist, a ritual of humility – a fetishistic gaze that eroticises the ritual and displaces it towards an object that will forever retain the echoes of its link with liturgy is evident. The question once more arises: who is the fetishist, Francisco or Buñuel? Probably both.

For Buñuel Catholicism is a source of perverse pleasure; and this pleasure is nothing other than the pleasure of sin. The more imperative the rule, the more intense will be the pleasure derived from the transgression. In Buñuel's words: 'When, in spite of all the prohibitions, this desire could be satisfied, the physical pleasure was incomparable, as it was always associated with this secret pleasure in sin' (1982, p. 52). Undoubtedly, there are Sadean overtones here, but limitations of space prohibit further commentary.

In reality, the hermetic, sophisticated and almost inextricable character of the liturgical ritual for the uninitiated is highlighted in several shots that show, among the worshippers who crowd into the church's nave, numerous Indians. These, being totally removed from the mysteries of the ceremonial, cannot participate in its eroticisation either. Buñuel, with his peculiar realism, introduces here traces of social criticism that denote an unexpected distancing in respect of the scene so intensely experienced.

V

Viridiana, at least in the first part, is full of religious references. The sarcastic nature of many of the allusions has been much studied (Sánchez Biòsca, 1999). Here, I shall limit discussion to the Angelus, halfway through the film.[6] Buñuel contrasts the tasks of modernising the countryside undertaken by the tractors under Jorge's (Francisco Rabal) orders with the evening Angelus led by the young Viridiana with the apparent devotion of all her beggars. The two life plans and the two destinies that unravel on Don Jaime's estate are thus in clear opposition, so much so that the praying appears even more anachronistic by being juxtaposed with the destruction of the countryside. Two worlds, two groups of people who seem not to exist in time, thus meet face to face through the work and artistry of the staging. The Angelus would have been a part of Buñuel's education and he undermines this by contrasting it with the productivity of the real world.

Buñuel here returns to one of the great feminine myths of Christianity: Mary's virginity. We know that the Angelus celebrates the archangel's Annunciation to the Virgin, in which she learns that she will conceive the Son of God in her womb. This already alerts the viewer to Buñuel's linking of sexuality and religion. However, the choice of the liturgical fragment is complex. Buñuel must have been familiar with the interpretation by his ex-friend and co-scriptwriter of *Un chien andalou* (1929), Salvador Dalí, in a classic study of Surrealism, *El mito trágico del Ángelus de Millet* (1978), concerning the enigmatic work of the pious nineteenth-century painter, Jean-François Millet, by whom, however, a number of pornographic drawings were later discovered. The reference to the prayer belongs, therefore, to a complex web of allusions ranging from Millet's iconography to Dalí's text and interpretation. The fact that Dalí's original text was lost in 1941, following the forced evacuation of Paris caused by the German occupation, and was only published in a first French edition in 1963, made for an additional problem: had Buñuel seen the text in its entirety? Was it chance that caused the convergence of both readings?

In any case, Buñuel and Dalí had already referred to this canvas of Millet's in the title and still that closed *Un chien andalou*, which showed the two characters half-buried in the earth at the onset of spring, a pose reminiscent of that of the couple in the painting by Millet. Furthermore, Dalí's thesis was in the public domain, independent of the diffusion or otherwise of the written text. As will be remembered, Dalí's was a strange reading of the Millet painting, in which he created and applied his 'paranoid-critical' method. Having been captivated by what he called a 'primary delirious effect' coupled with an incomprehensible and inexpressible anguish, Dalí reconstructed a series of secondary effects triggered by reappearances in his experience of the work in question. This led him to comment on the existence of mysterious similarities between the pious disposition of the feminine figure in the painting and the position of the praying mantis and the male at the moment of coitus and prior to the terrible absorption by the female that characterises her violent and deadly sexual relations. If this were confirmed, stated Dalí, the painting would constitute a ceremony of death, replete with erotic elements evoking castration, the canvas being readable as a collage of various scenes superimposed on the snapshot of the painting (the before, during and after of copulation).

Such a bold and brilliant interpretation led Dalí to ask for a radiographic analysis of the lower part of the painting deposited in the Louvre Museum, convinced that beneath the painted earth there must be something that would irrevocably refer to death and incidentally confirm his delirious intuition. In fact, the analysis reveals the existence of a parallelpiped – drawn and later erased by Millet – that could well be, according to Dalí, a coffin. This, in his opinion, confirms the accuracy of his hypothesis, according to which something sinister is projected onto the religious features, combining death and the act of sex.

This is not the place to comment on Dalí's reading of the painting. My aim is to show that Buñuel, by returning to the Angelus, sets off a chain of Dalíesque imagery that invades the film *Viridiana*, as the presence of necrophilic elements and the union of religion and sex demonstrate. Moreover, if we look, for example, at shot 108 of the film, which appears a few minutes before the recital of the Angelus, we find something unusual. Viridiana poses for El Cojo, who is completing a pictorial composition in which she represents the Virgin surrounded by little angels. The girl, dressed in black, with a wimple and scarf around her head, is sitting on a rustic wheelbarrow like the one that features in the Millet painting, with the leaning woman who in Dalí's interpretation evoked the praying mantis. The similarity cannot be coincidental. Neither, however, can the perversion, as the *Angelus Domini* embodies in the Christian liturgy, as already mentioned, no more nor less than the Annunciation by the archangel Gabriel of the fate awaiting Mary. Viridiana serves, in effect, as a model for the

Virgin, but does so bringing to the scene the motives of Millet–Dalí and under the eyes of someone who perceives her as a virgin, El Cojo, precisely the person who tries to rape her in the orgy.

Something further can be added to the above. While Buñuel films this canvas just as the 'devout painter' El Cojo sees it, Refugio, Viridiana and El Poca, in the presence of the blind man, engage in the following conversation:

> *Viridiana* (*to Refugio*): I need to know how long you've got before giving birth.
> *Refugio*: Why?
> *Viridiana*: To have the doctor prepared, of course.
> *Refugio*: I don't know. About four months, I think, but I couldn't swear to it.
> *Poca*: She doesn't know who the father is either. She said it was night-time and she didn't even see his face.
> *Refugio*: Shut up! I didn't tell you so that you could go around broadcasting it.
> *Don Amalio*: Enough! That's no way to talk, especially in front of our guardian saint, who is a decent person.

The specific subject of the conversation is maternity and virginity and its tone is perverse: just as the Virgin is conceived through the Holy Spirit, that is to say through divine grace, so too is Refugio ignorant of the identity of the man who made her pregnant. Buñuel's gesture is born of humour, not merely of blasphemy. In this respect, *Viridiana* is distanced from *L'Âge d'or*, as well as from Buñuel's intellectual French productions of around 1970.

VI

To conclude, as demonstrated in the examples discussed above, and also in others precluded from discussion for lack of space, the aim of *Él* is not to attack religion – as was the case, for instance, in *L'Âge d'or* – but to use one of its most essential elements, the liturgy, as a means of articulating the narrative. Liturgy relies, after all, on a ritualised symbolic universe, upon which the pervert can create, in turn, his own – though admittedly different – rituals. The pervert's mind invents scenes, in a process that eroticises the objects but in general is governed by monotony – of a type that perhaps only de Sade has been able to enliven. So Buñuel develops these scenes from previous ones, and remains surprisingly faithful to their symbolic function. The fact that desire is linked to specific expressions of Catholic ritual does not undermine their importance. On the contrary, it makes it a necessary condition of pleasure.

Of course, these are by no means Buñuel's only concerns here. The fantasy-fuelled assaults on the woman's body and on realism are also special targets. Nevertheless, the pleasure in perversity and the humour of many of Buñuel's films are totally incomprehensible without awareness of these rituals. When all is said and done, atheist or not, Buñuel is incomprehensible without reference to Catholic liturgy, before which he could never adopt an objective position. 'I am an atheist,' said the man from Calanda, 'thank God.'

Translated by John McCarthy

Notes

1. As is known, *Viridiana*, produced by UNINCI, Films 59 and Gustavo Alatriste was awarded the Palme d'or *ex aequo* with Henry Colpi's *Une si longue absence*. The prize was received by the Director General of Cinematography and Theatre, José Muñoz Fontán. But a furious attack published the following day in *L'Osservatore romano*, describing the film as obscene and sacrilegious, resulted in the summary dismissal of the Spanish official.

2. Popular naiveté – the Devil in the form of a dove who tries to hunt the Holy Spirit with a shotgun – that is not separate from brimming carnality and a reading of the aforementioned original sin as lust. Let us not forget that this is about the representation of original sin and that this is identified with lust.

3. A universe of reference that is not far from a certain popular vein in Buñuel: for example, *Susana* (1950) responds to this fairy-tale imagery which serves as an intertext for it and which is sustained throughout the film by the old maid. Without a doubt, this makes possible the exaggeration, as well as the humour this hyperbole entails.

4. Two texts precede Mercedes Pinto's: 'To Mercedes Pinto. By Way of a Prologue', by the legal adviser Jaime Torrubiano Ripoll, reflecting on the legitimacy of divorce, and 'Preface', by Professor of Psychiatry at Montevideo, Santín Carlos Rossi, who deals with paranoia. At the end of the story, two texts guard the volume with their science: an 'Epilogue', credited to Doctor Julio Camino Galicia, and 'A Final Opinion', by the legal adviser and writer Valero Martín. See Pinto (1989).

5. The ritual is as follows:

   > If the washing takes place during the Mass. After the homily the Priest goes to the seat and sits down; the holy Ministers, prior to genuflecting at the altar, go to the entry to the presbytery, or the church nave, near the pews, and invite the men chosen for the washing and guide them two by two to the designated place. They genuflect two by two and salute the Priest, then sit at their positions and bare the right foot. – Meanwhile the singing of the antiphons commences; these are sung throughout the washing, so that towards the end the eighth one, that is the hymn *Ubi caritas et amor*, is begun, the others being omitted if necessary.
   >
   > Martínez de Antoñana, 1957, p. 1007

6. The Last Supper, parodied through Leonardo da Vinci's painting, has been thoroughly dealt with by many critics, and needs no further commentary here.

References

Buñuel, L. (1982), *Mi último suspiro*, Barcelona: Plaza y Janés.

Dalí, S. (1978 [1963]), *El mito trágico del Ángelus de Millet*, Barcelona: Tusquets.

Martimort, A. G. (1992), *La Iglesia en oración. Introducción a la liturgia*, (French original 1984), Barcelona: Herder.

Martínez de Antoñana, G. (1957), *Manual de Liturgia Sagrada*, tenth edition, Madrid: Coculsa.

Pinto, M. (1989), *Él*, Montevideo-Buenos Aires: Agencia General Librería y Publicaciones, re-edited in facsimile by the Vice-consul of Culture and Sport of the Government of the Canaries.

Sánchez Biosca, V. (1999), *Luis Buñuel: Viridiana*, Barcelona: Paidós.

Luis Buñuel, or Ways of Disturbing Spectatorship

Laura M. Martins

> We should definitively renounce easy formulas such as 'fascism shall not pass'. It already has passed and continues to pass. In constant evolution, it continues to slip through ever more fine nets. It seems to come from without, when in reality it finds its strength in the heart of desire in each of us.
>
> Felix Guattari, 1995, pp. 171–2

Film-makers like Luis Buñuel are rare: an iconoclast always battling simultaneously on political, institutional and aesthetic fronts. Seldom have film-makers matched his sense of responsibility as an artist, a responsibility that is conscious, permanently grounded in political dissidence and in defiance of canonised aesthetic form. Only a few dare allow their work to be informed by the revolutionary potential of art. This leads to the question: how did Buñuel create one of the most irreverent artistic profiles of the twentieth century? I shall endeavour to answer that question by first turning to some key films. Throughout his career (1928–77), Buñuel dismantled the diegetic illusion by upsetting our expectations as hearing-seeing individuals who, distracted by artifice, are always placed in the more comfortable, familiar position, as defined by Burch (1990), of the non-corporeal spectator of the Institutional Mode of Representation (IMR). Burch refers to a special kind of naturalised discourse (the diegetic illusion), the Hollywood prototype that has established conventional processes of identification: the identification of the spectator with the camera and characters. The viewer's invisibility is achieved through avoidance of direct appeal and through prohibition on exposure of the credulity and complicity on which our gaze is based. Second, I shall concentrate on some of Buñuel's characters, such as Nazarín and Viridiana, and on various passages or lines of dialogue delivered by them, in order to observe how his films problematise issues related to Christianity. Buñuel vividly demonstrates how the image of a crucified rebel remains a key element in the formation of Western subjectivity. It could be said that the director of *Viridiana* (1961) anticipates the question raised by León Rozitchner in *La cosa y la cruz. Cristianismo y capital-ismo. (En torno a las Confesiones de San Agustín)* (The Thing and the Cross. Christianity and Capitalism [On St Augustine's 'Confessions']) as to 'whether the entire Christian religious foundation is … necessarily the foundation for domination precisely on the basis of its religious component' (1997, p. 11) (my translation).[1] Buñuel is aware that Western models of subjectivity – Jewish and non-religious individuals included – are firmly rooted in Christian culture.

In sharp contrast to the idea of the aesthetic as mere ornament, Buñuel's films are a contract of audiovisual reading. While they serve as a vehicle for com-plex issues, and for questioning artistic representation, they also claim the right to imagination in the light of 'the catastrophes of the public spirit that repression has caused and is still causing' (Negri, 1998, p. 20). In times of fear and apoc-alyptic beliefs – such as at the turn of this new millennium – one might draw inspiration from Buñuel's commitment to a sense of artistic responsibility. Jacques Derrida's claim in *The Gift of Death* that 'there is no responsibility with-out a dissident and inventive rupture with tradition, authority, orthodoxy, rule, or doctrine' (1995, p. 27) is perfectly applicable to Buñuel.

The most challenging enterprise Buñuel ever undertook was to construct a 'dialectic image', a critical image of image itself, 'an image that criticises the ways we see it' (Didi-Huberman, 1997, p. 113) because, as we look at it, it forces us to review our perception. In his attempt to show a void, Buñuel enunciates and denounces the fact that neither 'the object nor the viewing subject ever stop at the level of what is visible', because 'the act of seeing is not the act of a machine perceiving reality as a composite of tautological evidence' (ibid., p. 47).[2] Rather, seeing or making something visible is always a disturbing experience for the very act of seeing. It might even be possible to speculate that the inaugural image of the cut eye in *Un chien andalou* (1929) – an eye which is gazing at ours – would refer to the operation that effectively implies the act of seeing: an operation that is always agitated, restless and fundamentally unstable.

Paraphrasing Jean-Luc Godard's thoughts on the connection between modern painting and cinematography (1998, pp. 54–5), I argue that Buñuel's images are a 'thinking form' ('forms advancing toward the word'): his image defies us by returning our gaze. However, the image undergoes a major transformation in Buñuel's films. By exceeding and surpassing the rigid space provided by the frame, his images project onto the exterior of the viewing subject, foregrounding the 'invisible barrier' (Burch, 1990, p. 202) that seeks to preserve the viewer in that very state of invisibility. Buñuel's aim is to destabilise the viewing subject by breaking, for instance, with the naturalised notion of image imposed by the IMR. Most of his films – like *Los olvidados* (1950) – seek to expose the artifice as well as the rhetoric of film-making. This process also aims at unveiling the source of

Disturbing spectatorship in *Viridiana*

enunciation, the camera, as a way of unmasking the operations by means of which the film-maker exerts his power over the spectator.

In *Los olvidados*, Pedro (Alfonso Mejía), a ten-year-old child, is caught, at a progressive reformatory, stealing an egg. He turns around and, looking directly at the camera, furiously throws the egg at the lens. We see the yolk and the white of the egg slipping over the shiny, transparent surface of the lens. The egg's trickling motion clouds, de-forms and dis-figures the image. The violent and sudden attack with the egg should be viewed as a break with the naturalised notion of image proposed by the IMR. Something, then, appeals to us while looking at us defiantly. At the same time, we, the spectators, perceive that *visibility* – that gaze – as something strange (the strangeness of what ought to remain hidden). As Didi-Huberman notes, the experience of seeing/being seen by the gaze unifies two complementary moments, dialectically interwoven: 'to see how what is being concealed is both lost, so to speak, and uncovered' (1997, p. 159). Once again, Buñuel is performing a *cut* by revealing our credulity and our complicity as viewers and by the awakening of the act of seeing. Buñuel breaks the pact that underlies the relationship between the film-maker and the audience by unerringly aiming at the 'illusion of reality', because it functions as a mask that hides 'the existence of a rationally selective system of symbolic exchange' (Zunzunegui, 1991, p. 12). By exposing the processes of enunciation, he also seeks to distance the viewer from ideology, something that leads to constant identification with the point of view of the camera, with the gaze. How is this done? In a classical film, the diegetic process is maximised by means of the invisibility of the spectator resulting from the taboo prohibiting the actors from looking at the camera lens; we are being addressed as 'incorporeal individuals' (Burch, 1990, p. 250). Through the egg's descent over the slippery surface of the camera, not only does Buñuel disrupt the identification with the character (linked with the signified) and with the camera (linked with the signifier), but he also returns to us the corporality (the visibility) that the spatio–temporal mode of representation had removed. At this point, we are being addressed by what we see looking at us. This is achieved through the simultaneous and momentary manoeuvres of making explicit what was hidden (our awareness of film-making as an artifice), and of making us lose our credulity (our complicity).

Buñuel's search is directed towards the destabilisation of our gaze as spectators, but as I shall attempt to demonstrate, this is done not only in order to shake us out of that comfort zone but also to exhibit what Guattari would term 'molecularised fascisms' (1995, p. 170), that is, the 'fascist micro-crystallisations that keep proliferating in front of us' (ibid., p. 165) and that, disseminating into differentiated modalities, capture our libidinal energy. In his films Buñuel examines not only political fascism, but the fascism that is within us, that causes us to desire our own domination. The director of *Le Fantôme de la liberté* (1974) gives an account of the fact that fascism is not an historical error or a transitory evil but a deeply rooted phenomenon that goes beyond a strictly defined period. There are 'fascistising crystallisations' (ibid., pp. 163–5) entrenched in the structures of the State, in institutional, familial and individual structures. Such a conviction leads him to set the stage for situations in which despotism, frequently characterising conjugal, familial and other relationships, stem from the same type of libidinal *agencement*[3] found in the social domain (ibid., p. 154).

Susana (1950), for instance, may be read in the light of Adorno 's (1978) argument as a film where Buñuel corrosively makes visible the celebration of 'normality' as a permanent mask of oppression. Susana's (Rosita Quintana) entry as a stranger into a familiar/familial order jeopardises a perverted yet comfortable state of affairs. This order is identified with the phallocentric power of a couple, the relations of filial submission, and the power of the feminine super-ego in silencing passion. Having escaped the reformatory, Susana is once again sent into captivity, and with her expulsion from the exposed familial order, the previous stage of faked conjugal, paterno-filial, and domestic happiness, returns. What is revived is the celebratory illusion of alienated links that are nonetheless disguised in an appearance of normality. Buñuel unerringly shows a state of affairs that mainly relates to the fact that very frequently a woman 'carries her own Panopticon with her wherever she goes, her self-image [as] a function of her being for another' (Doane, Mellencamp and Williams, 1984, p. 14). Thus, Susana monitors herself and reproduces the very phallocentric structure which assigns her some sort of unified identity, that views her as a 'fixed signifier', an identity linked to the emotional, corporeal sphere, which makes her an individual existing in 'the metaphysical order of self' (Butler, 1998, p. 622). In *Susana,* Doña Carmen (the mother figure), accompanied by the maid Felisa (who shares her attitudes), seeing how her familial structure may be on the verge of collapsing, and in order to safeguard the *status quo*, evicts Susana, the intruder, by whipping her.

In the final scene, significantly presided over by a prominent crucifix, Doña Carmen reprimands her son as they sit at the table: 'Mi hijito, ¿otra vez sentándote a la mesa antes que tu padre?' ('My little son, are you once again sitting at the table before your father does?') Through her mediation everything falls back into 'place'. In disrupting family order and placing its mechanisms in the spotlight, this ending makes it clear that Susana is not the perverted one (without exception, everyone in the house makes that judgment of her, demonising and expelling her); rather, it is Doña Carmen herself who engineers the return to a state of affairs where a mode of production of subjectivity prevails that she, in her punctiliousness, makes certain to perpetuate. Once the command has been internalised, she fulfils it diligently and efficiently: the nurturing mother who, from within, safeguards family unity, protecting it from external evil. In *Susana*, and elsewhere, Buñuel portrays these relationships as being based on ownership, imprisonment and exchange, and, as such, they are the expression of the fascist structures mentioned earlier. In *Cet obscur objet du désir* (1977) the explosion at the end of the film seems like a fitting comment on such relationships.

It is a commonplace to maintain that virtually all of Buñuel's films draw on the abundant arsenal of Christian rituals and sources of symbolic production. Perhaps the origins and nature of his personal obsession should be sought in the historical survival of a religion based on universal expansion, convinced of its unique and absolute Truth, a religion that condemns Western subjectivity to definition through the image of a rebel crucified to death (Rozitchner, 1997, pp. 11, 15).[4] For Buñuel this is a type of subjectivity controlled by threat and death, one that is measured by fear of damnation, or by the protection of an ethereal, luminous world, available to all who are capable of suppressing those features that precisely define material humanity: desire, passion, enjoyment, fantasy, that is, the human condition itself. Detractors from this truth face irredeemable damnation. Christ's most dramatic act of rebellion 'also serves to deepen in submission and to transform it into the new instrument of the renascent power' (ibid., p. 51). As a consequence of having internalised this model of placated disobedience, he/she who dares subvert the established order dies through the power of the State (ibid., pp. 64, 95–6). Buñuel constantly elaborates on questions concerning the subjugation of the self.

Questions like this are given sharp focus, for instance, through the character of Nazarín (Francisco Rabal) who, as a 'holy man [is] no less harmful than the pervert or the degenerate' (Deleuze, 1986, p. 127) in partaking through his 'good deeds' in the work of degradation, trying to live by the Gospel through preaching and practising detachment and denial of passion. A seemingly irredeemable individualist, he is even capable of being a scab. Hungry from his pilgrimage in search of charity, he decides to begin working in front of a group of angry local workers who end up attacking him. The addition of this sequence as well as the spatial–temporal displacement to the Mexico of the *porfiriato* (1884–1911), produce radical changes to the original novel by Benito Pérez Galdós (1895), whose Nazarín is a character more attached to the idea of a contemporary resurrected Christ. The individualism of Buñuel's Nazarín's is again in evidence when, removed from the conflict he provokes, he hears several gunshots from the direction of the struggle between the foreman and the strikers while he – completely detached from and unmoved by these circumstances – continues to pick olive tree leaves. The powerful nature of this scene derives from the dialectic between the gunshots (out of frame sound and action) and the lightness of his gesture: regressive parasitism on the one hand, and perverse action on the other. Nazarín's individualism, his marginal position and his indifference to the capitalist system, as well as to the conditions of repression and persecution during Porfirio Díaz's dictatorship, suffocate all tendencies towards non-conformism, something that is taken to extremes in *Simón del desierto* (1965), where for years the protagonist perches, removed from the world, on top of a high column. By undervaluing their bodies, both Nazarín and Simón live without complaint, 'accepting the martyrdom that the capital, the state and the church impose on them, to certify that their fantasy is a divine commandment' (Rozitchner, 1997, p. 201). Protected in his imaginary subjective shelter Nazarín, a man defeated in life by death, remains aloof through disinterest and omission from all other outcasts on earth.

Among the many aspects of Christian theology scattered in Buñuel's filmography, one notes the links – as in, say, *Viridiana* – between the (ideo)logical premises of Christianity and capitalism. As Rozitchner points out, Marx had analysed the expropriation of the worker's body in the productive process, but he forgot to examine the prior, convenient 'mythic-religious' embargo 'of the living body, imaginary and archaic, which is … also presupposed in any economic relationship' (1997, p. 12).[5] Undifferentiated labour (required by a goods-producing system) stems from the devaluation of the body. It befits Christianity to undervalue 'the use of one's body', which the capital (value and price) will seek to expropriate. It is not surprising, then, that Saint Augustine remarks: 'by *saving* the flesh you will be able to *invest* in the Spirit' (cited by Rozitchner, 1997, p. 12) (my emphasis). 'Libidinal economy' makes a grand entrance. Materiality is denied. It must be avoided in order to prevent the collapse of the *ordo universalis* (Grüner, 1997, p. 10). From here, the passage to death as an instrument of social, historical and political order is narrow. Christian theology provides for that by centring on the figure of an individual who is tortured to death, and, in so doing, serves as a model for salvation as he is reborn in another life (collective rebellion is replaced by a religious, subjective, individual solution).[6]

On UNINCI's initiative, and thirty years after the beginning of his career, Buñuel directed *Viridiana*. The importance of this film lies in the fact that it was the first film he shot on Spanish soil as an exile. Although, *Viridiana*, like *Nazarín*, expounds a kind of subjectivity rooted in Christianity, it stages at the same time the novice's authoritarian side through the rites and rigid modalities imposed by her on the beggars whom she has sheltered. Even though Viridiana (Silvia Pinal) will later proceed to hide, then burn, the fetishes of crucifixion, at first, while surrounded by them, she accepts the dimension of death (her repressed carnality) inserted in her own life through religious ordinance.

Viridiana will go from the denial of all her passions to incipient self-acknowledgment as a desiring machine. The latter is possible as she moves from subservience from one kind of law to another: from the Oedipal territoriality of Christian law to the phallocratic power embodied in her cousin Jorge (Francisco Rabal), the heir to her uncle (Fernando Rey), who, thanks to his inheritance, plans the capitalist development and modernisation of the estate. In relation to the latter, we witness in *Viridiana* an evocative sequence uniting work and prayer (in a scene that also gestures to the painting of *The Angelus* by Jean-François Millet): the devout young woman calls the beggars for Angelus prayer while, not far from there, machines and tractors, shovels and wheelbarrows brimming with all kinds of materials, are busy carrying out the tasks of modernisation undertaken by Jorge. While the devout Viridiana and the poor souls she associates with are praying, the field becomes electrified and developed. To show this counterpoint, Buñuel resorts to the syntax of parallel montage: each long shot of the languid prayer with her motionless believers is followed by a close-up of the rapid, spasmodic movements typical of the new kind of productivity. However, rather than constituting, as Sánchez Biosca claims, a 'clear opposition' between 'two worlds, two groups that seem not to coexist in time [and who] appear, thus, face to face, through the trickery of montage' (1999, p. 71), Buñuel brings into play 'the (ideo)logical premises of the kingdom of Capital'[7] or, as noted earlier, the complementary nature of both premises, of Christian spirit and capital. In effect, after inculcating precepts, passing orders and establishing a rigorous programme of behaviour for the beggars that borders on the military, in this sequence, Viridiana is seen in prayer with them, that is, investing in the spiritual, saving the flesh (Saint Augustine *dixit*), preparing for eternal life. Viridiana is like a crypt, a sarcophagus, an in-sensitive body, whose expropriated identity is content to search for celestial dividends. Meanwhile Jorge invests capital to make the field yield material profit in order to enjoy its terrestrial dividends; he modernises his property because he intends to turn it from parasitic soil, from abandoned estate, to productive terrain through the efforts of all the workers. Through this counterpoint, aided by a clever use of images, Buñuel recreates the notion that capitalist order, much like the Christian subjectivity from which the latter derives, imposes a way of living for a mere quantitative system. Hence, it is possible to gather that each individual, as a function of that norm, must assume 'the control, repression and modelling mechanisms present in the prevailing status quo' (Guattari, 1995, p. 53).

Furthermore, some of Buñuel's characters are made to deliver significant lines that can cast light on one of his most obsessive targets: the relationship between drive/desire and Christianity. In *Abismos de pasión* (1953), for instance, Eduardo (Ernesto Alonso) discovers that his wife Catalina (Irasema Dilián) is still emotionally attached to Alejandro (Jorge Mistral), who has now returned to the *hacienda* after many years of absence. At that point, Eduardo has no problem condemning her by asserting: 'Me *engañaste con el pensamiento*' ('You *betrayed me in your thoughts*') (my emphasis). In *Viridiana* he once again uses the same notion when Don Jaime decides not to abuse the novice sleeping under the effects of a powerful drug that he had poured into her coffee. When she awakes, he confesses to his intended crime; at first, he lies to her by claiming to have consummated intercourse with her, but then he admits that this was not really the case. He uses similar terms as Eduardo to describe his desires: 'Sólo te *ofendí con el pensamiento*' ('I only *offended you with my thoughts*') (my emphasis). The repetition of this line is significant: not the act itself, but the power behind it; not the fact itself, but the intention or, rather, the sin of intention. Buñuel stages the most perverted comparison between thought and action, between subjective thought and objective reality produced by Christianity. According to this, the external legal order is internalised (Rozitchner, 1997, p. 17) and draws the individual – by feeling guilty – to refrain from fulfilling their most intense, spontaneous desires, to renounce their human condition without being able to experience it and 'to orient it socially' (Ibid., p. 17). This kind of religious affirmation and its veneer of spirituality terrorises our vital drive, that is, seriously affects life itself, for it neglects the materiality of our skin and flesh.

Yet, in his determination to counter the machinery of established power, Buñuel draws on his extraordinary imagination to develop his own aesthetic-political machinery. It is political because it stems from his understanding of cinematographic practice as 'an act of critical interpretation of forms and languages we are familiar with' (Haynes, 1999, pp. 8–9),[8] as a break from stan-dardised formulations that are cherished by and reassuring for the audience. If some part of the economic logic governing film-making leads the audience to buy emotions, sensations, experiences (something ideal, as Burch would have it [1990, p. 143]), Buñuel aims to dispense with that comfort zone by reclaiming the spectator's full attention, a kind of attention that never rests and is always nomadic. He does so either through images that refuse to disguise the opera-tions of power (as in *Los olvidados*), by displaying the nature of cinema as an artefact (as in, say, *Un chien andalou* or *Los olvidados*), or through provision of the necessary conditions for spectators, accustomed to the IMR, to search for their own answers (Tobias, 1999, p. 148), to discover the secrets hidden in the box that Belle de jour (Catherine Deneuve) is keen to open, or in the bag that is carried around rather unenthusiastically at first by the anonymous passer-by and later by Mateo in *Cet obscur objet du désir*.

Buñuel's aesthetic and political targets were clearly aimed at a form of despotic power that dictates how we have to look and what we have to listen to. They were defined by a kind of analytical practice founded on disrupting our certainty about what we see, and through a new approach to desire in order to intervene actively against the machinery of established power. Starting from there, he would point out unerringly that the strategic adversary, both histori-cally and internally, is fascism, which has nested deep down within us and through which we long for our own domination and exploitation. Hence, what truly matters, as a first step, is to acknowledge its prevalence in our daily exist-ence, one that does not remain hidden in the shadows, and that Buñuel made manifest through exposure, juxtaposition and his sharp inventiveness.

Notes

1. Henceforth all translations from languages other than English are mine.
2. The tautological form implies that 'what you see is what you see', which entails both the stability of the visual object (what is *is* what it is) and the stability of the viewing subject (you are you). A tautological verification would be found in an assertion such as: 'Vermeer's *The Lacemaker* is a lacemaker, neither more nor less', or like this: '*The Lacemaker* is nothing more than a plain surface covered with colours laid out in some sort of order' (Didi-Huberman, 1997, pp. 46–7). Although Didi-Huberman analyses the aesthetic and epistemic conditions for the visual experience as they related to sculpture (and, to a lesser extent, paintings), his claim can be applied to the cinematographic image. It is precisely the title of his book that I borrowed in another article to ascribe it to Buñuel's film-making (Martins, 1999, pp. 189–99).
3. I use this term as Guattari defines it, but as outlined by Gregorio Kaminsky in the

compilation and foreword he wrote for *Cartografrías del deseo* (1995): '[The *agencement* is] a wider notion than that of structure, system, form, process, etc. *Agencement* incorporates heterogeneous components from different orders (biological, social, mechanistic, imaginary, etc.). In the schizophrenic theory of the unconscious, the *agencement* is used to confront the "Freudian complex"' (1995, p. 201).

4. As I have argued elsewhere (Martins, 1999, p. 194), Buñuel would somehow point to the imperialistic nature of the first evangelical, Catholic religion in terms of its eagerness for universal expansion. And yet on the other hand, he did not propose a counter-truth, because that would imply relying on the same logic. Nor did his films attempt to provide correct answers; rather, he endeavoured to formulate problems that would challenge dogmatic views.

5. Marx illusorily thought that the advent of scientific rationality would bring about the collapse of myths and religions.

6. In fact, a new form of domination arises with Christianity: the Emperor Constantine realises that the new religion 'can appear by subjectively fulfilling that task of imaginary protection in each subject … Why not adopt a religion whose divine figure while turned into a Roman man appears crucified by the power of the State's law?' (Rozitchner, 1997, p. 267).

7. This syntagm is used by Eduardo Grüner (1997, p. 10) in his reading of the cited text by Rozitchner when he develops his bold argument that it is not necessary to wait for Protestantism to uncover such premises, nor for all the material conditions to be met, nor does it require the unfolding of the 'economic basis'. It is true, though, that one must return to the formation of a libidinal economy. For further details, see Rozitchner (1997, pp. 9–22).

8. Todd Haynes is one of the few American independent film-makers whose own practice is characterised by political opposition to 'totalitarian machinery'.

References

Adorno, T. (1978), *Minima Moralia: Reflections from Damaged Life*, London: NLB.

Burch, N. (1990), *Life to Those Shadows*, translated by Ben Brewster, London: BFI.

Butler, J. (1998), 'Variations on Sex and Gender: Beauvoir, Wittig, and Foucault', in R. C. Davis and Ronald Schleifer (eds), *Contemporary Literary Criticism: Literary and Cultural Studies*, New York: Longman, pp. 612–23.

Deleuze, G. (1986), *Cinema I. The Movement Image*, translated by H. Tomlinson and B. Habberjam, London: Athlone Press.

Derrida, J. (1995), *The Gift of Death*, translated by D. Wills, Chicago: University of Chicago Press.

Didi-Huberman, G. (1997), *Lo que vemos, lo que nos mira*, translated by H. Pons, Buenos Aires: Manantial.

Doane, M. A., P. Mellencamp and L. Williams (1984), *Re-vision. Essays in Feminist Film Criticism*, Frederick: University Publications of America and the American Film Institute.

Godard, J.-L. (1998), *Histoire(s) du cinéma*, Paris: Gallimard.

Grüner, E. (1997), 'Sobre *La cosa y la cruz. Cristianismo y capitalismo*', *La Gandhi. Argentina*, 2, p. 10.

Guattari, F. (1995), *Cartografías del deseo*, translated by Miguel Denis Norambuena, Buenos Aires: La Marca, pp. 171–2.

Haynes, T. (1999), 'El autor ecléctico', interview with J. Porta Fouz, *El Amante*, 92, pp. 8–9.

Kaminsky, G. (1995), 'Prólogo. Un bricolage existencial', in F. Guattari, *Cartografías del deseo,* Buenos Aires: La Marca, pp. 7–15.

Martins, L. (1999), 'Luis Buñuel: lo que vemos, lo que nos mira', *La nueva literatura hispánica*, 3, pp. 189–99.

Negri, T. (1998), *El exilio*, translated by Raúl Sánchez, Barcelona: El Viejo Topo.

Rozitchner, L. (1997), *La cosa y la cruz. Cristianismo y capitalismo. En torno a las Confesiones de San Agustín*, Buenos Aires: Losada.

Sánchez Biosca, V. (1999), *Luis Buñuel.* Viridiana, Barcelona: Paidós.

Tobias, J. (1999), 'Buñuel's Net Work: The Detour Trilogy', in M. Kinder (ed.), *Luis Buñuel's* The Discreet Charm of the Bourgeoisie, Cambridge and New York: Cambridge University Press, pp. 141–75.

Zunzunegui, S. (1991), 'Prólogo', in N. Burch, *El tragaluz del infinito* second edition, translated by F. Llinás, Madrid: Cátedra, pp. 9–13.

Filmography

As director

1969   *La Voie lactée* (*The Milky Way*)

1970   *Tristana*

1972   *Le Charme discret de la bourgeoisie* (*The Discreet Charm of the Bourgeoisie*)

1974   *Le Fantôme de la liberté* (*The Phantom of Liberty*)

1977   *Cet obscur objet du désir* (*That Obscure Object of Desire*)

As assistant director

1926   *Mauprat*. Director: Jean Epstein.

1927   *La Sirène des Tropiques* (*Tropical Siren*). Directors: Henri Étiévant and Marius Nalpas.

1928   *La Chute de la Maison Usher* (*The Fall of the House of Usher*). Director: Jean Epstein.

As executive director (Filmófono)

1935   *Don Quintín el amargao* (*The Bitterness of Don Quintin*). Director: Luis Marquina.

1935   *La hija de Juan Simón* (*Juan Simon's Daughter*). Director: José Luis Sáenz de Heredia.

1936   *¡Centinela Alerta!* (*Sentinel Alert!*). Director: Jean Grémillon.

1936   *¿Quién me quiere a mí?* (*Who's in Love with Me?*). Director: José Luis Sáenz de Heredia.

List of Illustrations

Whilst considerable effort has been made to correctly identify the copyright holders, this has not been possible in all cases. We apologise for any apparent negligence and any omissions or corrections brought to our attention will be remedied in any future editions.

L'Âge d'or, Vicomtes Charles and Marie-Laure de Noailles; *Las Hurdes*, Ramón Acín; Buñuel letters, Spanish National Film Archive; *Los olvidados*, Utramar Films; *Robinson Crusoe*, Producciones Tepeyac/Ultramar Films; *The Young One*, Olmeca Films; *Belle de jour*, Paris Film Production/Five Films; *La Voie lactée*, Grenwich Film Production/Medusa/Fraia Film; *Le Charme discret de la bourgeoisie*, Grenwich Film Production/Dean Film/Jet Films; *La Mort en ce jardin*, Film Dismage/Producciones Tepeyac; *Él*, Nacional Films/Producciones Tepeyac; *Viridiana*, UNINCI/Films 59/Gustavo Alatriste.

Index

Films and other works indexed by title are by Buñuel unless otherwise indicated
Italicised page numbers denote illustrations; those in **bold** indicate detailed analysis
n = endnote (indexed only for background information, not citations)